Bright Hope

BRIGHT HOPE

*Discovering Resilient, Sustainable Ways of Living
through Even the Darkest Times*

Ted Brackman

FOREWORD BY
Jim Wallis

CASCADE *Books* • Eugene, Oregon

BRIGHT HOPE
Discovering Resilient, Sustainable Ways of Living through Even the Darkest Times

Copyright © 2022 Ted Brackman. All rights reserved. Except for brief quotations in critical publications or reviews, no part of this book may be reproduced in any manner without prior written permission from the publisher. Write: Permissions, Wipf and Stock Publishers, 199 W. 8th Ave., Suite 3, Eugene, OR 97401.

Cascade Books
An Imprint of Wipf and Stock Publishers
199 W. 8th Ave., Suite 3
Eugene, OR 97401

www.wipfandstock.com

PAPERBACK ISBN: 978-1-6667-3081-4
HARDCOVER ISBN: 978-1-6667-2277-2
EBOOK ISBN: 978-1-6667-2278-9

Cataloguing-in-Publication data:

Names: Brackman, Ted, author. | Wallis, Jim, foreword.

Title: Bright hope : discovering resilient, sustainable ways of living through even the darkest times / by Ted Brackman ; foreword by Jim Wallis.

Description: Eugene, OR: Cascade Books, 2022 | Includes bibliographical references and index.

Identifiers: ISBN 978-1-6667-3081-4 (paperback) | ISBN 978-1-6667-2277-2 (hardcover) | ISBN 978-1-6667-2278-9 (ebook)

Subjects: LCSH: Hope—Religious aspects—Christianity. | Death—Religious aspects—Christianity. | Sickness—Religious life.

Classification: BT825 B65 2022 (print) | BT825 (ebook)

11/02/22

Unless otherwise indicated, all Scripture references contained herein are from the *New Revised Standard Version* of the Bible, copyrighted 1989 the Division of Christian Education of the National Council of the Churches of Christ in the United States of America, and are used by permission. All rights reserved.

To

all despairing people
and those who assist them.

Contents

Foreword by Jim Wallis | ix
Acknowledgments | xiii
Preface | xv

Section One: Hope Is a Reality We Live Into

1 What We Hope For | 3
2 What Keeps Hope Alive | 11
3 The Radical Origin of Christian Hope | 19
4 God's Future Now | 30

Section Two: Hope Transforms Human Personhood and Community

5 A New Way of Being | 41
6 Soul Work: Hopeful Body | 51
7 Soul Work: Hopeful Emotions | 63
8 Soul Work: Hopeful Mind | 79
9 Soul Work: Hopeful Personality | 89
10 Soul Work: Hopeful Spirit | 98
11 Soul Work: Hopeful Character | 112
12 Building Hopeful Community | 124
13 Healing Broken Community: Addressing Homelessness | 136

Section Three: Hope Gives Us a New Horizon

14 In How We Seek Healing | 157
15 In How We Endure Suffering | 171
16 In How We Face Death and Dying | 178

Afterword | 195
Bibliography | 199
Subject Index | 205
Author Index | 215
Scripture Index | 219

Foreword

IN THE FALL OF 1970, at Trinity Evangelical Divinity School in Deerfield, Illinois, I met Ted Brackman in a very diverse group of seminarians who found each other in our first few weeks at the school. We were in the midst of the student movements of our time—against poverty, racism, and war. Just months earlier, we had been through the historic student strikes and shutdowns of our universities after Richard Nixon invaded Cambodia and the Ohio National Guard troops shot and killed four protesting students and wounded nine others by firing live shots into unarmed students at Kent State.

Those were galvanizing times for our young generation. I had been directly involved in campus protests at Michigan State, as had Ted at the University of Washington. Others in our group had come from quiet Christian colleges where protests didn't occur. But when we met at seminary, we all felt called to put our faith into action by taking it to the streets.

Our small group became very close, with regular gatherings and prayer, convening public events for other students and young people, and marching in Chicago. We eventually started a tabloid and called it the *Post American*, a predecessor to the publication of *Sojourners*, which quickly spread around the country. I remember Ted being radical about the issues, passionate about his faith, and deeply invested in bringing the two together. I also remember his ready smile, his easy laugh, and his keen interest in a college girl across the street at Trinity College (whom he ultimately married).

Ted was an activist—I called him the guy who "just did it" when others were happy talking about it. Our group in Chicago eventually sojourned to Washington, DC to establish the Sojourners Community. Although Ted was deeply drawn to that vision of a radical Christian community and to coming with us to the nation's Capitol, he felt called to return to his beloved Pacific Northwest, where he loved the land and culture and his home community.

So of course, with his usual persistence and commitment, Ted began building a radical Christian community in the Seattle/Tacoma area. Although efforts grew by fits and starts, and an extended community was never sustained for very long, he organized successful events and conferences that brought in many of us from around the country to preach, pray, and practice radical discipleship. Locally, Ted was a trusted organizer and veteran mobilizer around the issues of homelessness, creating many sheltering ministries, and challenging local officials for compassionate and just policies.

Social activist Ted also went to graduate school in clinical psychology and soon established a very successful and trusted practice as a counselor. He seemed to move easily from listening one-on-one to a variety of clients with issues of mental and emotional health to public activism in the streets and in the local corridors of power. I knew few people who could accomplish simultaneously both a very personal and a very political mission. I think that integration of psychology and activism gave him a foundation to deal with the cancer which would later change his life.

I always loved hanging out with Ted and looked forward to coming out to speak at his conferences, or spend time together after a book event, or visit with his family, including two wonderful daughters full of his love for justice. Ted was fun to be with. Although he took seriously both his clients' and his country's struggles with illnesses, he still had time to smile, laugh, tell jokes, and have a good time. That, I now believe, also prepared him for the deep journey through cancer that was to come.

I was struck by how Ted was always ready to discuss the integration of psychology and theology. As he does so well in this book, he brought his theology into everything—personal, social, and political relationships. In our seminary years together, I saw how his deeply ingrained theological thinking and reflection shaped his vocation. Our own partnership and mutual vocations of justice were always deeply rooted in faith, leading to many theological conversations over a beer—back in seminary and out in the Pacific Northwest.

Ted's diagnosis of pancreatic cancer initially gave him less than a year to live—and that changed everything, as it would for any of us. I think of this book as his spiritual autobiography of how that one year was stretched into eleven, allowing him to watch his daughters get married and hold grandchildren in his arms with that same big smile on his face. All along the way he continued to practice his psychological therapy and homeless activism, continually deepening his integration of theology in both arenas.

FOREWORD

In our conversations after his initial cancer diagnosis, one of Ted's first questions was about hope: Where do we find it? What does it mean? How does it apply to our personal and political crises? We talked about hope all the time throughout Ted's pilgrimage into it psychologically, theologically, spiritually, and politically. One of his greatest attributes was perseverance, which sustained his decade-long "spiritual warfare" with cancer.

As you'll read in this book, Ted learned much about the difference between optimism and hope. Optimism is about feelings and moods and personality types, cups half-full and half-empty. Hope is a decision we choose based upon this reality we call faith. I best learned the difference between optimism and hope from Archbishop Desmond Tutu while I was in South Africa under apartheid. Even when there were no reasons for optimism in the face of such oppression and suffering, Tutu and the freedom movement never stopped making the choice for hope—and I watched hope win.

Ted and I often talked about the best biblical text for hope, Hebrews 11:1—"Now faith is the substance of things hoped for, the evidence of things not seen" (KJV). From what I witnessed in South Africa and in many other times and places, I have paraphrased that text as "Hope is believing in spite of the evidence, then watching the evidence change."

I watched this happen in Ted's life as well, as his experience became evidence of that kind of hope. He said to me again and again that it was very important to him to live well while dying. Living more deeply into hope helped sustain him while living more deeply into death from cancer. He believed that God's future is always coming to us, which is how he sustained his life-long activism for homeless and marginalized people, knowing how much they in particular mattered to God and belonged to the future God intends for all of us. The vision of God's future coming to us gave him a bright horizon even while seeing his own life coming to a physical end.

This chronicle of Ted's continuing reflection as psychologist, theologian, activist, and pastor is a rich legacy of life-sustaining resources amid death-dealing challenges. Ted always presented for me the bright hope that anything can be changed. I hope that reading his epitaph will help you to believe that too in your life and in your communities. God bless you, Ted.

—Jim Wallis

Acknowledgments

It may be apparent that composing this manuscript was a new experience for me. This project has taken me beyond what I had expected in time, energy, writing, reading, and consulting. I've learned and grown much along the way and, if I had to do it again, it would be easier and quicker!

I'm forever grateful for the contributions of many friends who have read, edited, and critiqued the manuscript in all its stages. Kathryn Helmers, an experienced agent, has most recently made a major investment, contributing to the organization, content, and editing of this project. Those who have also contributed significantly include Kate Hall, Arlyn Lawrence, Wes Howard Brook, Janet Guthrie, Linda MacDonald and our consultation group, Joe Roos and Cheri Herrboldt, Janele Nelson, Terry Gibson and the Pastoral Therapy Associates, Howie Davidson, Sandi Frood, and Sharon Mattson. Their comments and critical feedback have helped me shape and strengthen this manuscript. It's likely these gifted people will not agree with or embody parts of what I've said!

Similarly, I'm very thankful for the encouragement I've received in this endeavor from friends and family. In particular, I'd like to recognize and thank Al and Shari Shelton, Sue Ferguson Johnson, Art Hunt, Dr. Nick Chen and staff, Tristia Bauman, Jim Wallis, Dave Rodes, Mike Yoder, George Rodkey, Clara Davidson, Bobbie Petrone Chipman, Sandy Bremner, David Ortman and Ann Marchand, Dirk and Alicia Beckford Wassink, Meg and Peter Lumsdaine, Lisa Snow Lady and Jim Lady, Kevin and Marian Neuhouser, Pat Shaver, Becky and Ron McCorkle, Josh Lennox, Dale Helt, Janet Tran, Tina Kriss, Heather and Travis Ness, Norma Larson, Rachel Spang, Cathleen Herrera, Rhea Jason, Karolyn Ghosn, Jim Grant, Denny Hunthausen, Leeda Beha, and Tim Bean.

ACKNOWLEDGMENTS

We all have so many people who contribute to our hope. Dietrich Bonhoeffer has said it well: "In normal life, we hardly realize how much more we receive than we give, and life cannot be rich without such gratitude. It is so easy to overestimate the importance of our own achievements compared with what we owe to the help of others."[1]

To everyone who has contributed to mine: thank you, thank you, thank you.

---

1. Bonhoeffer, *Letters and Papers*, 109.

Preface

*Strength for today, and
bright hope for tomorrow*

FOR MOST PEOPLE, LIFE is challenging much of the time. What carries us forward in the midst of adversity is an abiding and sustaining hope. How do we find it?

I wrote this book during a season of stretching a fatal diagnosis with a three-month prognosis into eleven years. It has been particularly beneficial as I face mortality, relinquish personal attachments, and make difficult life adjustments. (Working on aspects of this project reminds me that I am a student, not a scholar!) But this project was created to assist anyone facing despair to cultivate hope, to be resilient and empowered, both internally and externally.

Along this journey, I've had opportunity to meet wonderful people, such as clients who came to me for counseling despite knowing that I had an aggressive terminal disease (I doubt I would seek out a therapist whose life expectancy is questionable!) and others in medical clinics who knew that any such insights were hard-won.

Completed in November 2020, this volume includes insights and stories I've collected over many years. Its actual genesis was a sermon on Christian hope I shared in 2012 while receiving chemotherapy, radiation, naturopathic, and acupuncture interventions for pancreatic cancer. Taking a Christian approach to this topic came from my experience that followers of Jesus have a wonderful, hopeful gift to share. For me, Christian faith just makes sense. As C. S. Lewis once remarked: "I believe in Christianity as I believe that the sun has risen, not only because I see it,

PREFACE

but because by it I see everything else."[1] Though written from a Christian perspective, there is much in this book that I believe can be used by people from different traditions or worldviews.

Organized around three sections, *Bright Hope* begins with recognizing the challenge of living with a dreaded adversity, the nature of hope, how it grows, and the foundation of a Christian understanding of present and future hope in both inner healing and outer action. The second section explores how hope grows in key dimensions of human experience and through personhood in community. The third section proposes the utility of hope for our happiness and well-being, its significance in dealing with social despair and injustice, the requirement that it make sense during acute suffering, and when we directly face our dying.

You'll notice that a recurring theme in this book is what Marva Dawn calls "being well while ill."[2] After my diagnosis, I realized I did not want to fight against the malignancy and treat it like something I had to battle with on a regular basis. Instead, it was much better for me to focus on living with cancer and making investments in my life or others that generated hope and a sense of thriving. Focusing on daily quality of life helped me maintain a positive focus and create forward momentum.

With limited life expectancy, I may not be around to share this material with you in person. However, anyone reading this book with growing hope will make this entire project successful for me—and so I am profoundly joyful and grateful to share this journey with you. My wish is that you discover an appropriate strategy for hope in your own life and enjoy the blessing of sharing it with others.

---

1. Lewis, "They Asked for a Paper," 164.
3. Dawn, *Being Well When We're Ill*, 7.

—— Section One ——

Hope Is a Reality We Live Into

1

What We Hope For

"Hope is both the earliest and the most indispensable virtue inherent in the state of being alive."

—Erik Erikson

Think of how often we use the word *hope* in our daily communications:

"I hope that I'll get there in time. . ."

"I don't know, but I sure hope so. . ."

"I hope you know how much I care. . ."

"I hope you have a good day. . ."

"We'll see—let's hope for the best. . ."

We use *hope* to express what we wish to happen but can't be sure will; to register our anticipation of what we're trying to make happen; to encourage others with good thoughts about themselves and their circumstances; to encourage one another when we are all facing an unfolding set of high-stakes events. *Something good can happen,* we want to affirm. *Hold onto that.*

It's hard to imagine a more basic component of being alive than hope—it's a requirement for any healthy, meaningful life; a necessity for a world facing threats from without and within. It is a basis for sustaining internal strength, for motivating us to move toward healing internally, for activating us to pursue reconciling action externally.

But where does hope come from, and how is it best understood? Is it mostly a human creation, or does it have a transcendent dimension? What gives hope, *hope?*

SECTION ONE: HOPE IS A REALITY WE LIVE INTO

Hope and Despair Can Coexist

Hope can generate a sense of trust in ourselves, the world, and the future. It is incredibly significant when we face adversity, when we need to see the world not simply as "it is what it is" or even what we'd like it to be, but rather as the possibility of what it may be.

When I was in the hospital for major pancreatic cancer surgery in 2010, I needed hope—badly. As I grappled for ways to help put the trauma I was experiencing into perspective, I recalled a story I'd heard of one person's struggle facing major adversity.

Daniel Berrigan, a Jesuit priest, was teaching a class at Union Theological Seminary. A student arrived for Berrigan's lecture, and Dan noticed he was very pale and looked rather sad. Berrigan asked him, "What's the matter?"

The student pondered how he might respond. Wouldn't it just be easiest to say, "It's none of your business?" But rather than shutting down, he opened up. "I'm dying. I'm dying of cancer."

Berrigan, without skipping a beat, simply responded, "That must be very exciting."[1]

What? *Exciting*? Shouldn't there have been sympathy or shock at discovering that a deadly disease was destroying this young man's body? Usually people respond to news like that with something apparently more comforting—like promises of prayer or encouraging clichés. At the very least, they maintain a polite silence. But . . . *exciting*?

Later, we learn that this student—in the late stages of cancer—reflected on Berrigan's response with insight: Yes! How true! This was perhaps the most extraordinary event of his life since birth. After all, he, like most of us, had never before faced death.

Despair is a normal response to a profound sense of powerlessness, hopelessness, and unresolved grief or loss. We can feel catapulted into the confines of the present in all of its harsh, cruel reality. Despair leads us to presume that, if we can't do anything about our miserable circumstances, then nothing and nobody can. It whispers that change can be destructive, that we are not up to continuing, and that our assets—both individual and social—are insufficient. It circles us, hems us in like a constellation of doom where all hope has vanished.[2]

---

1. Quoted in Forest, "Astonishing Hope," 67.
2. The phrase "constellation of doom" is drawn from the work of social psychologist

Viktor Frankl called despair "suffering without meaning,"[3] "meaning" being a deep-seated desire for ultimate significance in our experience. Despair tells us to give up and shut down. Hope tells us there are, still, exciting reasons to stay open to life.

The impulse to give up is often generated by the realization that cherished long-term goals have remained unmet. That loss can interfere with our ability to achieve more immediately realizable goals, and we turn a blind eye to opportunities that might improve our existence. We become so focused on the things that didn't happen—the miraculous cure to my cancer after years of prayer; relational disappointments; financial struggles; educational and personal projects; a pregnancy after years of trying; seemingly futile efforts to bring peace and social justice, or to reverse planetary warming—that we miss new things that can now happen.

Oddly enough, and as contradictory as it may seem, despair and hope may be concurrent as we respond to life's traumas. Actually, despair presupposes hopes that have not been, and cannot be, fulfilled. When hope is present, despair is not necessarily absent. Hope is simply the other side of despair, and when we are closer to one we may still recognize the other. When we bring hope and despair together, we create the potential for different approaches to ourselves and our life situation. Working alongside despair, hope pushes us to find how much of ourselves or others we can make use of in our current situation.

Sometimes experiencing a deep hopelessness or despair cannot be cured or talked away. It is important that we and others accept that there may be good situational or personal reasons for despair and that there may be more benefits in befriending despair than in resisting it. In fact, accepting despair—while being open to hope—may produce new perceptions and possibilities that were previously hidden.

It's possible that despair can be useful if we allow it to bring us to the depths of who we are, and it may help us find our deepest values and passions. Often, despair spurs us to let go of false hopes and investments that need to be relinquished if we are going to know ourselves more completely. Our darkness allows for a more nuanced and comprehensive search of reality. False hopes may have meant hoping for things that cannot happen, should not happen, or, perhaps, require resources we don't possess. False promises and hopes can lead to overlooking current responsibilities

---

Robert Jay Lifton.

3. Frankl, *Unconscious God*, 137.

and present realities and distract us from investing in quality of life. For instance, modern medicine has often suggested that it is bad to suffer and that we should do everything we can to take pain away. This may be a false hope if, in fact, suffering with some pain is inevitable and can actually make us more insightful or understanding.

As we discover more about ourselves or others, we can gain a sense of flexibility or freedom. We are freed from shallow optimism, cynicism, old behavior patterns that limit us, and the inappropriate goals that lead to our apathy, emotional numbness, or spiritual petrification. Private dreams that may have given us a false notion of our autonomy and independence can be reexamined in our darkness. Despair may break us free from an unreflective immediacy where we are entirely absorbed in our circumstances.[4]

Though we often find ourselves locked into the present and our immediate dilemmas, we can recognize that what was future a moment ago is now present, and what was present is now past. What is immediate is not static. Instead, life is constantly moving. We always have the possibility of something to look forward to. Life is constantly being re-created and renewed. Birth follows death, day follows night, spring follows winter. We are always changing, always becoming, individually and collectively. Each day is a challenge and an opportunity to be curious and explore more of who we are and what we have to work with, internally and externally, in our current situation.

What Hope Isn't (Optimism)

An important question we must ask ourselves regarding hope is not only what is realistic to hope for, but what is possible for us in the near future? Rather than certainty, short-term hopes are about possibility. After all, if we are certain about short-term goals, there is no need for hope.

Optimists want us to believe, naïvely, that the human future can be better and that progress will happen if we just strive for it. Optimists center on external realities and circumstances that generate a positive worldview, often eliminating the real struggles and contradictions of human life. When serious obstacles confront optimists, they often find their goals minimized or attenuated. When we need hope the most, when our situation is really terrible and not improving, optimists tend to look away. Optimism does not

---

4. See Eagleton, *Hope without Optimism*.

allow for the harsh and truthful reality of despair.[5] When we hear people say "I'm cautiously optimistic" about accomplishing or experiencing something, they are better served by simply saying "I'm hopeful."

Terry Eagleton, a public intellectual, points out that presumption is a pathological optimism.[6] By this he means that it is a fraudulent imitation of hope that leads us to believe we can simply take matters into our own hands with success. Eagleton maintains that optimists are typically politically conservative, believing that the corporate status quo is worth preserving. As such, optimism can be a component of dominant ideology. Indeed, in the United States, optimism functions as a national belief. For example, there's the notion that if we work hard enough, we can accomplish whatever we dream. Unfortunately, those who look comprehensively within and beyond our social and national borders will soon conclude that there are many people who work very hard and are unable to change their circumstances. However, in contrast to optimism, hope is not the conviction that something will turn out well, but the certainty that something makes sense, regardless of how it turns out. Hope tells us that even though all appears lost, we are not.

After optimism has eroded in the face of life's struggles, we may find an opportunity for a hope that is resilient enough to root itself in our innermost being and stand strong even through life's most tragic moments. Making sense of what we face in life creates the potential for people to work together more effectively: it creates space for community. It is a process of setting a specific goal and understanding the journey itself. Many times, small actions matter and ripple out in ways that cannot be predicted.

While hope and optimism are focused on our current reality, hope—unlike optimism—does not derive its inspiration from the circumstances of our lives. While optimists insist on the reality of progress, that the world will get better, those who have hope know that this world may not get better and that, instead, we can find a way of surviving through the darkness. True hope operates with a radical acceptance of our current situation and encourages us to make the most of the moment. Internal, intrinsic hope can emerge as part of our life and be nurtured at any point.

In *Intrinsic Hope*, Katie Davies writes that we live with the emotional paradox that, by acknowledging our fear, disappointments, anger, sadness,

---

5. Eagleton, *Hope without Optimism*, 4.
6. Eagleton, *Hope without Optimism*, 82–83.

and despair, we actually can become more hopeful. Ignoring these feelings allows for hopelessness to grow in us.[7]

Counselors and others can appreciate that there are sometimes good circumstantial reasons for despair and that despair may come to be experienced as more tolerable over time.[8] In fact, accepting despair—while being open to hope—may reveal new perceptions and possibilities that were previously hidden.

The project of hope is to make sense of what we face in life with something to look forward to that is not dependent upon whether circumstances turn out the way we want them to. Rather, we want to know that no matter what happens, we will find opportunities for a hope that is so resilient that even in life's most tragic moments, though our knees may give way, we know in our core that we have the strength to endure.

How Hope Works

We know that some circumstances will not change for the better: there are chronic conditions we simply have to tolerate or endure; fractured relationships impervious to mending, which continue to be very painful over time; uncertain or foreshortened futures; the threat of social disruption and the perennial struggle for positive change.

Acute anxiety or major depression may accompany us. We can wonder how we are going to be successful, or who is going to love us unconditionally, or whether we are really lovable at all. Looking forward, then, may bring us a sense of doom. Our deepest fears may involve a lack of meaning or purpose about who we are, individually and socially, and so then we question what it all means.

---

7. Davies, *Intrinsic Hope*, 14–19.

8. For caregivers, companions, and counselors alike, helping those they support to end states of despair can be stressful. After all, despair lacks a simple solution for most, and their mental, relational, and spiritual resources are often depleted before they seek help. What can inspire people who may have already given up? When we are exposed to people's trauma, how do we sustain ourselves and avoid feelings of our own helplessness, anger, or fear? Working with chronic despair can lead us to emotional insensitivity, diminished creativity, cynicism, simplification, and chronic fatigue. Do we have an adequate frame of reference consisting of beliefs, values, and social support that allow us to cope with secondary trauma? Can we maintain an attitude of potential and choice for ourselves as well as others?

Faced with very difficult or overwhelming circumstances, we can become alienated from our innermost selves and our legitimate hopes. We may wonder whether or not we are defective or deficient and presume that we're not worth investing in. Becoming increasingly critical of ourselves or others, and believing that we lack necessary endurance to go on, is disabling. The short-term easy route—resigning ourselves to self-pity or self-diminishment—is, in the long term, a downward spiral without hope.

With cancer, I've worked with small, practical hopes, such as finding the right treatment, paying for it, finding strategies to live with chemotherapy on an ongoing basis, hoping I could continue my counseling practice and community work, or hoping that I can maintain my strength and endurance. I've used short-term goals along the way for my day-to-day experience when there have been questions about my life with cancer, including my immune system continuing to tolerate chemo, whether or not I could handle nausea or pain, and wondering if I would maintain regular aerobic activity. These proximate hopes have required specific strategies and goals at different points. I've had to make adjustments and revisions as life with cancer has evolved. At times, I've had to resist well-intentioned but unhelpful advice. External goals were conditioned by many factors along the way, as sometimes these extrinsic hopes materialized and sometimes they didn't.

Proximate or provisional hopes can be as simple as the hope of living each day well or the hope of stepping forward when uncertainties abound. Perhaps it's as simple as hoping for the courage and wisdom that may be needed in the next hour or two.

By themselves, however, such short-term hopes have not been enough for me. After all, I do not control the process of this disease or how long my body can tolerate the treatment. There have been successes and failures along the way. If practical hopes did not materialize, I've needed a more general or ultimate hope that can sustain me when treatment may not be working. I've needed a transcendent hope that can give me confidence in something more permanent or unconditional, something that can sustain me in hopeless circumstances as the disease progresses.

My need is for an unwavering hope that is not subject to all the human limitations that I experience. I want to see a big picture that envisions something beyond the limitations of my life. This kind of transcendent hope would be intrinsic to me, something I can draw on at any point. Is there a way I can have a confident anticipation of the future, a hope that can inspire me to make the investments in practical day-to-day hopes when things seem dark?

Overarching hope is typically not something we create on our own. It likely exceeds our immediate functional capacity to hope and can only be received as a gift. For it to be sustaining, transcendent hope abides in the deepest, most central parts of ourselves. It is received externally but experienced internally. It incentivizes us to step forward with self-direction and creates the potential for any circumstance to be meaningful, no matter how ominous or unsettling. A transcendent hope toward a positive future can lead us to more effectively prioritize and shape practical hopes on a day-to-day basis.

Viktor Frankl survived a Nazi concentration camp and struggled with despair. In *Man's Search for Meaning*, Frankl writes, "In a last violent protest against the hopelessness of imminent death, I sensed my spirit piercing through the enveloping gloom. I felt it transcend that hopeless, meaningless world, and from somewhere I heard a victorious 'yes' in answer to my question of the existence of an ultimate purpose."[9] Later, he says,

> What was really needed was a fundamental change in our attitude toward life. We had to learn ourselves and, furthermore, we had to teach the despairing men, that it did not really matter what we expected from life, but rather what life expected from us. We need to stop asking about the meaning of life, and instead think of ourselves as those who were being questioned by life—daily and hourly.[10]

Philosopher Gabriel Marcel affirms that hope is not based on rational calculation, has no ultimate limit, can provide an unshakable assurance, tolerates disappointment, and exists with a sense of ultimate security.[11] A well-founded hope can bridge past, present, and future so that we can feel a sense of security and confidence at any time. It has been said that as long as there's life, there's hope. Perhaps it's better to say that as long as there's hope, there's *life*.

But what is our inner capability for hope, and how do we sustain it? How can it grow when we are most challenged?

---

9. Frankl, *Man's Search*, 51.
10. See Frankl, *Man's Search*, 111.
11. See Marcel, *Homo Viator*.

2

What Keeps Hope Alive

> "The character of hope is like a baby beginning to walk. It is in the practicing that we learn; we will gain confidence and hope as we enter more deeply into the practices of hope. Hope emerges out of the process of hoping, shaped by practices and nurtured by habits."
>
> —Dorothee Sölle

I'LL NEVER FORGET THE day I received a call from a local hospital social worker about a woman I'll call Jessica,[1] who had asked her nurses for a lethal dose of medicine so she could end her life.

Three days earlier, while driving home from teaching her first-grade class, she'd been hit head-on by a drunk driver. When this young, attractive, former college tennis player emerged from a coma, she couldn't recognize what she saw in the mirror.

Her injuries included severe facialced lacerations, a broken nose, a partially shut left eye, fractured ribs, a disfigured breast, a severely damaged pelvis, and a mangled right leg. It was unclear whether she would ever be able to walk again. The physical manifestation of the trauma she had faced filled her with self-hate.

When I arrived the first time, she could barely speak. When she did, she focused almost entirely on not wanting to live. All I could do—indeed, all I wanted to do—was listen, just listen, to why she wanted to die. She had lost her identity, her value, her sense of future, and her hope. I validated

---

1. In my counseling practice, I used fictitious stories as therapeutic assets, as do other mental health professionals, to help clients gain perspective and hope. Jessica's story is a composite narrative that has been useful with a number of client struggles.

her feelings of futility and powerlessness. We sat quietly most of the time, because talking required more energy than she could muster.

Jessica's immediate state of shock, disorientation, and disbelief soon shifted gears into anger at being a victim of circumstances out of her control. *How could this be? This makes no sense. This isn't right! Why me?*

Over several conversations, she learned that I accepted her as she was and was willing to accompany her in her despair. She began to open up and express rather than contain her distress. She was not alone. After a while she was able to respond to my suggestions about how we might seek hope in her life, simple slivers of encouragement built on an acceptance of where she was.

Early on, we began by setting simple, achievable goals. Her first goal? To feel less pain and find some comfort. With the nursing staff, we developed specific manageable movements, found some more helpful medications, and helped her to focus on lowering her discomfort in small steps. Slowly, she began to recognize that there were parts of her body that still worked and that she could learn how to move so as to make herself feel less discomfort and more alive.

She began to give voice to the psychic wounds from the accident. Fortunately, she was not subject to trite clichés—"Everything happens for a reason," "God is in control," "God will not give you more than you can handle," "things will work out"—that could have generated hostility, wishful thinking, or false hopes. Before too long, I saw her smile as she reflected on just how terrible she felt. Eventually, she even laughed at her own hopelessness.

After focusing on how she could feel a little better physically and mentally, we began naming positive qualities about herself and her life that still remained after the accident. She had an engaging personality and was liked by the hospital staff. Her mind still worked well, and she began to read stories of people who had survived disasters and to learn more about her injuries and how her condition might improve. Her body could still accomplish a number of coordinated movements. She would move forward.

After some physical therapy, she began to use a wheelchair to visit others around the hospital who were also recovering from major physical injuries. As she met more and more people, she recognized that she still carried certain values and convictions about herself and her life that were important to her. Yes, she realized, she was the same person she had been before her car accident. Only her body was different. This trauma survivor was experiencing a new normal as she began using a language of resilience and hope.

Then the next blow hit. Jessica's husband of six months, who had been visiting her regularly and who seemed supportive in wanting her to reach her full potential in recovery, came into her room one day with tears in his eyes. Distraught, he told her that their life was now different and, while he loved her, he didn't see how their marriage could continue. He wanted to get a divorce because they weren't going to be what they were, do the things they did, or practice the same lifestyle that had meant so much to the two of them before the accident.

I got another call from the social worker—once more Jessica wanted to end her life. Slowly, using the same strategy, she gradually pulled herself out of the depths of despair. Eventually, she was able to leave the hospital and lived temporarily in a rehabilitation facility, occasionally returning to the hospital just for doctor's visits.

One day, a man in rehab befriended her and eventually asked her if they could spend more time together. After all she'd been through, his invitation—and any desire for something more—frightened her at first. Though she distanced herself from him initally, he wisely looked past her first reaction and decided that it was support, rather than romance, that she most needed at that time. After several weeks, he decided to try again: would she meet him at the hospital Starbucks so they could get to know each other? Cautiously, this time she said yes.

After weathering four surgeries and continuing extensive physical therapy, today Jessica is back teaching at her school. Her wheelchair gave way to a cane and increased mobility. While she has had a few more facial surgeries, and does not look like she once did, she is every bit as liked, respected, and effective a teacher as she was before. She has strengthened key friendships and discovered activities suited to her physical limitations. She married the man she met through her time in rehab and feels an unconditional love from her husband—and, most importantly, an unconditional love for herself.

If she's asked about her accident today, she will say that it was a living hell. She will also maintain that she's a better, more complete person today than she was before.

SECTION ONE: HOPE IS A REALITY WE LIVE INTO

Hope Starts Early

In his book *A Rumor of Angels*, sociologist Peter Berger suggested that it is the mothering person who first communicates to the child that the world itself is dependable and thus worthy of trust and hope.[2] When a child wakes up in the middle of the night, perhaps from a bad nightmare, surrounded by terrifying darkness, trusted reality is upset and there's a sense of chaos. In such a moment, Berger wrote, the child cries out for its mother, the one who has the power to banish the chaos and provide reassurance with words and actions: *I'm here, it's okay, you're safe, everything is fine*. If all goes well, the child feels reassured and secure enough to return to sleep. The child experiences a secure attachment from a reliable caregiver.

This mother figure Berger describes—who may be a mother, a father, a grandparent, a foster parent, or another significant caregiver in the child's life—does not know that everything will turn out okay. What she does know, almost instinctively, is that her child needs to be reassured, that reality needs to be secure, and that hope needs to be real. The mother's messages to the child perhaps presume her own inherent hope that what is supposed to be will be. Ultimate reality, she communicates to her child, is good and purposeful. This de facto belief in the ultimate goodness of life is the ground for the child's growing hopefulness.

As children grow toward adulthood, hope becomes associated with a desire to initiate. Children learn to explore, experiment, and play: they discover their power to realize small, immediate hopes. Hopefulness becomes inherently rewarding for the child such that, even when some hopes are not met, the child remains expectant that good will come eventually. With increasing independence come greater capacity for children to let go of false hopes and transfer unmet hopes to better prospects. Over time, expectations become more realistic.

Consider the example of learning to ride a bicycle. Watching others pedal down the street, a hopeful child will desire to learn to ride even though there is risk. The youngster may know that attempting to ride a bike may involve falling off, getting bruised, scraping a knee—and embarrassment in front of others. At the same time, children who have had reasonably secure attachments and reliable care have a built-in tendency to take reasonable risks. And eventually, perhaps after extensive trial and error, they experience the wonderful feeling of riding all the way down

---

2. Berger, *Rumor of Angels*, 69–94.

the road and back without falling. I remember this moment in my own life—it felt like I'd just conquered the world! The accomplishment is exciting and serves as another foundation we can build on to step forward in a hopeful way with new challenges.

Sometimes, cultivating hope is about remembering your own inner-strength assets that may have been run over by trauma and its message of hopelessness. You might want to ask yourself, "Am I stoking a problem identity in thinking of myself as a loser or potential liability? What are the props, unrealistic demands, and inappropriate expectations I need to let go of?"

It's not easy to challenge old, self-defeating patterns or messages. We can expect that painful feelings will undoubtedly surface. The intensity of these feelings may test to the limits our efforts to recover hope. Most people want nothing more than to escape this kind of pain.

If you find yourself in this place, I encourage you to allow and even welcome all of the emotions you feel. They do not mean you are going crazy. Instead, express and acknowledge these painful emotions as creating potential for your journey toward healing and thriving.

How Hope Grows

According to Greek mythology, Pandora's box contained all the ills of the world and only one blessing: hope. The mission of hope was to help heal all the wounds inflicted by life's difficulties. It is the last virtue to die.

When we lose hope, it's natural to assume it will never come back. But just as hope begins early with infants and matures as children grow, we can grow into hope throughout our lives. We are not powerless in the face of adversity, disappointment, and loss. It just feels that way.

In over four decades of working with clients in mental health intervention and support, I see three key dimensions necessary to the growth of hope. These are choices we can make.

Hope is kept alive with patience. Hope is often learned and cultivated over time. Consider this metaphor from Albert Schweitzer, who faced extreme challenges in his initiative to provide medical services and start a hospital among people suffering under European colonialism in what is now Gabon:

We must become good plowmen. Hope is the prerequisite of plowing. What sort of farmer plows the furrow in the autumn but has no hope for the spring? So, too, we accomplish nothing without hope, without a sure inner hope that a new age is about to dawn. Hope is strength. The energy in the world is equal to the hope in it. And even if only a few people share such hope, a power is created which nothing can hold down—it inevitably spreads to others.[3]

Patience is a requirement of hope if for no other reason than when things are bad, desperation and panic typically make everything worse! Patience involves watching, being aware, alertness, and remaining awake. In dark times, if we are patient, light can emerge.

When we wait without complaining, we can be hopeful. Patience is the assurance that what is hoped for is worth the delayed gratification, frustration, and suffering incurred along the way. Patience creates space for acceptance, even when things aren't right. It gives us the room to recognize the things we'd hoped for but can't accomplish, and in the process discover what we can accomplish. Failure is not the enemy, but a teacher.

Patience should not be confused with indifference. If we are involved in an emergency situation, urgent action may be needed. We need to find a balance between urgency and patience, acting and waiting.

Hope is kept alive with community. This journey of hope is not a solitary one. In families and groups, people may pick up on each other's hopefulness or hopelessness. We rub off on each other. But our tendency when encountering adversity is to withdraw and isolate.

This inability (or refusal) to share with others what we are struggling with is one of the greatest obstacles to growing hope, individually and collectively.

In the individualistic United States, we have an epidemic of loneliness.[4] It's often the case that despair or hopelessness results in social withdrawal and that can be a direct contributor to despair. Though we need to feel connected, that we belong, are knowing and being known, nearly half of all Americans sometimes or always feel alone or left out. Twenty-seven percent of Americans indicate they rarely or never feel understood. Yet research shows that connecting with others can ease sorrow and increase hope.[5]

---

3. Quoted in Johnson, *Beyond Guilt*, 84.
4. Weddell, "Biblical Friendship," 30–31.
5. Weddell, "Biblical Friendship," 30–31.

No matter what kind of goals we set for ourselves, we typically need others' support in reaching them. The COVID-19 pandemic has taught us about our shared vulnerability and how we must draw support and endurance from each other, giving and taking as needed. Encouraging others to resist fear and hate is part of "doing hope" together.[6] Just as the effects of hopelessness are contagious, so too does hope have profound ripple effects. We might consider it a basic human need; just as food, water, and security must be equitably distributed, so must hope. Whether we offer or receive, co-create or imagine, we can all participate in active hope. Mutual belonging can be a source of real joy.

There are many reasons why we often feel personally unwilling to talk or seek help. For one, most of us don't want to complain, whine, or burden others. Sometimes, it may be an issue of pride, as it's often difficult to admit we can't solve our own problems. Additionally, many people find it humiliating to seek help financially or socially, or to solicit help with practical challenges. Finally, it may be that we just believe no one person or group can really do anything for us, anyway. It's too late, our situations are too complicated, our family, friends, and society are unable. This is when we most need to practice connecting in community in order to grow hope.

Hope is kept alive by looking toward the future. Human life is distinguished from other forms of life in that we have a built-in directedness toward the future, a fundamental conscious capacity for hope. Our existence is driven by cravings, urgings, desires, and strivings, all of which are essentially forms of discontent with the way things are. In every situation, there is always more that can be experienced or improved. To be healthy is to have a future. If we conclude that we have no future or that the future is bad, we will deteriorate physically, emotionally, relationally, and spiritually.

We think about the future routinely, often without even realizing it. We fantasize about the future. If our mental images of the future are difficult, then we may feel anxious or afraid. If our mental images are positive, then we may feel that our future is going to be better than our present. Lewis Smedes, a pastoral theologian, recognized that most of us have more hopes than we realize.[7] He observed that taking inventory of our hopes can be profitable because we always invest something of our happiness into every hope we have. Since we all are shaped by what we most

---

6. Weingarten, "Reasonable Hope."
7. Smedes, *Standing on the Promises*, 74–75.

hope for, taking an inventory of our hopes is a way of taking inventory of what *we are becoming*.

Smedes conceptualized that slaves do not move toward freedom because they are slaves; instead, they move toward freedom when they have hope that they do not have to be slaves anymore.[8] Hungry people do not change their condition because they are hungry, but rather because they believe they can find food. People who are homeless take initiative to change their condition only when they believe that housing is possible and worth working for. Societies don't improve unless people believe that social change is possible. Every good thing done in the world is done, finally, because someone held on to hope.

Our journey from despair is more than just about us: true hope visualizes thriving for all humankind. Of course, most of us have hopes that are simply wishes or desires for reaching private dreams that will enhance our own comforts, conveniences, or relationships. But true hope is more than just the anticipation of attaining personal goals. According to David Augsburger, it develops when we have caught a vision of values that will outlast our own lives, benefit more than our own kind, and serve those who may have little to offer in return.[9]

Indifference whispers that there is no more reason to look forward to a future that is brighter instead of darker. Despair makes everything look dark. If hope can grow, then how and where does it get planted to begin with? The good news of the Christian story is that hope comes to us as gift. Let's explore how receiving and acting on that gift can transform all of life.

---

8. Smedes, *Standing on the Promises*, 29.
9. See Augsburger, *When Enough Is Enough*.

3

The Radical Origin of Christian Hope

"No eye has seen, nor ear heard, nor the human heart conceived, what God has prepared for those who love him."

—THE APOSTLE PAUL, 1 Corinthians 2:9

"I AM PROFOUNDLY IMPRESSED with how the Bible is saturated with trauma and survival of it," writes David M. Carr. He continues:

> If the Bible were a person, it would be a person bearing the scars, plated broken bones, muscle tears, and other wounds of prolonged suffering. It would be a person whose identity, perhaps average at one time, was now profoundly shaped by trauma. This person would certainly have to endure everyday life, but she or he also would bear, in body and heart, the wisdom of centuries of trauma survival.[1]

Christian hope is often stereotyped as a pie-in-the sky escape from suffering. But biblical hope is generated out of human struggle. It is founded in the reality that God created all things out of sheer love and joy. God made all of it good. God's love and joy led God to create people with complete freedom to order their lives individually and collectively and form relationships in any way they choose. With that human freedom comes wonderful achievements in myriad fields, including philosophy, medicine, film animation, rocket science, and athleticism. However, human free will also is joined by great tragedy, deep hatred, and substantial grief. In many cases, it is in this tragic dimension of life that despair can take us over, both individually and collectively.

---

1. Carr, *Holy Resilience*, 250.

With infinite wisdom and mercy, our loving Creator has left for us a particular special and unique revelation of hope, which we find as we explore and investigate the Old and New Testaments of the Bible. From Genesis to Revelation, we are confronted and inspired by a God who works with a particular people in an unfolding drama of salvation and liberation. The Bible contains written narratives and poetry describing centuries of mission and outstanding communal resilience. In the Christian Bible, this redemptive history culminates in the life, death, and resurrection of Jesus Christ, and the establishment of Christian communities.

Christian hope is rooted in this very powerful story, which is revealed even in the deepest despair.

Jeremiah's Rupture of Faith

In the Old Testament, we find the prophet Jeremiah caught up in a story of loss, displacement, brokenness, despair, and incredible hope.

Jeremiah wrote before and during a devastating assault by the Babylonians and King Nebuchadnezzar on his country and the city of Jerusalem in the sixth century BCE. Both the temple of Jerusalem and the city itself were severely damaged by the attack, crumbling the peoples' lives and dashing their confidence in the presence of God. Jeremiah is an anguished and wounded man, just like his community, in the grip of a catastrophe.

How was he so anguished? The Babylonian assaults drained the population in violent struggle, starvation, disease, deportation, and the creation of internal refugees from warfare. Most inhabitants were exiled, never to return, dying on foreign soil. There were children starving in the streets, nobles who appeared like walking dead, and mothers cannibalizing their own children for food.[2] Jeremiah struggled to deal with displaced and homeless people in a world where irrationality, violence, and loss were suddenly, overwhelmingly real. Jeremiah faced these devastating circumstances firsthand, as a number of threats were made on his life, and he was attacked, captured, and beaten. His language throughout the narratives exudes pain, confusion, and extreme disappointment. He writes in Jeremiah 4:17, "My anguish, my anguish! I writhe in pain!"

What is it like when people face overwhelming violence, chaos, and disaster? Kathleen O'Connor, a leading Jeremiah scholar, helps us understand the powerful message of this prophet and his relevance for our

2. Jer 7:32—8:3 and 19:9; Lam 5.

finding hope in great adversity. As O'Connor has described so well, traumatic violence often results in a terrifying disruption of normal physical and emotional processes.[3] Social resources are depleted, and any sense of safety evaporates. Memories are repressed or turned off in an emotional and spiritual deadening. Images of traumatic violence imprint themselves in the brain like a powerful ghost that returns again and again, haunting daily life. Words to describe the trauma fail, as it often seems unspeakable. Reality itself is incomprehensible. Such trauma and disaster can destroy a person's trust in God, other people, and the world. Often, traumatic disaster victims experience no apparent protection from God, no answer to prayer, and are no longer able to believe.

Like so many of us who may experience horrific circumstances, Jeremiah despairs and feels utterly hopeless. At one point, he exclaims, "Cursed be the day on which I was born! The day when my mother bore me, let it not be blessed! Why did I come forth from the womb to see toil and sorrow and spend my days in shame?"[4] In his outrage, he calls God a traitor and an impostor who has forsaken him: "Truly, you are to me like a deceitful spring, like waters that fail."[5] Jeremiah brings his deepest accusations against God with abrasive, hyperbolic cries: "O Yahweh, you have seduced me and I was seduced. You have raped me and you have prevailed."[6] The ultimate violation and rupture of faith that often accompanies disaster are riveting in Jeremiah's laments.

These responses are common. Before hope can emerge, survivors of trauma and disaster have to find language to share it; they have to grieve the accumulations of terror and loss and begin to place catastrophe in larger frames of meaning. Being able to acknowledge and talk about trauma is the first step in moving toward coping. Hope often arrives in fits and starts, a painful alternation of despair and trust.

Then, when there is no way forward, when the future is cut off and death appears to be winning, hope can appear unexpectedly, and the universe expands in surprising and shocking ways. In the depths of hopelessness, Jeremiah still clings to God, even when it feels like God is nowhere. Though God does not rescue him, Jeremiah keeps talking and praying and imploring. He keeps God alive when God is hidden in the deep, unending

3. O'Connor, *Jeremiah*, 1–34, 47–91.
4. Jer 28:14–18.
5. Jer 28:14–18.
6. Jer 20:7.

wound. Jeremiah's cries, bringing dreadful suffering into the light, allow room for hope to emerge in the midst of crushing circumstances.

Eventually, Jeremiah envisions a reconstituted community, restored to health for all the displaced and broken. This vision of the future arrives when he least expects it, bursting through the dark demoralization and utter hopelessness.[7] Because Jeremiah could see the future in new ways, the future changed who he was in the present, despite what happened in the past.

When we recognize God's presence and future victory, that active vision changes our perspective. These unpredictable, novel messages of God's future, coming in the middle of profound emotional distress, provide a new energy, a new resilience, a new courage in the very midst of deep darkness and despair. Hopeful people make a habit of hope, watching and continuing forward until the evidence itself changes.[8]

Jesus and Systemic Evil

Jesus knew well the history of prophets like Jeremiah, Isaiah, and Ezekiel. In Mark 1:15, he taught his Galilean audience—subjugated by an imperial, often tyrannical power—about the arrival of God's kingdom. For Jesus, God's kingdom was to transform the world according to God's purposes. It was for earth as well as heaven.

Peasants, degraded by Roman soldiers and faced with double taxation and substantial debt, were inspired by Jesus' ministry, his vision for a new social order, his healings, and his unconditional love and grace. People could see just how intimate he was with God and they looked to him for social change, a new jubilee, peace, justice, a godly temple practice, and relationships of reconciliation and forgiveness. He taught the people of the land how to live the life of God's inaugurated kingdom and went about building a new community based on teachings, such as what is collected in his Sermon on the Mount.[9]

Following a dramatic procession into Jerusalem, Jesus disrupted the corrupt temple operation and predicted God's judgment on the nation's self-interested, hypocritical leaders. He was summarily executed by Roman soldiers in a torturous, violent, unspeakable way. Crucifixion,

---

7. Jer 20:3.

8. My friend Jim Wallis is known to say, "Hope is believing in spite of the evidence and watching the evidence change."

9. Matt 5–7.

ultimately, was meant to intimidate and suppress any opposition to Roman domination through torture and trauma. His followers witnessed the rigged legal proceedings and brutal execution, which shattered their hopes for a messianic intervention by God that would eradicate Roman occupation and reorder Jewish society. Betrayed, demoralized, and hopeless, most of Jesus' disoriented followers snuck away from the cross, traumatized by the horror of what they had experienced. The one in whom they had placed their hope was dead. What had happened? Why hadn't Jesus delivered their nation? What now? Reality seemed like a closed system where oppressors had the final word.

Serene Jones helps us imagine the life-changing experience of two witnesses of Jesus' death.[10] They meet outside the walls of Jerusalem. Each is living in a world of traumatic grief. The first woman, Rachel, has lived with the trauma of a state-sponsored massacre in Bethlehem, where she witnessed the slaughter of innocent baby boys, including one of her own. She carries vivid, awful memories of traumatic violence. She has lived with a sense of powerlessness, underlying depression, and emotional numbness, attempting to keep away intrusive memories of her son's murder. Rachel likely suffered from what we now know as post-traumatic stress disorder, experiencing flashbacks, nightmares, hypervigilance, and patterns of avoidance.

The other woman is Mary, the mother of Jesus. She, too, has lived in a society dominated by Jewish elites and violent Roman power regimes. She has likely witnessed or heard about other crucifixions of rebels, bandits, or revolutionaries. Jesus' mother experienced a male-dominated society as a female peasant. She is a woman marginalized by gender, class, and political oppression. Her son narrowly escaped death in the Bethlehem massacre, but now, thirty years later, she has witnessed the horrible crucifixion of that same son.

Both Rachel and Mary had envisioned a world in which sinful power structures would be overturned and the people given their land and freedom. Both these women longed for a world in which, as Mary said, God would send the rich away empty, bring down the powerful, fill the hungry with good things, and lift up those of lowly status.[11] Rachel's son was killed in the search for Mary's son. Both women now struggle to hope in the depths of their minds and bodies, their grief testifying to the slaughter of innocents and the longing for a salvation to make things right. They

10. Jones, *Trauma and Grace*, 107–25.
11. Luke 1:46–56.

are united as victims of traumatic violence, and both struggle to find some order, coherence, and stability, some hope that life can be good.

From Friday's execution until Sunday morning, grief and fear overwhelmed Jesus' traumatized followers. Afraid of both the Romans and temple authorities, they stayed out of sight.

An Unprecedented New Reality

Then, early on Sunday morning, fearful women, including Jesus' friends Mary Magdalene; Mary, mother of James and Joseph; Salome; and Joanna, went to Jesus' tomb to prepare his body for burial. Upon their arrival, they were shocked to find that Jesus was not there. Their executed leader, placed in a tomb secured by Roman guards, had risen from death.

Through their shock and bewilderment, these women found themselves faced with something not analogous to anything comparable in this world. What they experienced forced a new mode of knowing, an unprecedented new reality beyond anything they had ever encountered. These faithful, incredulous women reported what they had seen to Jesus' disciples.[12] They courageously described not a general Christian hope, but the reality that something transformative had happened to the crucified Jesus where, in the middle of human history, he had risen from death—shockingly—all by himself. The knowledge of bodily resurrection meant that a physical phenomenon generated a reality that must be rejected or, if accepted, demanded a different worldview.[13]

Picture this story: two of Jesus' followers walk along a road to Emmaus, traumatized after their leader's torturous execution. They replay the scene of horrific crucifixion over and over in their minds, knowing that their hope in the future has collapsed. These journeyers attempt to come

---

12. Keep in mind that women who saw that Jesus was resurrected were not regarded as credible witnesses in the ancient world and could not testify in public. Though they were initially treated skeptically and with disbelief by Jesus' other disciples (Luke 24:11; Mark 16:11), these women later gained functional apostolic status. They had walked and worked alongside Jesus in his ministry, torturous death, entombment, empty tomb, and resurrection. Mary Magdalene, Mary the mother of James and Joseph, Salome, and Joanna, could each courageously now testify: "I have seen the Lord" (John 20:18). Richard Bauckham (*Gospel Women*, 257–304) explains that these women became principal sources and trusted agents who interpreted and shaped the astonishing stories of Jesus' death and resurrection for the earliest followers of Jesus.

13. Wright, *Surprised by Hope*, 58–76.

to terms with an overwhelming catastrophe that traps them in shock and confusion. There is no return to a state of normalcy. The promised Messiah is dead, and their hope for a new social order has died with him. Instead, they're trapped in a living nightmare.

As they walk, a stranger comes and joins them, and they repeat the story of Jesus' life and crucifixion to him. Their account of Jesus' life and death sparks a conversation with the stranger, and they invite him into their home for a simple meal. During the conversation, the newcomer takes the bread and blesses it and gives it to them. In this moment, they recognize the stranger is Jesus himself, and they discover he has done something unprecedented.

Before leaving their home, Jesus teaches them of God's faithful providence and that the future of life in the face of death is God's overarching moral purpose. He helps them understand his resurrection by referencing a number of prophetic statements from the Old Testament. In Isaiah 26:19, the prophet says, "Your dead shall live, their corpses shall rise. O dwellers in the dust, awake and sing for joy! For your dew is a radiant dew, and the earth will give birth to those long dead." In Daniel 12:1–3, they read that "many of those who sleep in the dust of the earth shall awake . . . and those who are wise shall shine like the brightness of the sky." While the Isaiah passage notes the transformation of creation, the Daniel passage highlights that resurrection will transform God's people forever.

Like the women discovering the empty tomb, these two disciples knew in that moment that the reality they had once known was now completely inadequate.

Eventually, many other followers also encountered the risen Jesus, and, through careful explanations of the Hebrew Scriptures, he continued to help them understand the trauma of crucifixion in terms of God's action of salvation and hope.[14] These disciples came to an understanding of Jesus' sacrificial death, modeled from the suffering servant foretold to them in Isaiah 53. The very cross the Roman government had used to torture and oppress became, for Jesus' followers, a symbol of profound hope.

Jesus' resurrection upset social reality in another way: his resurrection was against the law! Most followers of Jesus remember that he was officially crucified for blasphemy and sedition by Roman executioners, and his body was placed in a state-secured tomb monitored by Roman guards. To remove the stone and break the tomb's government seal was a crime.

---

14. Luke 24.

When God raised Jesus from the tomb, it immediately overruled the laws used to justify his execution and burial. All the Jewish and Roman officials involved were therefore guilty of crucifying an innocent man, a conviction that carried a death sentence. Jesus' resurrection, however, overturned the very law that would result in their execution, and, in God's amazing grace, they could be saved from the consequences of their own tragic mistakes. This divine action displays the reality that human law, when it is unjust or corrupt, should not be considered binding on faithful followers of Christ. Jesus' resurrection confirmed that he had power over secular authority.

Saul of Tarsus was widely known for persecuting Jesus' followers[15] until he, too, faced an incredible new reality: a dramatic encounter with the risen Christ on the Damascus Road. After suffering collapse, extended blindness, and the inability to eat or drink for three days,[16] he came to believe in the one whose followers he had once persecuted. Paul learned that Jesus' death and resurrection were signs of the beginning of the end of the world. He faithfully recorded the earliest testimony of hundreds of eyewitnesses to Jesus' bodily resurrection.[17]

In his witness to the resurrected Christ, the apostle Paul experienced the power of nonviolent sacrifice and love through trials, including stonings, beatings, shipwreck, and imprisonment. Jesus' crucifixion became a model for his own suffering.[18] As with Jesus, Paul would achieve true personal power through weakness.[19] This radical faith sustained Paul through his entire ministry and eventual execution, likely at the hands of Emperor Nero.

Jesus' followers were given a new way of life that radically changed the way they thought, felt, and acted. They heard how Jesus experienced godforsakenness, eternal damnation, and eternal death. His resurrection destroyed the hopelessness of hell. In the darkest, most despairing time of Jesus' crucifixion, his followers understood that God was present and creating new life. The hope that had been crucified was resurrected. Evil was not the final word, death could be overcome, and the future was open instead of closed. It was not the Roman and Jewish authorities who had the power to define reality, but God. The end of Jesus was the beginning of life, as resurrection displayed the victory of God over the absence of God at the cross.

15. Gal 1:13.
16. Acts 9:3–22.
17. 1 Cor 15:1–8.
18. 2 Cor 11:23–29; 4:8–11.
19. 2 Cor 12:7–10.

The power of Jesus' resurrection opened a radical novelty, a faithful disbelief in present assumptions. Not everything is as it appears. God acts in the darkest times and in periods of urgent need. With this inescapable new reality, Spirit-led followers of Jesus gave up everything—their vocations, families, security, and even their lives—so they could share their spectacular hope with others. They found the strength to deal with great adversities such as persecution, poverty, dislocation, imprisonment, and even torturous death. Courageous followers of Jesus stood against Roman occupation and elite Jewish collaboration and insisted on living an alternative new life together. Through faith in his resurrection, Jesus' followers were enabled to face intimidation and death threats made by tyrants who themselves were threatened by disciples of the living Lord. Fear of death could no longer be used to manipulate or control Jesus' people.[20]

Jesus' bodily resurrection was public, open to the world, universal, and began the new creation of all things. A new age, a new epoch, had truly begun. God's future was more real than present circumstance, and God was in the process of making all things new. What's more, the resurrected Jesus was with his followers to empower them in their radical, new, unprecedented lives!

Jesus promised his followers that he would personally return to transform all of reality. Resurrection was the beginning of a universe where God would be recognized in everything. When the resurrected Jesus returns, heaven and earth will be joined in a new way, open and visible to each other. People are headed toward an eternity where there is unlimited, simultaneous, and perfect enjoyment of life. It will be God's loving, unrestricted, inexhaustible, and creative fullness.[21]

Jürgen Moltmann has maintained that if we know that Jesus is coming, he is already in the process of coming. The kingdom that he embodied is relentlessly underway. In the power of hope, Jesus' followers could open themselves and all of their senses to experience his arrival. In other words, the future Christ was already present without ceasing to be future. Jesus was both absent and present. God's space and ours, heaven and earth, though different, are actually not far from each other. God's space and ours interlock and intersect in a whole variety of ways, even while they retain separate and distinct identities.[22]

---

20. Carr, *Holy Resilience*, 26, 50, 75.
21. Moltmann, *In the End*, 152–64.
22. Moltmann, *In the End*, 157, 158; Wright, *Surprised by Hope*, 105, 111, 116, 134–35.

Jesus taught his disciples—and teaches all of us—not to take things as they are, but to see them as they can be, in light of God's future. We are given the opportunity to envision what is taking place through resurrection eyes and engage in what is happening through resurrection's power. The kingdom of God that Jesus embodied is revealed as real not only by what is in place and before our eyes, but by what is taking place and coming to pass from God's future.[23] His crucifixion demonstrates God's investment for our proximate practical hopes and his resurrection shows the basis for our transcendent hope. We can engage the world strategically with small, realistic proximate hopes, knowing that we are ultimately confident and secure in God's transcendent hope.

Through Jeremiah, Jesus, the women who discovered the resurrection, and the experiences of Paul and the early church, we find some of the most important truths about hope. No matter how we come to despair, whether by our own actions or by those of others, by circumstance or by the nature of a disordered world, we are never alone. Our loving God embraces us. Even in death, we are held in the presence of the One who has conquered death for all time.

We learn that God's future rarely develops out of the old. Instead, God's future is about creating all things new and transforming what has gone before. We are never stuck or trapped. Instead, we, like Jeremiah and the prophets, like Jesus and his followers, like the apostle Paul, are called to live in the reality of what is in the process of coming from the future. Even in darkness, we are to live looking for the new, unpredictable, surprising, and novel. Every circumstance carries potential and possibility for healing and reconciliation, peace and joy. Even when we don't know what to do, we can be certain that God personally knows our pain, is ever with us. It is *kairos*, the moment of Jesus' immediate, resurrected presence, that creates the potential for our healing and reconciliation.

The crucified One is near to us and all who are brokenhearted, disenfranchised, or feeling godforsaken. As Jesus practiced solidarity and identified with poor and downtrodden peasants, so we are led to a similar alignment with the least among us today. We learn from Jesus that God's power is made perfect in weakness and surrender. With hope, we can say *no* to the wrongs of the past and present and declare *yes* to what is coming and what needs to come. This hope is both individual and corporate, meliorating inner distress as well as sociocultural injustice and violence.

23. Morse, *Difference Heaven Makes*, 107, 121–22.

God's sometimes inconvenient hope may lead us to engage with people that we don't like or be involved with actions that may seem counterintuitive. Indeed, hope understands that life emerges out of despair, death, and grief. Every defeat, every catastrophe, every end, can signal a new beginning. Peace can emerge from violence, justice from corruption, love from hate, and joy from sorrow. Because Jesus lived from the future to the present and from the bottom of society up, our hope is not tied to immediate circumstances or the expectation that all temporary hopes will materialize. Our hope, finally, is dependent solely on God's freedom to fulfill promises in God's own fashion.

So, despair and trauma can lead us to new possibilities and a new life. Our old life, without the power of resurrection hope, says we must work it out with our own energy. Our new life says we may not control circumstances, but we do control how to find transcendent hope in the midst of circumstances. The old life says that we don't have the assets that we need. The new life says the victory has already been won and we can be secure doing what we can.

The old life says we are stuck. The new life says the resurrected, crucified Christ is bound to us forever. Our old life says former friends and activities must continue. The new life says freedom comes with people who share our hopeful vision. The old life says there's not much, if anything, that we can do. The new life says resurrection hope leads us to step forward and take responsibility for our life with proximate practical hopes. The old life says we are determined from where we've come. The new life says our past is being transformed as we move forward. The old life says what we have is what we have to work with. The new life says we are free to look for the unexpected, the novel, beyond business as usual.

May we all be carried with an unrelenting confidence in the ultimate victory of Jesus over everything that assaults human life.

4

God's Future Now

> "What awaits us is the unending exploration of the inexhaustible riches of God, a pilgrim journey into deepest reality that will always be thrilling and life enhancing."
>
> —John Polkinghorne

GOD ACTS IN HUMAN history to create a new reality for all of us. This is the same newness that was demonstrated in the creation of the world, a creation out of nothing, *ex nihilo*. Though Jesus' resurrection occurred in human history, that phenomenon transcended its circumstances and brought a reality entirely new. In Jesus, God's future is visible ahead of time. Divine power is experienced in our world as the power to bring something new for all of us. We need what is new to overcome all that we experience. God's future involves the consummation of our time and space, the gathering up of all that has been part of our history into an incredible eternal life.[1]

The strength of our life, then, comes to us from the future, from God's future. Our hope can't be based only on temporary, momentary experiences, but instead it must come to us from a certain future where there is a final completeness and fulfillment. We can live fully in the present, moment to moment, because of our dynamic dependence on God's power to complete our lives.

In many ways, our ability to operate with overarching hope depends on the mental pictures we form when we think about what God's future looks like in comparison to our earlier assumptions. It is important for us to have reality-based, dominant images of our bodily end and God's new beginning. We find the true meaning of life only by being able to

---

1. Peters, "Terror of Time."

comprehend its end and review our life story in light of that end. In the words of Paul in Philippians 3:13: "I forget what lies behind and strain forward to what is ahead."

In the power of hope, we already participate in the eternal life of God's future world. God's time, *kairotic* time, has no beginning or end, no before or after. It is not bound by chronological time, space, history, or future projections based on the past. There is no measurement of God's time. *Kairos* is eternity in the midst of what is transitory and a prelude to what is coming. The presence of eternity often comes as we immerse ourselves fully in the moment and remain wide awake.

Bright Future

God's promises about the future always line up with God's character. It is a future of joy, justice, peace, mercy, and unconditional love. Every act of love, passion, gratitude, and justice; every work of art or music inspired by God's love and delight in the beauty of creation; every minute spent contemplating the goodness of our self, others, and our natural environment; and every experience of real happiness and joy will be made complete and unending in God's future.[2] All victims will triumph and all perpetrators will experience the justice that puts wrong to right. All pain and suffering, all death and dying, all grief and despair, will face the transforming message:

"Behold, I make all things new."[3] God's radiant glory will illuminate everything and all created beings will be able to participate in God's never-ending celebration. As Paul wrote, "God will be all in all."[4] What we have loved, what we miss, will all be part of God's resurrection future.

In the book of Revelation, John's vision of the new creation includes the descent of the holy city, the new Jerusalem, from heaven to earth. Through its descent from heaven, God's presence with the new Jerusalem shifts from heaven to earth: "See, the home of God is among mortals. He will dwell with them as their God; they will be his peoples, and God himself will be with them."[5] Just as God is pictured planting a garden in Eden, so God will build the city of life.[6] Kings and nations will bring their glory and

2. 2 Pet 3:13.
3. Rev 21:5.
4. 1 Cor 15:28.
5. Rev 21:3.
6. Rev 21–22.

honor into the city, including all the best of what humans have cultivated over time.[7] In the new universal creation, we find all people, including cultural and national diversity, and all created life. In Revelation 7:9, John envisions a great multitude that no one could count, from every nation, from all tribes and peoples and languages. Heaven and earth will be filled with the knowledge of the glory of God.[8]

God wants never-ending jubilation, where human beings delight in their joy in God and God is overjoyed to be at home with all of life. Indeed, everything in its unique character will dwell together: not just individuals, but the whole community; not just human beings, but all created things, in heaven and earth. In the end, God gathers everything into God's own self, the divine and the earthly become one, unmangled and undivided. God is present as pure livingness and love of life. As Jürgen Moltmann maintains, God will dwell in the world in a divine way and the world will dwell in God in a worldly way.[9]

In *The Coming of God*, Moltmann writes of the new creation:

> The fullness of God is the rapturous fullness of the divine life; a life that communicates itself with inexhaustible creativity; an overbrimming life that makes what is dead and weathered live; a life from which everything that lives receives its vital energies and its zest for living; a source of life to which everything that has been made alive responds with deepest joy and ringing exultation. The fullness of God is radiant light, light reflected in the thousand brilliant colors of created things. The new heaven and new earth, God's new creation, will be like a great song or a splendid home or a wonderful unending dance. The laughter of the universe will be God's delight. It is the universal Easter laughter.[10]

Our hope in God's future is based on our Creator's unlimited grace and not in our own righteousness. Jesus' death on the cross took all human rebellion and sin into God's own Trinitarian self. God will be "all in all" in the new creation's flourishing, and all creatures will be empowered with divine love. When we see Jesus Christ face to face, we will witness victory over all evil, including our own. God's unconditional love overwhelms, in the end, even the most horrendous evil. All people will surely

---

7. Isa 60:11.
8. Isa 11:9.
9. Moltmann, *In the End*, 58.
10. Moltmann, *Coming of God*, 339.

say *yes* to God in response to God's unsurpassed *yes* to them. Who would not want to be part of this future?

God's ultimate redeeming action, the new creation, the new heaven and earth, involves all of us, our world, and the entire cosmos fully enlivened by God's Spirit, continually regenerating in God's presence.

God's Future Now

Many times, God's hopeful presence contradicts the reality of our daily life. God's reality, the complete truth, is both with us and something that we can fully look forward to in the new creation. Through the power of hope, we never give up and we remain unreconciled and unaccepting in an unjust and often deadly world. With spiritual power of the age to come dwelling within us, we participate in God's new creation and act with expectant desire.[11] Sometimes, Christian hope is a hope against hope, or a hope where there is nothing else left to hope for in our immediate situation. We have a passion for the possible, with an inexhaustible hope until Jesus comes to complete it for all of us and all of creation.

The good news of heaven is that it's less a place where we go than what comes to us. It's less about a postmortem afterlife than about life here and now. We recall that heaven is the opposite of that which is passing away; instead, it is simultaneously coming to pass and taking place right now. It is at hand but not in hand.[12] As Christopher Morse explained in *The Difference Heaven Makes*, "the out there" of heaven is "here" without ceasing to be "there."[13]

Heaven has been created, as has earth, to be central to our flourishing. It is the place of our citizenship. It is close to what is familiar but exists beyond our preconceptions. As our most inescapable reality, heaven overtakes chronological time (*chronos*), as time and space are subject to history-making events and experiences from God. Our hopeful imagination prompts us to see more of reality than simple scientific facts. Based on God's arriving future, we can fully live in our current situations and question secular authority.

Christian hope can generate an explosion of resurrection grace and an uprising of liberation and freedom. It is always at least a little out

---

11. Heb 6:5.
12. Phil 4:5; Rom 13:12; Jas 5:8.
13. Morse, *Difference Heaven Makes*, 107.

of order and out of place and provides the genesis for new life-giving thoughts and actions. Followers of Jesus are often misfits! Hope is never wishful thinking or blind optimism. The coming new creation motivates our social action in current affairs. This reality gives us ability to deal with the worldly issues through a power greater than death itself. What facing reality calls for, the reality facing us calls forth.[14]

The real world is Christ taking form in all things.[15] It is Christ who helps us find meaning and significance in our ordinary experience. The world belongs to Christ, and it is only in Christ that the world is what it is, and only in the midst of the world that Christ is Christ.

When we perceive Christ in our daily experience, already there, already acting, we develop the ability to discern and respond. Responding with Jesus to those who suffer, to those who are victims or powerless, comes from the doing of heaven on earth. As Paul said: "I worked . . . Though it was not I, but the grace of God that is within me."[16] It is not so much that we hope as that God hopes in us.

Isn't it nice to be relieved of the ultimate responsibility for what is possible or not in our current circumstance? Instead, reality now is our free movement toward the future with anticipation, inventiveness, wonder, and change. Unexpected developments are to be expected. Some say that those with Christian hope carry a vision like advanced explorers, dashing ahead and then coming back to point the way forward. They carry confidence that life explodes with the overwhelming victory of God.

So, hope does not only derive from inherent potential or possibilities in the moment, but from the capacity of God making all things new. God's commitment to our present experience is not necessarily observable, but rather is experienced in our perseverance of hope.[17] Jesus comforted his disciples, "I go to prepare a place for you and will come again and take you to myself."[18] Paul similarly spoke of the reality that awaits in stark contrast to present events: "I consider that the sufferings of this present time are not worth comparing with the glory about to be revealed to us."[19]

---

14. Morse, *Difference Heaven Makes*, 94.
15. Col 1:17.
16. 1 Cor 15:10.
17. Heb 13:1–3.
18. John 14:2, 3.
19. Rom 8:18.

In life and in death we face a passing away and a coming to pass that is stronger than all death's opposition. As Christopher Morse writes, "We are called to be on hand for that which is at hand, but not in hand, an unprecedented glory of not being left orphaned but of being loved in a community of new creation beyond all that we can ask or imagine."[20]

Christian hope begins with Jesus' announcement that the kingdom of God is at hand. That kingdom is our future and is also inaugurated through the power of God's Spirit. Based on the life, death, and resurrection of Jesus and the Pentecostal experience, we are enabled to recognize that God's future is bright for us and the coming new creation is embodied by Christ.

Followers of Jesus are confident of God's culminating work for all people and are equipped with the Spirit to a daily empowerment for destiny-congruent experience and behavior. Our daily empowerment provides opportunity to live out practical, temporary hopes with resiliency, knowing that, while they may not all materialize, there is a sustaining, transcendent hope that is our most intimate experience.

This hope dynamic is circular, beginning with Jesus' inaugurated eschatology, providing hope that is transcendent, internalized by the Spirit, and creating daily movement in us as we live into God's coming future.

The Difference It Makes Today

I believe it's helpful to develop many different attractive and inspiring images of the new creation. We can start with virtually any area of our life where we see the good and the beautiful, those things we experience to be life-giving. Perhaps it's our family or intentional community relationships, or our meaningful accomplishments, or the experience of nature's grandeur, or deep experiences of calm and peace. Multiple examples in these areas and others can be coupled with the glorious majesty of the One who gives us life. Listing these images of God's future and reviewing them regularly helps us live with general hopeful anticipation.

An example of mine is the joyous experience of regularly attending the Washington State Fair in my hometown of Puyallup. When my daughters were young, we attended the fair a few times each year. When they were in grade school, we pulled them out of class one day each year to enjoy the fair's midway and its celebrative, exuberant environment. Together, we spent all day eating fair food and enjoying the many rides. It became a profound and

---

20. Morse, *Difference Heaven Makes*, 121–22.

inspiring image for my daughters to picture their future with God as including a giant fair where all the rides are free, all food is shared, all games and gadgets available, and all their friends join in their fun.

Our future transcendent hope is only beneficial if it creates ways for us to experience each moment more fully. Meeting proximate hopes is important if they shape us to be part of God's future with Christ. With this vision of the new creation, we may ask people in states of despair or hopelessness questions that focus on what is coming: Have you thought about a meaningful future, full of possibilities? What kind of a future have you always wanted to live? What is the work you need hope to do for you? What would be different if you carried hope all day long? Can you appreciate the pain and limitations of the present, while knowing that God is already working in us to anticipate a better future? May it be that you have yet to know yourself or others fully, but will?

I often asked individuals who were currently experiencing the depths of despair to write themselves a letter from God's future. I asked them what sort of advice they would give themselves today from a future that is full and complete. "If you were living your way into God's future, what would you be doing or thinking at this very moment?" This concept is powerful, because it prompts people to think about their despair from a perspective that is not their customary big picture. In fact, their transcendent "big picture" only exists in God's future, and it includes whole personhood in community (this is elaborated in section 2, chapters 8–14).

I also asked those same people: Since Jesus experienced the depths of darkness, the bottom of the bottom, do you have confidence to face your darkness in hope? Can you recognize that hope is not simply accomplishing a goal, but also aiming toward it? Can you picture that any life-giving temporary hope you accomplish today may be a feature of God's new heaven and earth? Can you pay attention to what is hidden as much as what is present in your circumstance? Could God be more at work in the darkness than in the light? This is the true logic of hope: letting go may be gain, pain may lead to healing, adversity may lead to resiliency, death will lead to life.

We are provided two assurances from God. First, no matter what our past, we can be forgiven and are loved unconditionally. Second, God will be with us in life and death. All other expectations risk false hope.

What does it take to live into these assurances, to experience the change and growth that comes individually and in our relationships when our transcendental hope opens up our ability to experience each moment more fully? In the next section we will explore human personhood, both individually and collectively, as *soul*, to see how hope grows in every dimension of our lives. Our soul is relational and dynamic: fashioned from the dust of the earth and stars, brought to life by the breath of God. We are called to become caretakers together with God, stewards of soul in ourselves, in our communities, in all of human life. Growing into hope is an active process. There are things we can *do*, gladly and gratefully, to live into God's future already coming to us in Christ.

—— Section Two ——

Hope Transforms Human Personhood and Community

5

A New Way of Being

> "The human problem is not to be who we are, but to begin being who we shall be, to be re-oriented beyond our present reality toward the God who is to come, who makes all things new, who forgives the sinner and raises the dead."
>
> —Rodney J. Hunter

ONE OF THE MOST startling discoveries we have as humans is the experience of our unique existence. *We are aware that we are.* This capacity for self-reflection and our desire to be uniquely ourselves was and is created by a Designer who has the capacity to call all of who we are and all of what we experience into being. We are built for relationship—with God, with ourselves, with others, and with the world.

From the beginning of time, as we read in the book of Genesis, we learn that the Designer has put ingredients in place for relationships to thrive, for life to abound. Humans are given the freedom and responsibility to practice dynamic relationships with God, themselves, and others in such a way that life will be hopeful and flourish.

Relationship with God

The biblical narrative tells of a God who literally loves us into being and delights in having a relationship with all creation. The Creator shares a relationship with each person in a unique fashion, such that we have a resulting desire to know and be known, to love and be loved, and to walk together as an essential feature of our experience. We are continually invited into a divine relationship that is life-giving and life-enhancing in every respect.

Jesus taught that that we are loved unconditionally (see, for instance, Luke 15:11–32), that all we are is to be cherished. Nothing more delights our Designer than flourishing individual relationships and community.

Our initial ability to know ourselves comes in many respects through the history of how we have been treated, the messages that we have received, and the attitudes that have been shown toward us. There is a kind of dialectic that exists between our experience of ourselves and our experience of others. As we encounter ourselves, we are encountered. As we think about ourselves, we are thought of. We are acting and being acted upon. Our capacity to hope is about our evolving relationships to others and the earth. This relational experience determines much of how we feel about ourselves and about others.

We can conceive of ourselves, others, and our Creator as a relational enterprise that provides the basics of meaningful and purposeful life. If we are called into being with intention, rather than presuming that all we are and see is random and accidental, then our most primary relationship will involve our Creator. We know ourselves in the best sense when we know the Designer of who we are. It's easier to be intentional in our relationship with ourselves and others if we know the intentionality of our design.

As we reflect on our existence, we find we exist in a web of life so intricate, beautiful, and comprehensive that we never get tired of our encounters with creation. All of life surrounding us is part of us, displaying wonder and sacredness. We require a life-giving environment, and we engage our environment with every breath we take. Our health is tied to earth's water, soil, air, vegetation, and animals. We act on our environment and are acted upon by our environment. Like our inner selves, each part of our environment has a unique place and is immediately interacting with all the other parts. Our earth creates all the potential for us and others to live and reflects design and beauty for all who can perceive it.

Hope as a way of life allows us to focus on what is most important in life: first, simply to respond, receive, invest, and share the gift of life in all its dimensions. And second, to cultivate these relationships on a regular basis.

Relationship with Ourselves

Our "self" is a gift from God to us; our Creator brings us into being and entrusts us with the stewardship of our personhood. To be a steward is to be caring, supportive, responsible, and understanding, much like we would be with a very dear friend. We want to know our innermost selves and we want to develop our life because our Creator has said that this person is sacred and that life is a treasure.

We all want surprisingly similar things: to feel well, enjoy who we are, like ourselves and be liked, feel at peace with who we are, and be able to take care of ourselves or others. Although our relationship with ourselves is a critical dimension of our experience, it is often neglected in American culture. This may seem a strange thing to say, because we all want to think that we know ourselves better than anyone else. But most of us are not focused primarily on our own internal experience. Rather, we look outward for our main stimulation in life—to vocational or financial success, to what kinds of relationships we have with others that give us validation and social status, on intimate relationships we expect to meet our deepest needs and give us a sense of purpose and meaning.

We will live with ourselves for the rest of our lives as the most primary experience and relationship that we have. It is, in many ways, our most intimate encounter, yet very few of us are comfortable just being still with ourselves without some kind of external stimulation. When we get home, we flip through channels on the TV or the latest releases on Netflix. We scroll through the latest news or messages on our phones when we can't sleep at night. Having an external focus can be an escape from the self rather than honestly facing who we are on the inside.

When we are still and quiet, it may feel strange just to *be* as opposed to *do*. And it can produce anxiety—what if we feel flat and dead inside? What if uncomfortable thoughts or feelings surface within us that are too difficult to endure?

Most people want to feel a sense of serenity or peace. But they look in all the wrong places to achieve that. True peace, or shalom, is achieved, in part, when we relax and accept and value ourselves.[1] Here is a way of encountering and perceiving ourselves that has been helpful for myself and others:

I begin by considering this verse, Psalm 46:10: "Pause a while and know that I am God."

I choose to collect myself for a few minutes in a state of acceptance and grace. I am in a "being" state instead of a "doing" state. Knowing my hunger and spiritual yearning, it is God's presence that I relax into. I want to connect with my core self and the life in me. All my inner parts,

---

1. For further discussion of shalom, see Yoder, *Shalom*.

past and present, can be held with compassion. I imagine myself slowly descending a mountain, or going down into the water, as in a deep pool, to help reach the center of myself.

I sit straight and relaxed, close my eyes, and become attentive to my breathing. I notice the space between each of my breaths. After a few moments, when I exhale, I silently count "one"; I continue counting with each exhale, "two, three, four . . ." When I become aware that my mind is wandering from breath counting, I gently reattend to my breathing. I do not try to keep away thoughts, feelings, or images, only to be alert and focused on my breathing. I do breaths counting to twenty.

All thoughts, feelings, noise, images, or movements are welcomed and accepted. I recognize I do not have complete control over what comes into my mind, and I allow myself to be distracted, returning to engaging myself and resting in God's grace. When difficult emotions emerge, I accept them without panic. I allow waves of emotion to pass over and through me, no matter how painful.

In encountering my own imperfections and strangeness, I don't attempt to understand or fix them. This is an encounter with my own depth, my true self, the essence within, my spiritual core. There is a connection between mind and body, intellect and feeling, belief and action. Knowing now comes by inner experience. As I sit with my inner self, my external false self becomes more apparent. I simply accept it and allow it to be.

I descend into my spiritual center and seek my inner world. All attachments that gratify my ego, whether titles, learning, gifts, accomplishments, charity, intellect, or imagination, are let go. Underneath and beyond my immediate thoughts and feelings is the Spirit of God. I choose not to comprehend God and simply let God be. Openness to my own inner self brings a participation in God's holy presence. I look for new ways of experiencing and knowing myself in God.

In the reception room of the Spirit, there is a purer awareness and attunement, a place of security and oneness, a unity with all life in the creation, an openness to surprise and change, a willingness to let things be and let things go, a freedom from attachments and addictions, a desire to receive love and to love, a sense of inner spaciousness and wonder.

I do not strive for an inner sensation but simply practice being centered and allow my true self to slowly emerge in the presence of God. I commit to embracing all of myself—without control or manipulation or expectation—as God embraces me.

Peace is allowing myself to be in this state of grace. In rest, I remember that I am a human being, I am a human doing, allowing me to accept God's love in my past and my present, in mystery and complexity. Best of all, this intimate, internal experience can continue and develop indefinitely. Someday, this is how I want to die—in a state of peace and acceptance, simply enjoying God's loving presence and delight.

Relationship with Others

Our relationship with ourselves cannot and does not exist without others. From the moment that we know we exist, we also perceive our relationship with others. Others bring us into this life and nurture us along the way. People relate to us in ways that tell us who we are and how we are.

Our relationship to others is similar to our relationship with God and with ourselves in that it requires intentional practice. Without regular investment internally, time spent together, careful loving conversation, and understanding, this relationship will not grow and the inner emotional benefits will not develop. In a growing friendship with our innermost selves, we enjoy getting together as best friends. Honest conversations about personal and even intimate subjects may occur. In a relaxed and graceful manner, we are free to be our true selves without judgment, demand, or self-blame.

It is important that we recognize the intrinsic dialectic between our inside and our outside, being and doing, action and reflection. To embrace our inner selves as God does, to bring together the many different parts of who we are, to support, affirm, and protect ourselves in all our parts, allows us to intimately know ourselves. Our rich inner world can then be shared with others in meaningful ways. We have much more to work with in relationships with others if we know and use the strengths of our own thoughts, images, feelings, sensations, personality, character, history, and spiritual life. If we know how to nurture ourselves and recognize our capabilities, and we are closer to ourselves than others, we are free to be ourselves and to let others be themselves. We will move to deeply respect who we are and ask that others respect us as we respect them.

Becoming more sensitive to our inner world allows us to become more empathetic toward the inner worlds of others. Respecting the great gift and treasure that our life is means we will not ask other people to love us better than we love ourselves. Instead, we hope others will love us as we love ourselves and we will love others as we love ourselves. Durable hope can begin and be maintained on the inside.

Healing from Difficult Relationships

What do we do with memories that are deeply wounding, emotions we don't know what to do with, people from our past we can't engage with? Perhaps we have spent much of our life avoiding neglectful and painful people, memories, and disturbing associations from the past. It is often tempting to use drugs or alcohol and drift into addictive or compulsive behavior in order to distract from or avoid inner emotional distress.

In healthy families, children who experience hurt are given support and encouragement to express how they feel, to describe their emotional or physical pain. Their caregivers embrace them, listen, empathize, reassure, and help them develop strategies to better understand what happened and what can be done to avoid that pain in the future. The experience of this love, devotion, support, affirmation, and protection empowers them to face the prior hurtful situation with more self-respect and confidence.

Internal healing work (e.g., inner-child therapy, trauma processing, family-of-origin work, and many other modalities) can open up possibilities for us to create hopeful, healing experiences with our difficult memories and resulting emotions as we learn to become more accepting of our inner struggles and more at peace with how we respond to our past. Our bond with God and with ourselves can provide a steady sense of emotional sufficiency even when others are mistreating us. Because we radically accept ourselves and are close with who we are, we have the capacity to love others when they don't love us. Since we can be at peace and don't need others to make us happy, we may engage others with a freedom that is self-directed and nonreactive without losing ourselves. This, in turn, encourages the people we interact with to take more responsibility for themselves and their relationships.

Hope from the Inside Out and the Outside In

Hope gains strength and durability in this inner space of calm harmony in our relationships with God, self, and others. Hope both creates desire for inner peace and is itself nurtured by inner peace. Hopeful people can live from the inside out.

This inner strength enables us to look outward at the world and see it not through despair and fear, but through the expectation of what God is doing, and how we are in relationship to that redeeming work of God. The hope rising from our inner life meets the hope coming to us from beyond ourselves, giving us a new way of being—grounded in God's future, coming to us now in the present.

Because our hope in Jesus begins with the future and works back to the present, it is a catalyst for action. Theologian Ted Peters writes:

> God will not fail. God has the power of resurrection. The burden of our errors and evils, although heavy, will not last forever. The good news of the Christian evangel is that sin is met by forgiveness, that hurt is met by healing, that death is met by new creation. The new humanity and new ecology for which we yearn will not ultimately be stillborn. Our visions are not vain illusions. Our praxis is not without meaning. The new world will finally come. It will come with God's power.[2]

One of the beauties of Christian hope is that it incorporates a dynamic interplay between the absolute unconditional reality of God's coming with very realistic and practical steps that activate hope in the present. We know that evil triumphs when good people fail to act. If we are not engaging in hopeful action, however small, we will not become hopeful people.

Hope is not a passive wish-list for what others can bring about. It necessarily involves stepping forward, being active participants in bringing about what we hope for. We engage the world strategically with proximate practical hopes, having ultimate confidence and security in God's transcendent ultimate hope.

We owe it to each other, and we owe it to those we advocate for, to cultivate hope. It is infectious. Hope inspires even without words. We cannot be healthy, either individually or collectively, without hope, because it creates the motivation to take the next step forward no matter our circumstance. This requires our willingness to be patient and steadfast through despair while remaining open to emerging possibilities. We can remind ourselves that there is always a way, starting on the inside, to picture things constructively and take some small step forward (some days this might mean just getting out of bed). Then we can celebrate! Even the smallest achievements can create forward momentum.

---

2. Peters, *God*, 376.

SECTION TWO: HOPE TRANSFORMS HUMAN PERSONHOOD AND COMMUNITY

We tend to overlook our personal strengths and the capabilities we have to work with at any given point. Our greatest asset is our attitude, our hopeful perspective. I like to envision how this asset is present in what I consider our six dimensions of human personhood—mind, body, emotions, personality, character, and spirit:

- Our *mind* is able to entertain new, accurate, and hopeful thoughts. It facilitates our memory, is a reservoir of information and experience, and can help us project forward. Our capacity to learn is a fundamental mental asset.
- Our *body*, with its mobility and sensual apparatus, even in our pain, is life-giving and incredibly functions for us as we move through each day.
- Our *emotions*, even the difficult ones, give our life depth and insight, enhancing our experience. We can remember pleasant emotional times and the fluctuations or patterns of our feelings. Emotional sensitivity, soothing, and empathy are strengths.
- Our *personality* gives us the ability to communicate with others and use our social skills effectively. We can remember how it has helped us navigate many prior circumstances.
- Our *character* embodies the values and convictions that are important and can guide us each day. Some of these values are so substantial that we may actually be willing to sacrifice for them.
- Our *spirit* facilitates finding meaning and purpose in any moment, any activity. It keeps us mindful of ultimate concerns.

What ultimately saves us from despair and encourages active hope is an internal locus of control, living from the inside out, where our hope is anchored. Contemplative theologian Thomas Merton wrote, "Do not depend on the hope of results . . . You may have to face the fact that your work will be apparently worthless and even achieve no result at all, if not perhaps results opposite to what you expect. As you get used to this idea, you start more and more to concentrate not on the results, but on the value, the rightness, the truth of the work itself."[3]

And when we are living from the outside in, we notice the contrast between what is promised by God for the coming new heavens and new

---

3. Quoted in Forest, "Thomas Merton's Struggle," 27.

earth, and what is real today. If in God's future there is no more war, then why have war now? If in God's future the hungry will be fed and the poor provided just opportunity, then it is imperative that we now care for the hungry and practice solidarity with those who struggle in poverty and loss. If God's future involves the lion lying down with the lamb, then we should all be moved today toward harmony with and care for all of nature. This tension between reality and redemption is an important catalyst for taking steps of hope forward into God's future.

I have slightly adapted Ted Peters's picture of God's redeemed, new humanity that we can point toward:

- God will bring about a humanity capable of a single collaborative planetary perspective.
- All will be united in devotion to God's will.
- It will be sustainable within the biological carrying capacity of the planet and harmonized with the principles of the ecosphere.
- It will be organized socially so that people's dignity and freedom are respected and protected.
- It will be organized politically to preserve the just rights and voluntary contributions of all people.
- It will be organized economically so that the basic survival needs of each person are guaranteed.
- It is dedicated to advancing the quality of life on behalf of all generations to come.[4]

We are reminded that the *who* of the kingdom of God is us, and the *what* of the kingdom of God is what we do. There is one new heaven and earth for all people and all of nature to share.

In this intergenerational community that is coming with God, we are mindful that we have not only inherited the earth from our ancestors but are borrowing it from our children.[5] When we picture God's kingdom, each person is an end and not simply a means. People experience their sacredness or dignity through being respected, honored, loved, or served. Dignity itself is dependent on the web of interconnectedness that eventually will

---

4. Peters, *God*, 366.
5. Peters, *God*, 370.

unite all things. The biosphere has dignity because of God's promise that someday the lion will lie down with the lamb rather than devour it.[6]

To live and work in anticipation of this coming reality inspires and conditions followers of Jesus as representatives of humanity's future. With our continuing impulse for change, we are preparing ourselves and the world for something more, something new. Our labor is not in vain.

The good we do in the present—by painting, preaching, singing, sewing, praying, serving, teaching, building hospitals, cleaning, digging wells, planting crops, campaigning for justice, writing poems, caring for the needy, loving our neighbors as ourselves, forming community—will last into God's future.

Soul Work

Our body, emotions, mind, spirit, personality, and character each play an essential role in how we function. While I list them as individual parts, they actually exist in symbiosis and mutually benefit our life experience. Their interplay forms a gestalt, a totality greater than the sum of its parts that establishes our identity as people. Together I designate them as *soul*. While the person can be designated as soul, so too can the person in a covenant community. Our humanity and hope are both individual and communal. We are called by God to be stewards of ourselves, our communities, and all life. In this process, we take initiative and responsibility to maintain a covenantal relationship, entrusting ourselves together to our Creator in a bond of faithfulness with one another as we agree to journey together with the Lord.

The following chapters address "soul work"—that is, how we can cultivate hope in body, mind, and spirit. Our choice to engage in this work is individual, but we do it in partnership with one another, deeply embedded in, with, and for our common life.

---

6. Peters, *God*, 373.

6

Soul Work: Hopeful Body

"Brain researchers now believe that what happens in the body can affect the brain, and what happens in the brain can affect the body. Hope, purpose, and determination are not merely mental states. They have electrochemical connections that play a large part in the workings of the immune system and, indeed, in the entire economy of the total human organism. In short, I learned that it is not unscientific to talk about a biology of hope."

—Norman Cousins

WHAT DOES HOPE—WHICH HAS much to do with our overall perspective—have to do with our physical body? Quite a bit, as it turns out. Hope is undeniably good for our physical well-being, and a number of studies have illustrated the relationship between hope and healthier bodies. Hopeful people are more physically active, eat more nutritious food, deal more effectively with stress, maintain fewer bad habits such as smoking, can better tolerate pain, more readily accept their body image, and often live longer.[1]

People who are in a state of despair or hopelessness, on the other hand, typically become distant—or even alienated—from their body, their physical self. When we operate without hope, we can step out of rhythm with our body's needs and signals, including appetite and sleep. We may eat too much or sleep too much, or, on the opposite end of the spectrum, end up undernourished and sleep-deprived. We can become more critical of our body, blame it for our despair, and find it difficult to invest in physical life-sustaining activities.

---

1. See Lopez, *Making Hope Happen*, 58–60.

Our body may become a chore for us to take care of. Worse yet, it may be a source of increasing discomfort. We may have a hard time appreciating what it does and wish that it were somehow different: an extra inch to reach the top shelf, a couple inches less around the waist to squeeze into the suit at the back of our closets, the strength to pull ourselves out of bed in the morning. We may actually be afraid of our own body, particularly about its aging and illness. If we are disfigured or have a serious disease, we may be inclined to avoid even looking at our body. Fear can cause us to be hypervigilant about what is wrong or could be wrong with our physical selves. We may lose the desire to care for our bodies as we lose the desire to care for ourselves in general. When we are alienated from our bodies in any of these ways, we also may be alienated from other parts of ourselves.

Accepting Our Imperfect Bodies

Oftentimes, when we are alienated from our bodies, we will look to external opportunities to find pleasure or comfort, including entertainment, social media, work, money, exercise, food, sex, and drugs. We may try forcing our bodies to be different than they actually are in order to fit with some external criteria of success. Without a fundamental appreciation and loving of our physical selves, we carry an inner restlessness, a sense of conflict with our own body.

Living in a culture where media-savvy corporations make billions of dollars in profit by telling us that our bodies are not good enough simply compounds the problem. It makes acceptance of our physical selves challenging in many ways. Accepting ourselves and loving our bodies may feel like something we shouldn't be doing at all!

We may feel like we need to look like people on the magazine covers at the local grocery store checkout stand. We are told we need to lose weight, tone up, buy different cosmetics, and wear different clothes. We are sold multiple (and often conflicting) weight-loss products and strategies. We are encouraged to join a gym. We are given examples of plastic surgery that will allegedly make us look more youthful and attractive. Photos everywhere—on magazine covers, social media, and advertisements—are presented in such a way that makes us think something is wrong with our bodies. It's very difficult to look at ourselves in the mirror and not immediately find our flaws. Extra weight, stretch marks, scars, wrinkles, and blemishes make us feel less adequate. This is simply unrealistic and untrue.

Our cultural understanding of dating is particularly difficult for people who do not accept their bodies. When we meet someone on a date, what do we see? What physical features of the other person are attractive or not? What does that other person think about our body? Since dating or socializing is about putting our best foot forward and doing impression management, we may carry significant anxiety about our physical appearance. Online dating networks encourage a focus on profile pictures, and we often make a decision about whether to even consider dating someone based on their physical appearance. These preferences extend to friendship, too: it can be very difficult to develop a relationship and know a person behind their physical selves if they do not match our cultural stereotypes of outward beauty.

Unfortunately, most of us engage in relationships and social or professional circles in which our identity is often based on our outward appearance. It is, after all, the first part of us that people observe. Because of this, we are more likely, then, to focus on, critique, or blame our body when it's not working or looking the way we perceive others would accept.

As we read in Jessica's story (chapter 2), getting sick or becoming disfigured in an accident can be challenging for people who have put considerable value on a certain physical image. It can seem to be our body's fault when we have cancer or some other threatening or debilitating disease. Is our body against us or defective? After all, if our body was truly our friend, wouldn't it keep us from disease or death? It's easy to degrade our body for aging and for any progressive physical deterioration we experience.

The fact is, our bodies are remarkable creations, and most of us tend to take them for granted. Our physical selves are life-giving in function and help us navigate each day. Very rarely do we acknowledge and thank our body for what it actually does.

Human bodies can be a source of great division and conflict in our world. Throughout history, weight, height, age, and racial appearance, among other factors, have acted as indicators of status and acceptability. Racial division and injustice have fueled hostility, hate, and violent conflicts. Black, indigenous, and people of color (BIPOC) know the awful reality of white supremacy in the United States and around the world. BIPOC are disproportionately impacted by hunger, poverty, homelessness, infectious diseases, disasters, nationalism, and climate change. It may be that the more different a person looks from us, the more difficulty we will have relating to the person beyond their physical appearance.

During our early years, we simply wore our bodies. Our skin was our primary sensory organ, and, as infants, we felt what our body felt, and knew what our body knew. As we developed, the construction of our self-image moved from *being* our body to *having* a body. Our body became an instrument to be used for our personal advancement. We learned to fashion our physical selves so as to fit culturally derived norms for attractiveness or performance. To feel good about ourselves, our bodies became an appearance project. We developed from a primary experience of living with our physical selves to the experience of having separate bodies, viewed and evaluated by others.

With this shift, we unconsciously constructed a "body image" based on our feelings or perceptions about our body's appearance, its sensations, and the feelings or perceptions of others. We learned to evaluate our body based on its external presentation, or how we look, and its utilitarian value, what it does. Our identity became, quite literally, fused to our body.

Until we can accept and embrace our bodies, it will be more difficult for us to operate confidently with a more secure physical foundation.

Our Bodies Connect Us to the Earth and One Another

Though the Bible is not interested in giving a detailed anthropology of our personhood, it does describe our human relationship with God, one another, and the creation. We are embedded in God's physical creation, and our physical life is connected to the earth and its life-giving dynamics. There is no existence that does not involve our body and the earth. A recent lecturer has reminded us that, "Nature is not something to look at, but something in which we dwell. In fact, we are that part of the Earth that is conscious of itself." He continued, "Humans depend for their existence upon a nested hierarchy of systems, from the smallest atom to the largest galaxies, the simplest creatures to the most complex life forms."[2]

We cannot physically exist without water, air, plants, animals, and other humans. We are complex, interactive persons with brains that are formed through a kaleidoscope of daily experiences. Though genes contribute a rough blueprint of brain wiring, the rest of our development is based on continued feedback from our own interaction in the world. The growth of our intelligence, personality, and character, while influenced to

---

2. Heard at a lecture on February 22, 2019 (Morris, "Therapeutic Approaches to Extinction Anxiety").

some degree by our genetics, mostly takes place through complex interactions with our environment. Exploration, give-and-take, and trial and error with our physical world and social milieu fundamentally impact us at the level of our neurons, particularly when we are young.[3]

Our bodies impact the world in varieties of regular encounters. In our capitalistic society, we are tempted to engage our natural environment as though we have ultimate control and an unlimited right to extraction and consumption. Our physical appetites may lead to unwarranted attempts at disproportionately accumulating the world's resources and have contributed significantly to our current carbon-induced ecological crisis. It is important for us to recognize that our bodies belong to the same world as plants and animals and are just as dependent as they are on the natural environment. Our physical embeddedness in the natural environment should lead us to be more accepting and less consumptive, with a reverence toward nature.

Christians believe that our physical self is a gift from God and should be cherished. In the early creation story, God breathed the breath of life, *ruach*, into people and all creation: "God fashioned Adam of dust from the soil. Then he breathed into his nostrils the breath of life, and Adam became a living being."[4] Originally, "Adam" meant human or earthling, a creature of God's earth.

The *ruach*, or breath of life, is the life force of God's presence. "By the word of the Lord the heavens were made, and all their host by the breath of his mouth."[5] Through the Spirit, God is in all things and all things are in God. True spirituality involves the restoration of love for all of life. God's Spirit is present everywhere sustaining, nourishing, and revitalizing every living thing, including our bodies.[6]

Since people have been animated with the *ruach*, human bodies are connected to both heaven and earth. Our creation includes both God's life-giving Spirit and our physical selves.

The Christian Scripture also tells us that our body reflects God's image, which suggests that we are connected to God, created for relationship with God, called to represent God, and designed to be accountable to God.

---

3. For a deeper analysis, consult Brown and Strawn, *Physical Nature*, 51–70.
4. Gen 2:7.
5. Ps 33:6.
6. Moltmann, *Source of Life*, 117.

God's image is also communal, reflecting God's Trinitarian being. We are intrinsically social and function best in healthy relationships.

The fact that our physical body is created in the image of a loving God also speaks to the fundamental sacredness of human life. Our bodies and our lives are not our own but are authored by and ultimately sustained by God. The apostle Paul reminds us, "Do you not know that your bodies are members of Christ himself?"[7] God entrusts us with our bodies, and we are charged to be stewards of our Creator's gift.

Christians believe that Jesus, living with a human body, showed us how to physically navigate our life.[8] As God in human form, Jesus experienced the same bodily sensations, feelings, and thoughts that we do. He had to eat, clean, sleep, eliminate, clothe himself, manage his hair, handle his sexual desires and erections, deal with sickness and physical injury, and generally pay reasonable attention to his physical appearance.

Jesus made daily decisions about his physical self and took care of his body until his crucifixion. On the cross, Jesus endured pain and suffering, demonstrating his willingness and his Father's willingness to share our physical illnesses. The resurrected Jesus, with physical scars from an imperial slaughter, shows us God's commitment to human flesh and blood.

Jesus' crucifixion and resurrection saves and heals our bodies as well as the other dimensions of ourselves. Our physical selves are eternally significant. When we follow Jesus, we make our body parts available to God as servants of righteousness. God invites us to receive our body on a daily basis, take care of it, and use it for good.[9] Neither random nor accidental, our bodies have a natural beauty and are intentionally designed. Though there is no perfect body, and we are each flawed to some degree from our history of human faithlessness and destructiveness, our physical selves yet remain amazingly designed—true works of art and awe. We all should be hopeful in how we picture, use, and treat our physical body.

Compassion for Our Physical Selves

We can actually enjoy a friendship with our bodies. After all, we have a 24/7 intimate relationship with our physical selves. Each part of our body constantly works with all the other parts to be life-giving and life-enhancing.

---

7. 1 Cor 6:15.
8. See, for example, Rom 8:11.
9. See, for example, Rom 6:19.

Instead of taking our bodies' efforts for granted, our discipleship should include maintaining tuned-up and fit bodies that function with energy and strength, enabling us to live healthy, hopeful lives.

How we treat our body also reflects our appreciation or gratitude to God. Do we give thanks for our body? Can we appreciate our senses? Can we present our physical selves to God daily as a living sacrifice?[10] Can we make sure our body is nourished each and every day with good food, restorative sleep, peaceful reflection and relaxation, aerobic exercise, and adequate stimulation, and that it is appropriately shared with others? Do we pay attention to its watershed location, food supply, interaction in the natural environment, encounters with pollutants, etc.? We know that our bodies function best when they experience a daily rhythm, from significant activation to quiet relaxation. If we believe that our bodies are a gift intended with purpose and design, then we can make a lifelong compassionate commitment to our physical selves as part of our following Jesus.

Our imperfect bodies deserve our compassion and gratitude. It's been particularly helpful for me to recognize that my body functions best with cancer if I value it the same way I would treat it if I didn't have the disease or was cured. If anything, my body needs more appreciation and care when it is sick or injured.

With that in mind, we should step outside of our culture's often misguided perception of what makes a body beautiful or lovable and ask instead if we can find natural beauty when we look at ourselves. Since our body is a reflection of God's beauty, there are multiple ways we can help ourselves gain this appreciation.

As our bodies are embedded in creation, the natural environment, it can be helpful to be more attentive to our physical world. We can explore nature and seek out an old-growth forest, meadow, or another area relatively untouched by humans where we can walk, hike, or bike. In this place, we can find life-giving splendor everywhere we look. There is something fascinating about looking at an entirely natural setting. The trees, the ground cover, the plants and animals, the many colors, and the fragrances and sounds generate a feeling of aliveness throughout our bodies. This natural state captures our wonder and awe. It is a sanctuary of God's presence, teeming with life.

As we take in the beauty of a forest or meadow, we should closely examine the many varieties of foliage, flowers, insects, animals, trees, and

---

10. See, for example, Rom 12:1.

ground cover that together make up such a life-giving ecosphere. Upon closer inspection, we might find that every aspect of life in a forest has flaws, disfigurations, lack of symmetry, and is part of a birthing, developing, aging, and dying process. The flaws we observe do not diminish the natural beauty of God's earth.

Then, we can take that appreciation for God's creation home with us. When we stand in front of our mirror, bathing, showering, dressing ourselves, or getting ready for bed, what do we see? Do we find the natural beauty that is part of God's design in us every bit as much as God's design in the natural, old-growth forest or meadow? Do we carry any less beauty, as a part of nature, than the plants and animals? Do our flaws or disfigurations compromise our ability to view and revere the beauty of our own body in its life-giving state?

Another helpful opportunity to appreciate our bodies is simply observing them in involuntary action. Our heart is beating, lungs oxygenating, blood circulating, muscles moving, and brain working without any of our own prompting: with no conscious effort, our bodies give us life throughout the day.

A useful personal exercise is to stand naked before a mirror and look at each visible body part, from head to toe. Can we find in each of our body parts what is life-giving? Can we determine how each body part equips us to live each day? Is there a natural beauty about how all the parts of our body work together so that we may exude vitality, animation, and movement? Rather than stopping at a skin-deep analysis, viewing our body functionally moves us to value how it works in so many amazing ways every day.

A challenging opportunity is to look in the mirror at the body parts that function for us 24/7, including hair, eyes, nose, ears, hands, mouth, neck, arms, stomach, genitals, legs, and feet, among others, and identify two affirmations for each of these. To grow gratitude for our body, we can uncover its many assets empowering us to walk through our days.

If we have difficulty appreciating or affirming our body when we look in the mirror, we can imagine that Jesus Christ stands next to us. Ask him to help us look at our body the way he does. What might he tell us about us our body's design, intentionality, many parts, and potential for life and health? What might he tell us about how he has cared for his own physical self and how he dealt with the limitations of his own body? Perhaps interacting with Jesus—or others who know him—can help us receive our physical selves as a gift every day. I imagine he would remind us that our body, as a treasure of life, "the temple of the Holy Spirit," works for us as a dear friend.

Caring for Our Bodies

Once we appreciate how our body wants to work for us, we may decide how we are going to specifically take care of its parts each day. If our body were to speak to us now, what advice would it give us regarding its care for the day? How are we going to feed it, exercise it, rest it, keep it relaxed, give it necessary sleep, and stimulate it well? Can we make a commitment to our physical selves each day to invest in the care it needs to be well and do well? Since it does so much for us, we want to keep it fit and help it do its life-giving work.

Here are some considerations as we contemplate ways to help our body be well.

Relax. Our bodies ask us to live relaxed instead of stressed. When we relax, we have reduced muscular tension, reduced metabolism and oxygen consumption, slowed heart rate, lowered blood pressure, warmer skin temperature, and increased alpha brainwave activity. We suffer less migraine and tension headaches, hypertension, ulcers, chronic anxiety, and recover more readily from illness.

It's beneficial to set aside two to three times each day for meditation, prayer, and progressive muscle relaxation. Through progressive muscle relaxation, we recognize the sensation of muscular tension and learn to release tension by separately tensing and relaxing each of our sixteen major muscle groups for five seconds at a time. Relaxation can be enhanced with biofeedback, yoga exercises, and autogenic training.

Be attentive. We may set aside time each day to focus on our body. Often, when I lay in bed, my body can truly rest. I desire to be present to my body and its parts, holding each of them in a state of gratitude and appreciation. Each part of my body can be sensed merging with the bed, slumping, sagging, and sinking into grace. My body can feel heavy, floppy, and peaceful as I enjoy its many sensations in the moment.

Condition your brain. Autogenic training exercises can help us recover from anxiety, stress, and tension. People who practice autogenic training twice a day fall asleep better and sleep more deeply. They also think more clearly.

Find a quiet place where you feel comfortable. Repeat every phrase, silently and thoughtfully, three times. Each phrase will help you shift your focus to a different part of your body. Pause after each phrase and notice how you feel. Focus on your feelings for two or three breaths. Practice each set of exercises until you are familiar with them.

Set 1.

"I feel quite quiet. . . . I am easily relaxed. . . ."

"My right arm feels heavy and relaxed. . . . My left arm feels heavy and relaxed. . . . My arms feel heavy and relaxed and relaxed. . . ."

"My right leg feels heavy and relaxed. . . . My left leg feels heavy and relaxed. . . . My arms and legs feel heavy and relaxed and relaxed. . . ."

"My hips and stomach are quiet and relaxed. . . . My shoulders are heavy and relaxed and relaxed. . . ."

"My breathing is calm and regular. . . . My face is smooth and quiet. . . . I am beginning to feel quite relaxed. . . ."

Set 2.

"My right hand is warm. . . . My left hand is warm. . . . Warmth flows into my hands. . . . My hands are warm. . . ."

"My right foot is warm. . . . My left foot is warm. . . . My hands and feet are warm. . . . Warmth flows into my hands and feet. . . ."

"My eyes are comfortably warm and peaceful. . . . My forehead is soft and my eyes are warm. . . . I am warm and peaceful. . . ."

Set 3.

"I am beginning to feel quite relaxed. . . . I am learning to feel calm and confident. . . . I think about what I appreciate and I feel confident. . . ."

"I appreciate myself and others. . . . My life has many blessings I overlook. . . . I am beginning to see my own blessings. . . . I appreciate more and more. . . ."

Set 4.

"My breathing is calm and regular. . . . My heartbeat is calm and regular. . . . I am at peace. . . ."

"Sounds and sights around contribute to peace. . . . Peace goes with me throughout the day . . . There is nothing to bother and nothing to disturb. . . ."

Set 5.

"I am not required to think now. . . . I don't have to think now. . . . Thoughts are not important now. . . ."

"There is nothing to bother or disturb me now. . . . I am not interested in thinking now. . . . There is nothing to bother and nothing to disturb. . . ."

Whenever I feel particularly good, comfortable, or confident, I notice that feeling and welcome it. I'm grateful for prompting that relaxed feeling. I'll remember this experience because cultivating good physical feelings is like learning music: the more you practice, the more skilled you become.[11]

Use sensory stimulation. People who battle with despair and hopelessness may find it helpful to gain appreciation for their body by using sensory stimulation. The best forms of it for reflection and relaxation are unique to each person. For many, there's little better than soaking in a warm bubble bath with candles burning and music playing. Simply allowing our body to feel immersed in warm bathwater can be a very pleasant physical experience and contribute to our peacefulness. Other sensory stimulations for the body's pleasure include short walks, dancing, naps, or massages.

Reflect and re-evaluate. It's often difficult to appreciate our body when it is suffering or limited. When we find ourselves at odds with our body, we can reflect on what it has done for us in the past. We can reflect on all the experiences it has taken us through. How many times has it navigated strenuous activities or projects? How many times has it allowed us to travel? How many times has it been able to play, individually or with others? How many times has it labored to produce needed items and support our livelihood? To conceive and birth our children?

---

11. Johnson, "Happiness," 51.

Get moving. Our bodies are able to respond and develop strength if exercised appropriately. For instance, we can set certain appropriate physical goals for ourselves, just like I did in preparation for climbing Mount Rainier (chapter 7). Since I—like most—was not a professional mountaineer, I had to develop a training timeline and involve others in my training, both as coaches and cheerleaders. Even if your mountain is metaphorical (strenuous hiking, a ten-minute mile, a 100-mile bike ride, or a 3,000-yard swim), you can and should still develop a plan to meet your goal. The goal is reachable provided we have a pathway of carefully laid-out steps that slowly build our strength and endurance. It is very rewarding to watch ourselves gain strength and energy.

Physical fitness isn't just for the young. We know that ninety-year-old nursing home residents can be involved in an appropriate exercise program perhaps three days a week. Led by an experienced geriatric trainer, residents often discover, after three months of regular activity, that their strength has noticeably increased, their energy improved, their relationships have become more engaging, and they have grown into more alive and hopeful people.

Our bodies are remarkable organisms, yet many people take better care of their cars than they do their own bodies. Just as our vehicles need regular tune-ups, fueling, and care, our amazing bodies deserve respect, reverence, and compassionate care. We do exist in a 24/7 intimate companionship with our physical selves.

When we accept and invest in our bodies, we become more positive and hopeful in general. Bodies that are loved and fit give us more potential to cultivate life, share it with others, and contribute to our community and earthly home.

Let's move from perceiving hopeful bodies to experiencing hopeful emotions.

7

Soul Work: Hopeful Emotions

"We are held safely in the hands of a God who knows better
how we shall live toward wholeness, well-being, and joy."

—Walter Brueggemann

WE ARE ALL EMOTIONAL people. When we think about and describe our life experience, we typically state how we *feel* about our life concerns: a good day, an exciting moment, a meaningful conversation. For our general purposes, "emotions" and "feelings" will both be synonymously describing our felt experiences. Emotions and feelings are central to our lives. Without emotion, life would feel dead, flat, and black and white. Can you imagine going through a day without feeling anything?

Our emotions are composed of sensory, motor, autonomic, and mental components. As a basic part of our personhood, our emotions are always active and tell us much about ourselves and what we consider to be important. It's wise that we discover our emotions as friends and guides, telling us how we are and what we need. We all hunger for emotional connection and fear isolation or abandonment. Our worst fears and our deepest desires are developed in response to our feelings in relationships with other people and ourselves. Specifically, emotions impact our communication with others, the manner and content of our memories, our performance, and our choices. Emotions are communal as well as individual.

Emotions provide us with important information that shapes our response to various stimuli. We often describe our emotional sensitivity when we experience intensity and stress. We may sense that the hair is standing up on the back of our neck, chills are running up and down our spine, or our heart is skipping a beat.

SECTION TWO: HOPE TRANSFORMS HUMAN PERSONHOOD AND COMMUNITY

In combination with our inner dialogue and perception, emotions can, in a variety of circumstances, be accurate or inaccurate, too sensitive or not sensitive enough. They may occur with little or no evaluation, emerge spontaneously, and often require little mental effort. Our unreasonableness at times suggests that emotions can be irrational. Feelings can be immensely enjoyable or terribly painful, acutely intense or very mild. Emotions may reveal truths about ourselves and our beliefs. They can help us understand where change may be necessary and whether or not we are resolving our conflicts or making good decisions. Emotions enliven our memories and bring us a deeper sense of connection with the past as well as the present.

Emotions can be thought of as polarities of experience in which different emotions represent opposite ends of a continuum: from hate to love, sadness to joy, shame to grace, fear to hope. We all have identifiable primary emotional or feeling states, including anger, hurt, sadness, joy or happiness, guilt or shame, anxiety, love, and peace. Each of these feeling states is related to our thoughts. Though distinct, we cannot entirely separate thoughts and feelings, as they are interconnected and interdependent. Thoughts have great impact on feelings and feelings have great impact on thoughts. It's easy to confuse thoughts and feelings. When we say, "I feel that," we are talking about thoughts. When we say "I feel," and we name a particular feeling, we are directly expressing emotion.

Positive emotions, according to Barbara Fredrickson and others, tend to contribute to thinking that is more creative, inclusive, flexible, and integrated. They tend to broaden our attention and action so that we can find more positive interpretations of difficult situations. Positive emotions may increase our attentiveness, socializing, and physical activity.

God is emotionally sensitive and wants us to experience enjoyable emotions such as love, joy, gentleness, calm, and hope.[1] Our moral choices need to be both reasonable and emotionally sensitive.

Some emotions are reflexive and hardwired. Infants, long before they develop mental capabilities, can demonstrate a number of states of feeling, such as sadness, anger, fear, hurt, calm, or pleasure. The entire human emotional repertoire is available by about the age of two.

In the 1990s, psychologists coined the term "emotional intelligence" to describe the ability to monitor our own or others' emotions, discriminate among them, and use this information to guide our thoughts and

---

1. Rom 5:5; Gal 5:22.

actions.² Generally, psychologists recognize five dimensions to emotional intelligence: (1) awareness of our emotions, (2) managing them, (3) generating motivation to work with them, (4) recognizing emotions in others, and (5) using them effectively in relationships. Emotions contribute to our processing of life events in four typical steps: from (1) an initial sensory experience to (2) emotional responses, (3) thoughts that provide a framework for our experience, and (4) action.³

Paying attention to people's tone of voice, physical gestures, facial expressions, and movements may give us clues about their emotional state. We have more than 100 muscles in our face that can move in predictable patterns to express certain emotions. It only takes 100 milliseconds for our face to reflect our emotional state and 300 milliseconds for someone else to recognize it. Indeed, it's important for us to interpret body language since at least 80 percent of all human communication is nonverbal and it often expresses a variety of feeling states.⁴

Empathy, a closely related concept to emotional intelligence, is the ability to sense how other people feel, recognize our own emotional sensitivity for them, gauge the impact of our behavior on them, and respond compassionately to their concerns. Our capacity for being moral people is dependent on our ability for emotional empathy for others. We know that our empathy for others is based largely on our own internal emotional sensitivity and insight. In other words, it's hard to sense others' emotions if we aren't sensitive to similar feelings in ourselves. In sum, our emotions are an expression of what is going on inside us and others, and our task is to manage them for everyone's benefit.

Emotional Decision-Making

Managing our emotions can be a challenge for all of us. When we feel distressed or distracted, our decision-making can be negatively affected. Distressed feelings can lead to escapist external gratifications, unreasonable projections, superficial pleasures, impulsive or compulsive behaviors, substance abuse, and anxious attachments. An example of misdirected attempts at self-soothing, artificially attempting to feel better, is overeating.

---

2. Oswalt and Jacobson, *Emotional Intelligence of Jesus*, 1–2.
3. Oswalt and Jacobson, *Emotional Intelligence of Jesus*, 27.
4. Carbon, "First 100 Milliseconds of a Face," 859.

While eating should bring a natural comfort or fullness, we live in a culture that encourages overeating, which in turn has generated a significant amount of obesity, diabetes, and other related physical complications. For most of us, food is available almost anywhere at any time. Eating has become a rapid, indelicate process: Americans tend to eat both quickly and excessively. We often consume second or third helpings, dole out oversized portions, or simply graze between meals. Many people find that they are more prone to compulsive overeating during evening hours, beginning with dinner and proceeding until bedtime. Eating can feel good and satiation can give a sense of fullness that masks our emotional hunger or distress.

I have often advised compulsive overeaters to take five minutes before consuming food to explore their emotional state and reflect on a series of questions. What level of distress are they experiencing? Are their muscles tense? Do they feel restless? Are they eating for emotional reasons? What would it take for them to feel calm on the inside? What would happen to them if they did not eat at the moment? How would they feel or think? On a scale of 1 to 10, can they recognize the intensity of their urge to eat? I often advise clients to refrain from eating if the intensity of their urge to eat is at 5 or higher. We should reserve our consumption of food for authentic hunger, since it won't satisfy emotional hunger or distress. If we take the necessary time to emotionally calm ourselves, we can eat with more satisfaction and enjoyment. Similarly, there may be a deeper sustenance available mentally, emotionally, and spiritually that we need to experience ahead of eating. Our distressed emotions often signal larger issues we should address.

When we approach our meal emotionally settled and relaxed, we can choose to eat more slowly, chewing our food several times before swallowing. The meal we consume has certain textures, smells, colors, and tastes, and we should savor this gift. The food we consume is a product of the earth and human labor. Where does it come from? How is it harvested? What trade and labor dynamics are involved in bringing it to our local store or restaurant? Are we able to eat this food with a genuine sense of gratitude and appreciation? It's important for us to check with our body and ask our heart for advice about what kind of food to eat and how much to eat. If our doctor or dietitian were sitting next to us, would it change what or how we're eating? If Jesus Christ were physically sitting next to us and wanting to enjoy this table fellowship, would it change our behavior? Are we living to eat or eating to live?

This approach to eating, focused largely on our emotional readiness before and during meal consumption, can be very successful. I have observed a number of clients, with a history of compulsive overeating, change their approach to food by doing appropriate emotional regulation and soothing their feelings. Before eating, their goal is to only eat calmly and slowly, eat nutritious food, savor what they eat, and appreciate where it comes from. In combination with an appropriate exercise program, their weight tends to stabilize or lessen without the stress of restricted dieting or weight-loss drugs. They are not deprived of food, but rather endowed with potential to consume it responsibly.

The basic procedure we follow regarding compulsive overeating can also be modified to mitigate any number of compulsive behaviors, including shopping, drugs and alcohol, gambling, sex, and screen attachments. We can say that virtually all addictive processes and compulsive behaviors can only be treated successfully if people first develop emotional freedom, peace, and hope on the inside. When we feel driven or compulsive, can we delay gratification, allow the emotional distress, and embrace our emptiness? By taking personal responsibility for self-compassion, people can become effective emotional regulators, enhancing their prognosis for recovery from compulsive or addictive behavior.

Emotional Struggle and Hope

But how do we handle complex, difficult emotions? Despair, fear, shame, hurt, sadness, and anger leave us feeling mired in hopelessness, yet, when we learn to manage them effectively, they lead us to strength and hope. We will briefly explore some of these.

Despair. Despair is both an emotion and a mindset. As we discussed in chapter 1, despair feels like we are powerless and stuck in an impossible reality. It can feel like abandonment, loss, impaired desire, and futility. Loneliness is often the breeding ground for despair. With emotional despair, people may expect nothing from life except more of the same. Despair typically results in an inability to derive pleasure from even the most positive of situations. People may feel afraid to hope again, as hope could invite further disappointment, loss, and emotional distress.

Yet, in despair, we have an opportunity to discover, as Jesus did, the paradox of God's presence in the midst of God's absence. We may newly look for the divine after we have given up attempting to manipulate our spirituality. If our desire is for our true self and God, then despair can give us motivation for healing.

For many people, it may come as a surprise that profound despair or depression, the utter absence of any sense of hope, exists in the Bible. Psalm 88 describes perhaps the most dark and despairing place in Scripture. The psalmist cries out to God day and night. His soul is full of trouble, and his life draws toward the grave. His body has no strength and is decaying, moving to join those who are dead. He does not remember what it feels like to be well. God has forsaken and abandoned him, and he feels God's anger resting heavily on him. He is isolated, having lost his closest friends. There is a sense of collapse that feels like the land of oblivion. He feels destroyed by God's terrors, and without the comfort of hope, darkness is his only reality. Crying out to God brings no relief.

This brutal, frank, desperate lament to God is actually the one paradoxical element of hope that the psalmist retains. The very act of crying out, of lamenting, allows for a kind of authentic communication with the divine. Eventually, the dark lament of Psalm 88 is followed in Psalm 89 with a new sense of confidence and hope.

In the Bible, there are several examples where the emotion of despair has to be fully and completely experienced by crying out to God before, eventually, there is some ray of hope for relief (just as Jeremiah found, as we saw in chapter 3). All of our cries are heard, even our questioning of, or anger at, God. When we feel despair, we can pay attention to its intensity, its origin, its connection with other feelings, thoughts, behavior, physicality, and social interactions. Is our despair brief or chronic, and does it reflect a pattern or history over time? Has emotional despair ever evolved into something more hopeful?

Fear. Neurotic, self-defeating fear is another common feature of emotional distress. Neurotic fear can constrict us, take away our confidence, and instill dismal images of what's coming. Fearful images of the future typically involve pain and suffering, loss, or tragedy. Sadly, fear not only creates morbid images of our future, whether daily, weekly, or yearly, but also makes those fearful mental scenarios feel like they are happening or about to happen right now. Despite being "all in our heads," our worst-case scenarios generate adrenaline, muscular tension, and shallow, more rapid breathing. In this sense, fear, as a future-oriented emotion, negatively impacts the present and gives us the sense that the anticipated, dreaded future may actually feel more real than the present moment.

Biblical hope rebukes this neurotic fear that tends to diminish people. We are told to "Be not afraid" ninety-five times in the Scriptures. Furthermore, the Scriptures tell us that God brings the good and can overcome our fears, including the fear of death. Instead of obsessive, stifling "what-ifs," hope allows us to embrace the present moment and step into each day with confidence. The more our confidence grows, the more our fear diminishes.

Shame. Whereas fear is a future-oriented emotion, shame is a past-directed experience. Shame is a contradiction of God's intention for humanity. It suggests that we haven't just made a mistake, but we *are* a mistake. Shame-based people tend to have an alienated relationship with themselves and are tormented by their prior losses and failures. People carry shame both physically and emotionally: someone who feels shame will have often have downcast eyes, a drooped head, and slumped shoulders, and they will struggle cultivating self-forgiveness, self-acceptance, and self-esteem. People carrying shame will have difficulty in relationships, since they don't feel deserving of acceptance and project that they will not be acceptable.

Shame can be overcome with God's amazing grace. The divine capacity to absorb all of our faults, worst mistakes, or sins is displayed by Jesus at the cross. Resurrection faith is a guarantee that grace and hope will always be victorious. We know shame is being overcome as we experience gratitude for our past and accept ourselves today, no matter our flaws.

When fear and shame are being transformed, we can join with Dag Hammarskjöld and say, "For all that has been—Thanks! To all that shall be—Yes!"[5]

Hurt and anger. Two other emotions common to all of us are hurt and anger. Hurt and anger are two sides of the same emotional experience. Hurt is the deeper emotional feeling that can give rise to anger. When we are hurt, healthy anger is there for us to set appropriate boundaries, protect ourselves or others, and energize us to change the circumstance that hurts us. While protective anger does not bring healing or reconciliation, people who work constructively with their hurt can experience deep healing. Healing our hurts can diminish our anger.

---

5. Hammarskjold, *Markings*, 89.

The ways in which we experience and manage these emotions vary greatly based on a number of factors, including gender, age, and cultural background. In the United States, it is generally more difficult for men to express hurt and more difficult for women to express anger. Traditionally, when women are hurt, they tend to display sadness and tearfulness. Women emotionally heal their hurt if they process their pain. When men are hurt, they tend to show anger. Men who have anger control issues typically have been hurt historically and have not been able to find healing.

Each of these emotions and reactions exists on a spectrum, and everyone's healing, regardless of gender, comes through addressing and resolving our wounds.

There are a number of ways that people can learn to soothe their emotions, beginning with radical acceptance, understanding, and appropriate hopeful self-talk.

The emotional dimensions of hope bring about a feeling of vitality and vibrancy. Hope generates energy, drive, strength, and a sense of inner buoyancy, because what is hoped for is of supreme value. Hopeful people are more alert and awake, experiencing life more fully, showing greater interest in others, and anticipate that good is coming. Their underlying confidence and security contributes to their resiliency when things are going poorly.

Hope's motivation and emotional energy allows us to invest in the present while anticipating the future. Hopeful people reach out and are expansive. Because life is moving toward a positive climax, there is an inner desire to celebrate, share, and grow. Emotionally hopeful people are more determined, inspiring, and encouraging in all aspects of their lives.

There is a necessary connection between emotions and the Christian story, because positive emotions can come from experiencing the good news of Jesus. God is love, and love is the most basic of emotions. God is personal, God is emotional, and God feels all the emotions that love can produce. We are created by love, in love, and for love. In love, we are drawn to whatever is valuable and dear. Our love for God and others should come from the center of us and be resolute.

Jesus' followers can be filled with hope that life is bigger than death, that resurrection is coming, and that we are unfailingly accompanied by the One who is already risen from the dead. Our hope is not tied to our immediate circumstances, but to a good and loving God whose presence and promise of a glorious future has power to transform us emotionally. Hope is sure, for our God is behind hope's promise. The divine desire for us is to be full of hope, a hope that gives confidence in hard times, the hope that fills the heart with gladness, the hope that brings joy, gratitude, compassion, and peace.[6]

For emotionally mature Christians, the expected new creation is the focusing goal of life, and everything else is framed by this goal. It's important to distinguish hope and expectation as they come from different viewpoints. Despair may happen when proximate practical hopes become expectations that are not accomplished and are given too much emotional significance. Unmet temporary goals do not generate distress if we don't overinvest in them and create rigid expectations. There is often emotional risk in setting expectations, but never a risk expecting God's future. In many ways, Christian emotional resiliency is based on habits of seeing the world as God does. When God's overarching hope transcends our finite hopes, we can have an authentic joy in life.

Jesus as an Emotional Example

Pictured in the Gospels, Jesus showed himself to be a model human being, someone whom we can emulate and follow. A picture of emotional health, his predisposed state was a loving intimacy with his father. The inner core of his personality was a perfect trust or confidence in God, whom he affectionately called *Abba*, My Father. He loved God with all his heart, mind, and spirit. His obedience and strength led to a deep inner peace and an underlying emotional stability that was reflected throughout his challenging ministry. While he experienced all human temptations and emotionality, his inner core connection with God kept a harmony and emotional equilibrium intrinsic to his personality.

The love that Jesus experienced in his abiding fellowship with God meant he would not be negatively influenced by fear or those in power. As a beloved Son, his experience of his Father's love meant he then could cherish and treasure his own self. We find him enjoying his life, building relationships with people, appreciating God's creation, and taking breaks from ministry to relax, meditate, and play. His love for others never superseded his love for himself or God. We see evidence in the Gospels of a personality balanced between strength and weakness, love and anger, highs and lows, action and reflection.[7]

6. For more on hope, see Rom 12:11–12; 15:13; Gal 5:22–23.
7. Shostrom and Montgomery, *Healing Love*, 26–42, 68–81.

Life among the peasant population of Jesus' day could be emotionally taxing. Most Palestinians probably had a scarcity mentality, living in constant fear of loss, powerlessness, and questionable ability to meet their immediate and long-term needs. In contrast, Jesus brought the peasants of Capernaum and Galilee his abundance mentality based in God's graciousness and generosity. Cautioning against living in the fear of not having enough, he joyfully suggested that God provides what we internally need, but not what we may want. A demonstration of his abundance mentality was feeding the multitudes with a couple of dried fishes and five pita breads.[8] He taught people to pray for their daily bread and said that "an abundance of possessions" would threaten people's future.[9] The kingdom of God, for Jesus, was holy, fulfilling, and free.[10]

There was a deep congruence between Jesus' words and his deeds. His emotional intelligence allowed him to understand the situation of his people and generate hope. An abundance mentality meant people were able to be happy, positive, and future-minded in a time of injustice, scarcity, and hunger.[11] People had opportunities to change their despair and fear into a more hopeful, balanced emotional life with Jesus' kingdom-first mentality.

In contrast to people's hypocrisy and self-centeredness, Jesus taught the Golden Rule: "So in everything, do to others what you would have them do to you."[12] He displayed a substantial empathy, sensing other people's thoughts and feelings and responding effectively to them. To be effective with people, Jesus was adept at reading people's voices, gestures, facial expressions, and body language. He was not afraid to get close and touch people who were considered unclean or demon-possessed and responded with emotional sensitivity based on the amazing graciousness of God, who loves all people.[13] God's love was so unconditional and abundant that those who felt it could even love their enemies, including tyrants, slave masters, and unjust creditors.

Though homeless and dependent on others, Jesus abounded with a sense of God's joy and richness.[14] He was a person of great equanimi-

---

8. As recorded in Matt 14:13–21; Mark 6:30–44; Luke 9:12–17; John 6:1–15.
9. Luke 12:15–21.
10. Shostrom and Montgomery, *Healing Love*, 19–22.
11. Shostrom and Montgomery, *Healing Love*, 22.
12. Matt 7:12.
13. Matt 5:45.
14. Matt 7:7–8; Luke 12:27.

ty.[15] People who were emotionally upset, carrying major burdens, were promised rest through trusting God.[16] Peasants were encouraged to stand up for themselves in the face of oppression, trusting God and each other for their security. Jesus countered peasant humiliation, resulting from imperial domination, by advocating for the sacredness of their lives and striving for their empowerment.[17]

Another example of Jesus' emotional sensitivity was his practice of forgiveness. Forgiveness, for Jesus, meant letting go of past guilt encumbrances, canceling unhealthy obligations, and setting people free from shame. Jesus believed that human acts of forgiveness were also divine in that forgiveness allowed a victim to be healed of the emotional burden of bitterness, resentment, or anger. Repentant perpetrators were to be released from guilt. Jesus recognized that emotional healing required the triumph of God's grace, such that relationships in Jesus' community always included opportunity for healing through acts of forgiveness.

Jesus' final act of forgiveness happened at the point of his death when he forgave his executioners, who were living in utter darkness. "Father," Jesus asked, "forgive them, for they don't know what they are doing."[18]

Jesus shared love and compassion on a regular basis. He showed compassion to lepers, children, the sick, the poor, foreigners, prostitutes, oppressors, and the oppressed. He encouraged his followers and opponents alike to seek first God's coming new regime. Since there was a great deal of empathy in Jesus' healings, people could trust him.[19] Healing with an authority that came from God involved not just the ill person but also the person's family and community.[20]

Jesus' emotionality also displayed anger and outrage. He castigated the corrupt temple aristocrats, Sadducean authorities, and the hypocrisy of the Pharisees. At the end of his life, Jesus' faithfulness to God's kingdom spurred his outrage in holy civil disobedience, calling out God's judgment and disrupting the corrupt temple operation.[21] On another occasion, he was profoundly angry and disturbed when his dear friend Lazarus, whom

15. Shostrom and Montgomery, *Healing Love*, 72.
16. Matt 11:28–30.
17. Wink, *Jesus and Nonviolence*, 8–37.
18. Luke 23:34.
19. Mark 1:35–42.
20. Mark 1:27; 3:15; Luke 7:8; see Wink, *Jesus and Nonviolence*.
21. Mark 11:15–19.

he loved, was dying.[22] He could be very frustrated at his disciples when they showed a lack of understanding, such as not allowing children to be brought to him.[23] Contradicting religious practices by healing people on the Sabbath reflected both his compassion for the sick and ongoing anger at religious hypocrisy.

Because of an ultimate sustaining relationship with his Father, Jesus could experience weakness and vulnerability without it overwhelming him. There were occasions when he deeply struggled in his mission. At Gethsemane, he was troubled, sorrowful, anguished, and terrified.[24] Jesus wept openly on a number of occasions.[25] Perhaps the most striking picture of Jesus' weakness, though, is found in the procession to his crucifixion. By this time, Jesus had undergone so much trauma and torture that another man, Simon of Cyrene, had to bear the cross to Golgotha.[26]

Being vulnerable and tempted in all ways, whether with bread, power, fame, or fortune, required a complete reliance and surrender to God's coming kingdom. For Jesus to be tempted as we are, he had the freedom to compromise his faith as easily as any of his followers. That he did not do so is an indication of his incredible, unique, unbroken, hopeful fellowship with God.

Balancing Jesus' experience of weakness was his resiliency. He is pictured at times in the Gospels as a prophet, teacher, and master of incredible strength. He announced that the Spirit of God was upon him, and he boldly articulated his mission to liberate the poor, blind, and oppressed.[27] On other occasions, Jesus calmed the sea, preached to the multitudes, brought the dead to life, attacked the demonic, and pictured Satan falling. In difficult circumstances, he maintained joy and also loved being alone with himself and his Father.

The fundamental interactive dynamic between himself and others was maintained by setting boundaries. He could say "yes" to some and "no" to others. He experienced a balance between being and doing, giving and taking, expressiveness and containment, immediacy and

---

22. John 11:3, 33, 38.
23. Mark 10:14.
24. Matt 26:38; Mark 14:33; Luke 22:44.
25. For example, during his lament for the wayward city of Jerusalem (Luke 19:41) or at the death of Lazarus.
26. Luke 23:26.
27. Luke 4:18–22.

goal-directed behavior, connectedness and isolation, conformity and individuality. Jesus could be entirely surrendered and be completely in charge. He experienced great empathy and compassion without losing capacity for healthy, righteous anger.

The Gospels illustrate many examples of how Jesus kept himself well. His commitment to love himself the way he was loved by his Father moved him to live life with routine exuberance. Jesus did not go to Jerusalem at the end of his life as a feeble, frail, fragile, codependent Messiah. He went, instead, as a well-nurtured human being who freely chose to lay down his life for others. It is because he willingly surrendered and sacrificed his healthy body and mind that we can say that he was a perfect sacrifice for his people, including all of us.

In summary, Jesus' unbroken bond with, and trust in, his Father was at the center of his life. His relationship with God was entirely open and transparent, such that he was authentic in every way. There was a congruence, harmony, equilibrium, and balance to his emotional life that coalesced around this bonded relationship with God. Through his relationship with, and love for, God, and God's love for him, he was able to experience and manage the full spectrum of human emotion, and he lived with great joy in body, emotion, mind, soul, personality, and character.

Working with Our Emotions

Our challenge, then, is to transcend an emotional life solely based on our own personalities and historical experience to one that includes being conditioned or shaped by the hopeful personality and experience of Christ. Being able to experience, from our spiritual core, the entire range of emotions, feel resolved about them, and be able to express them appropriately as Jesus did, is our goal. This is especially true when we are despairing or feeling hopeless, as it is usually unhealthy to suppress emotions.

Even in the most intimate confrontation with death or tragedy, we can experience hope.[28] Suffering can encourage us to stabilize our hope and help us remember that current earthly existence is not going to always satisfy our desires. The follower of Jesus who recognizes how suffering can be meaningful is in a position to experience a hope that will not disappoint. Our true self can emerge in suffering.

---

28. See Rom 5.

Our emotions help us connect with our past as well as our present. Most of us have repressed or suppressed emotions that were unacceptable during childhood years. Failure to access painful emotions may make it difficult for us to understand and manage current sensory or emotional experiences. As we observed in chapter 6, if a suppressed feeling is aroused and appropriately expressed, there can be a release of physical tension and an opportunity to better understand our current experience.

Since our emotions allow us to re-experience the past, we can look back and actually feel or sense similar emotions to what we may have experienced during childhood or early adulthood. It's helpful to regard uncomfortable feelings as coded messages to be deciphered. This gives us an invitation to work at integrating our past, reinterpreting painful experiences, processing shut-down or distorted emotions, and re-experiencing past events with a sense of healing empowerment or victory.

We are created with emotions that move toward resolution, both past and present. It is important that we trust this God-given, inherent desire to complete unfinished or unprocessed past experiences. Usually suppressed or unfinished emotional experiences are connected to trauma, parents or caregivers, adult authority figures, intimate partners, and siblings. Are we aware of the many different emotions, of varying intensity, generated in our interactions with them? Will we radically accept our feelings and let grace defeat shame?

Identifying emotions that have been denied or suppressed is enhanced by paying attention to our physical sensations. We might notice changes in our voice, throat, physical posture, or breathing, or we might recognize pain in our stomach, tightness in our shoulders, or soreness in our jaw. Sometimes, we may even experience difficult emotions in cycles. When stimulated, there can be a buildup of emotional intensity that reaches a peak point of expression and then recedes as we appropriately express our emotions. Are we aware that we can direct our feelings to be more intense or calm? This process can repeat many times. Self-awareness and insight into these changes are crucial so that we can be honest with ourselves, God, and others about our inner experience.

Journaling is a simple, effective way to regularly work with our emotions. We should start by jotting down our predominant emotional states each day in a print or digital diary. Journaling about our feelings can assist in activating our emotions. Our felt resistance to certain feelings may be explored and even exaggerated for further insight. If we prefer not to write, sometimes it may work to physically act out our emotions or express them through drawing or coloring. Some people find helpful emotional expression through music—singing, dancing, or even writing songs.

Our body can be used to elicit suppressed emotions by pretending or role-playing our involvement in painful situations. In doing so, we can practice moving our many emotional descriptions from tentative to definite, from disowning to owning, from can't to haven't, from questions to statements, from incomplete to complete sentences, from you to I. Again, as people centered in Christ, our goal is to experience the entire range of our emotions, accepting and expressing them appropriately in a variety of contexts.

It may be helpful, at times, to let our emotions consume us. Other times, it's wise to think or act beyond our feelings. As we have observed, a worthy goal is to not allow an emotion, like unhealthy fear, to have a pattern of making decisions for us. We are emotionally at our best when we have adequate stimulation each day, pay attention to our thoughts and behavior, and follow healthy daily routines. If we are able to make discerning choices and act without simply being driven by feelings, then we have healthy self-direction.

Hopeful emotions do provide depth of meaning and experience to our life. God knows our emotions and can meet us in their felt weakness as well as in their strength. It may be that God is revealed more in emotional struggle than in happiness.

The emotion of peace is living with the assurance that things will sooner or later work out. Shalom, the biblical word for peace, identifies the holistic nature of inner and outer harmony, as well as goodwill.[29] When love, joy, and peace are predominant states of feeling, then fear, anger, or hurt are not so distressing.[30]

Can we emulate Jesus' emotional life? *Yes*. We see examples of Jesus' followers displaying incredible emotional resiliency. Jesus' apostles were arrested, imprisoned, and beaten for announcing the good news.[31] Arrest, imprisonment, and beatings are not typical occasions for joy and hope among people. Most people, when faced with such adversity, perceive the situation as tragic and are likely to feel distressed, angry, fearful, or miserable. In contrast, the followers of Jesus responded with joy and hope because they saw themselves as having suffered disgrace for Jesus'

---

29. See Yoder, *Shalom*.
30. See Yoder, *Shalom*, and Swartley, *Covenant of Peace*.
31. Acts 5:41.

sake. Their persecution was, for them, an opportunity to share God's good news. Emotional freedom and hope, for followers of Jesus, comes out of seeing and seeking God's new order first, which affects understanding and feelings toward God, ourselves, and others.

Closely connected with our emotional experience is our amazing mind. We explore that next.

8

Soul Work: Hopeful Mind

"The natural flights of the human mind are not from pleasure to pleasure but from hope to hope."

—Samuel Johnson

OUR MINDS AND BRAINS are inexorably intertwined. Our brain is an absolutely incredible organ that can be visualized as a stream of constant informational flow, with 100 billion neurons and trillions of synapses working together to send and receive messages. There is an intimate relationship between our brain and our mind, as our mind utilizes our brain for conscious awareness.

Our general consciousness involves both hemispheres of our brain, yet we depend on different parts of our brain to accomplish different tasks. Generally, we consider the left hemisphere as the site of mechanical, linear, competitive, and focused thinking. Our brain's right hemisphere includes our spontaneous, creative, abstract, and visionary thinking. With both hemispheres of our brain working in unison, we are able to engage life with all of its complexity and connections.

We have learned from brain research that our nervous system has the ability to respond to stimuli by reorganizing aspects of the brain's structure, function, and connections. From moment to moment, elements of our brain can be strengthened or weakened depending on how it's used. When cells in the brain are actively used, messages are transmitted more efficiently and more connections are made with other cells. If we repeatedly activate certain areas of our brain, those capabilities can grow. Inactive brain cells, however, are starved of the nutrients and oxygen they need to survive as our body directs resources to more active regions of the brain. This means that each of us, to some extent, has the capability of changing the structure and function of our brain. Brain researchers call this process neuroplasticity.[1]

When we are aware that there is "something on our mind," we are usually referring to our thoughts. By thoughts, we mean all the ways that we are conscious of ourselves, others, and our world. Our thoughts include memory, general collection of information, perception, learning, language, imagination, projection, and synthesis of ideas. Decisions are made from our thoughts about the circumstances of our lives. A goal of our thoughts is to accurately describe our experience and the reality of our life. Our mind allows us to picture our past, present, and future, testing our assumptions and previous hopes. Ultimate concerns usually generate many of our thoughts.

There is a sense of freedom when we can direct our thoughts. Our mind can expand and develop if we pay attention to the kinds of thoughts, images, and concepts we entertain. What we repeatedly think about, observe, or hear affects what we do and what we will continue to think about. Our identity and capacity to be hopeful people is generated by what matters to us and what we are committed to. If our mind is not properly exercised and nurtured, it is likely to stagnate and simply recycle old patterns.

How we focus our thoughts, then, determines much of our reality. What are we thinking about ourselves and our relationship to God and all creation? The apostle Paul taught that only through renewing and transforming our mind can we discern the will of God.[2] We should, in other words, regularly review what's going on in our mind and be intentional about what we put in our mind so that we can find what is good, pleasing, and complete in the eyes of God.

In his book *Who God Says You Are*, Klyne Snodgrass summarizes the assets our minds bring to us:

> If we thought about our own identity more, about our remembering, our values, and our internal and external dialogues, we would find first a sensitivity to God, then a sense of direction, energy to engage life, freedom to be who we are supposed to be, rebellion against cultures' manipulation of us, appreciation of community and its importance for life, and the realization that life is not merely about oneself. We would be on the way to being who God

---

1. See Southwick and Charney, *Resilience*, 13–16.
2. Rom 12:1–2.

says we are, and we would have a healthy internal self-interpreting, self-directing memory.[3]

Our very being, Snodgrass maintains, is at stake in how we think, remember, value, judge, and converse with ourselves, with each other, and with God.

Addressing Emotionally Unhealthy Thoughts

Since the 1960s, there has been a substantial amount of interest in, and research on, the relationship between people's conscious thoughts and their emotions. When people are in states of hopelessness or despair, researchers have found that negative streams of thought actively contribute to their despair. In the world of Winnie-the-Pooh, humans tend to be a bit more like Eeyore than Tigger, ruminating more on negative experiences than positive ones. From an evolutionary perspective, this has helped people avoid danger and react quickly in a crisis. From a practical perspective, these negative thoughts can be emotionally and psychologically distressing.

When we try to control—or even micromanage—our troubling thoughts, worry or obsessions can take root in our minds. The best way to address negative thoughts isn't by shoving them aside or stuffing them down, but through active recognition and acceptance. By accepting that we have these thoughts, we can step back and examine the validity of despairing thoughts and gain a more accurate and hopeful perspective.

Hopelessness involves negative routine thoughts about ourselves, the world, and the future. Despair and hopelessness often trigger the following kinds of automatic thoughts:

> "I feel hopeless, so it must be true."
>
> "My life is not worth living."
>
> "I have felt this way for a long time and will never get better."
>
> "I feel worthless."
>
> "I'm no good. I've made too many mistakes."
>
> "I'm a failure."
>
> "I'm dumb."
>
> "I'm a poor student."
>
> "Nobody likes me."

3. Snodgrass, *Who God Says You Are*, 132.

"My life is a disaster."

"This world is going to hell."

"My situation is too much for me to handle."

"My situation will never change."

"I'm a failure at relationships."

"I don't deserve any better."

"I hate what people have done."

"I hate what I have done."

"I hate my body."

"I will never get out of debt."

"People I care about will eventually leave me."

"I will never be healthy."

To work constructively with our thoughts, it's better to be still, quiet, and turn inward. We can accept our thoughts, knowing that we are working to change for the better. If we feel despair or hopeless, when is it the worst? What are we saying to our self, or picturing in our mind, when we are feeling so sad or anxious, when life seems futile? It is a helpful practice to write down what's going through our mind when we are feeling the worst. Indeed, feeling worse can function for us as an emotional experiment that we can investigate and dissect. There is no thought that we cannot work with—even the ones that may be ugly or horrible or shameful. Writing them down is a way of accepting that they exist, and that is the beginning of learning how to change them.

Once our thoughts are written down we can look for these key characteristics of unhealthy mental patterns:

- **All-or-nothing thinking** reduces everything to black-and-white categories, as if shades of gray do not exist. If our situation is not perfect, we see it as a total failure or an overwhelming problem.

- **Overgeneralization** takes a negative event, failure, or mistake and makes it about our entire self or that of others, now or in the future.

- **Mental filters** screen out or ignore positive thoughts and focus entirely on the negatives so that our general picture of life is dark.

- **Discounting the positive** diminishes our personal aspects or positive experiences by insisting that they are an exception and don't count for much. We are undeserving or worthless.

- **Jumping to conclusions** produces arbitrary and disturbing predictions about what's coming that will likely go badly for ourselves or others. We presume to know what others are thinking and feeling without giving them an opportunity to clarify their thoughts.
- **Magnification/minimization** exaggerates the negative and minimizes the positive. When we're hopeless, we tell ourselves that things will never change, that our problems can't be solved, and that we will be in despair forever.
- **Emotional reasoning** misleads us into presuming that our emotional despair reflects accurately the way things really are. If we feel hopeless, then it must be hopeless.
- **"Should" statements** declare that things should or must be different with ourselves, others, our circumstances, or the world, and we don't face what actually is.
- **Labeling and mislabeling** tags ourselves or others with words that are diminishing, degrading, and emotionally upsetting—e.g., "I'm such a jerk."
- **Blame** assigns fault in ourselves or others for our difficulties, evading the need to identify the true causes of the issue and working to solve the problem.

In *Feeling Great,* David Burns suggests that thoughts falling into one or more of the above categories will contribute to our despair and hopelessness.[4] By paying attention to our thought patterns and how they lead us toward despair, we can rehearse our responses to our customary negative self-talk two or three times a day. Initially, one of the best ways to respond to repetitious thinking mistakes is by writing out exactly what's going through our mind and following it with a strong rebuttal that challenges and cracks the initial mistake. It might be helpful to treat our distorted thoughts as if they were being told to us by someone trying to disturb us. If we can maintain this practice for about a month, it's likely that we will begin to automatically revise and restructure our thinking into something more healthy and beneficial.

---

4. See Burns, *Feeling Great.*

Interrogating Thinking Mistakes

To adequately interrogate thoughts that fall into those ten categories, we might ask ourselves strategic questions. For example, if we tell ourselves that the future is hopeless, we can recognize that thought as part of "jumping to conclusions" or "all-or-nothing thinking." Telling ourselves the future is hopeless may also involve categories of mental filter, discounting the positives, and emotional reasoning.

Since we know this self-talk about the future is associated with emotional distress, we can challenge ourselves to answer the following questions: What is the evidence for this thought, and where did it come from? What are the positive or negative consequences for us thinking this way? What if this thought is false? What might we do differently today if we were not saying that to ourselves? How would our thoughts be different if we were at a party or talking with a supportive friend or jogging or working on a project right now? Would a counselor or close friend be able to give us evidence that some of our hopeless thoughts are not 100 percent true?

By exploring why we remain stuck with hopeless thoughts, these questions give rise to rethinking. How is it comfortable or beneficial to continue thinking this negative thought? For instance, perhaps our despair is preventing us from "getting our hopes up" and then being disappointed again. Will we have to accept something about our self or others that requires change? Is it possible for us to arrange an inner dialogue where our despairing self is in conversation with our hopeful self?

Humbly facing our issues and unhelpful thoughts honestly and without condemnation is a step forward. Facing despair shows our strong will to change and we may discover values or standards that are important to us in the process. We can be sensitive to the emotional struggles of others and discover both empathy and the importance of hope.[5]

Hopeful people do have a different way of talking to themselves than despairing folks. Rather than falling into patterns of unhealthy thoughts, they respond to adversity by viewing their current circumstances as temporary and limited in scope. They are more likely to use words such as "sometimes," "lately," or "right now." They learn what they can through struggle. Rather than diminishing themselves, they take credit for investments made toward the outcome. Gratitude for help received is part of hopefulness.

---

5. Burns, *Feeling Great*, 280.

Creating a vision toward personal growth and continuing the desired behaviors are ways in which we can step forward.

If our despair is tied to specific losses, can we identify them and respect our grief? Is it possible to grieve without blaming ourselves? Are losses part of our life to navigate? Do any current losses merge with previous losses? How do we want to remember our losses? Is there wisdom to be gained from them? It may be necessary to grieve multiple losses at once and understand how these losses interact and influence us. Grieving through our emotional pain, with real self-compassion, can be an investment in the quality of our life. Just as hopelessness may lead us to hope, loss can lead us to gain.

Maximize—Don't Minimize—Assets

When we think despairingly or hopelessly, it's easy to doubt or diminish our assets, strengths, or capabilities. When we find ourselves falling into the trap of hopeless thinking, we can pivot our mental energy to constructing statements of truth we can affirm each day, enabling us to focus and believe in what is strong or good about us.

I recommend building an asset list summarizing several personal strengths: mental skills, emotional capabilities, spiritual resources, physical strengths, personality traits, and enduring values and convictions that make up our character. Create the largest asset list you can, and consider asking others for their input as well. Make it your goal to be an asset-based person instead of a liability-based person; "I can do" instead of "I can't." Include assets from your surrounding community as well.

After I came home from a nine-day hospital stay for cancer surgery, I felt confused, shocked, and despairing. It was hard to reflect on my strengths when I felt so weak. But I recognized that I was falling into thinking mistakes, and I decided to construct a spiritually based affirmation list to help myself deal with the reality that I had pancreatic cancer and was told I would likely die within a year. Eleven years later, I continue to repeat the same personal statements of truth each morning and night:

1. This is the day the Lord has made. Rejoice and be glad in it.
2. You are generating life in me now.
3. You want me whole and well.
4. You are closer to me than my own breath.

5. You are closer to me than the cancer and death itself.
6. Your presence is my first and most intimate reality.
7. You have borne it on the cross and will bear it with me.
8. You give me sufficiency in the moment. I can find a calm center.
9. You are the first and last lover of my life, and I will surrender.
10. I will love myself today the way you do.
11. If this is as good as it gets, it's good enough for me.
12. My body is your gift and my friend. Your Spirit embraces, transforms, heals, and enlivens each cell.
13. Your healing is coming sooner or later.
14. I am cultivating life.
15. I can picture healing occurring.
16. There is a life force within.
17. I will be in the moment and live from the inside out.
18. Fear and its what-ifs are my biggest enemy.
19. Fear is defeated by your Spirit with love, power, and a strong mind.
20. There is a way.
21. I am not a victim.
22. I am my own statistic and not a mythical average.
23. I will picture the medicine being directed to any evil cells.
24. There is redemptive power in the treatment.
25. I'm going to live today well.
26. I am in the hands of a loving God.
27. My illness gives me a ministry.
28. I am not my disease.
29. Your victory is my foundation, whether I am living or dying. It infuses all parts of my experience. I am a resurrection person with an underlying confidence and security.
30. The battle is yours.
31. You call me to live as a winner.

Changing Negative Scripts

Creating new convictions is not the only way to change our negative patterns. When we are struggling with hopelessness, it's crucial for us to act in ways that are stimulating and nurturing. Consider making a list of self-nurturing activities you can do several times a day, such as: listening to favorite music, going for a walk, praying, calling a friend, practicing "belly" breathing, doing stretching exercises, laughing, finding a few things to be grateful for, riding a bike, working in a garden, soaking in a bathtub, drawing or painting, recalling a few enjoyable memories, taking a nap, looking at nature's beauty, playing as if we were a child, petting an animal, watching a favorite TV show, reading the Bible or other motivational literature, reflecting on what we most value, practicing a new hobby, looking for God's presence.

It's important to remember that we all have underlying, often unconscious assumptions or attitudes about life that stem from messages we received as children from parents or authority figures who became part of our internal world. Our basic core beliefs about life, our value, the nature of relationships, the world in which we live, and the future may influence the automatic self-talk that we have previously considered. Left unchallenged, they undermine our sense of value, significance, worthiness, lovability, and capability, making it difficult to receive grace and forgiveness.

Some of us are all too familiar with scripts we learned in childhood, such as "my value as a person depends on what others think of me" or "the world is a dangerous place and my safety is up to me." But often these messages lie hidden. One way to surface them is by asking clarifying questions:

- What are my deepest fears?
- What can hurt me the most?
- What is a childhood belief I acquired from early experiences that is causing me distress or despair?
- What did I learn at a young age about God and how God relates to us and the world?
- What were my early expectations about relationships, and how did I adjust myself to fit what my parents or other authorities were encouraging or requiring?
- What messages kept me from appreciating myself or life in general?

Changing our core beliefs is not easy, because it involves reconsidering aspects of our basic identity and relationships. Just as we can reset our thought patterns to avoid thinking mistakes, so too can we shape new, productive core beliefs and attitudes. It's often useful to write more accurate and healthy core beliefs as thoroughly as possible in contrast to the earlier inaccurate messages that we were taught and absorbed. When facing difficult circumstances, we can compare how our old attitudes fit with new, more reasonable core beliefs. How might more hopeful attitudes and assumptions lead to more positive outcomes?

Finally, we can hold up our earlier views about our loving God and God's divine agenda for us and test them against basic scriptural themes to consider how our faith is imbued with—and imbues us with—hope.[6] What do we glean from Christian Scripture about ourselves, our relationships, and the future? What do the Scriptures teach us about hope? How did Jesus' followers find hope, and how might we?

Our mind, indeed, is a powerful instrument that provides us an opportunity to relate to ourselves, God, and others hopefully. We *do* have the ability to change our thinking mistakes and underlying assumptions that generate despair or fear. This does require regular practice, much like regular physical exercise is needed to strengthen our muscles or endurance. It is important that we respect the life of our mind by infusing it with thoughts that are more truthful, life enhancing, and hopeful.[7]

---

6. See, for example: Ps 103:13; Matt 6:31–34; John 3:16; Rom 5:8; 8:28, 35–39, 12:1–2; 1 Cor 10:13; Gal 3:28; Titus 3:4–7; 1 John 1:9.

7. Phil 4:8.

9

Soul Work: Hopeful Personality

> "True personality lies ahead—how far ahead, for most of us, I dare not say—it will come to us when we occupy those places in the structure of the eternal cosmos for which we were designed or invented. . . . We are marble waiting to be shaped, metal waiting to be run into a mold."
>
> —C. S. Lewis

PERSONALITY IS OUR SOCIAL, interactive self. Relationships are the great projects of life. God created us to be loving, social creatures, and God's design for each of us is to develop life-giving, engaging personalities that are unique, vibrant, and relationally effective.

We establish our personalities through living and working with different people who help us think and develop social skills beyond ourselves in an expansive and constructive fashion. Through exposure to different people, we open ourselves up to growth, development, and healing. In fact, it's often the people we have most difficulty relating to that are the very ones that provide us the most opportunity for our healing and formation.

Here's an easy way to know that our personalities are effective: when we can compassionately interact with other people, no matter how different they are, and not let them shake our inner security or hope, regardless of how they behave. It's imperative we use our social skills with others to find the beauty within them, as opposed to manufacturing an agenda for the relationship or being judgmental. Truly hopeful personalities release other people to be freely themselves, and do not fear being hurt or controlled. They give and receive love freely.

SECTION TWO: HOPE TRANSFORMS HUMAN PERSONHOOD AND COMMUNITY

I am speaking here of personality in the context of Christian hope. Because we are drawn toward God's future relationships and are accompanied along the way by the resurrected Christ, an understanding of personality can be inherently hopeful.

Understanding Personality

In psychological terms, personality represents a pattern of deeply embedded and broadly enacted mental, emotional, and behavioral traits that persist over extended periods of time. At the core of our personality are two processes:

- how we interact with ourselves and God
- how we interact with our day-to-day environment (including others)

A hopeful, healthy personality allows us to function independently and competently, adjust to our environmental challenges effectively, provide a sense of contentment and satisfaction, and fulfill our potential. We do not rely on others to make us feel fulfilled, and we are resilient in change and adversity. Psychologist Theodore Millon maintained that personality is the psychological equivalent of physical appearance: a person grows up with both, and although each might get a facelift, they remain essentially the same throughout our entire lives.[1]

In general, personality has to do with the familiar patterns of engagement that typically feel most comfortable for us. We develop our methods of interacting by cultivating sets of social skills that can be used to greet people and grow relationships. We cannot be human by ourselves, and we need other people to find out who we are and how we fit with others. Jesus taught that our relationships are central to our identity and how we treat others reflects on our relationship with him.[2] The quality of our relationships determines, in many ways, the quality of our life. We are social beings through and through.

---

1. For a traditional understanding of personality, see Millon and Everly Jr., *Personality and Its Disorders*, 4–21.

2. Matt 18; 25:31–46.

SOUL WORK: HOPEFUL PERSONALITY

People we spend the most time with are continually influencing who we are, and we return the influence toward them. Together, we help develop each other's personality.[3]

How Our Personality Is Formed

At birth, we are all malleable and, like sponges, open to being shaped by our environment. Babies are not complete personalities. They undergo a process of relational sculpting in order to become more complete people as they grow. While the world has no innate meaning to an infant, their mental system becomes increasingly complex and intelligent by constant sensory and motor interaction with others.

We observe personality developing when infants imitate the facial expressions, voice, and touch of the people around them. Children observing the actions of others have similar brain activity as they would from performing an act themselves. They infer the mental states of adults based on their behavior over time. The child's personality also develops by sharing attention and receiving a common set of sensory experiences of objects, persons, or events with his or her primary care providers. Through these interpersonal interactions, children grow into more complete people.

Caregivers who provide a dependable, trusting experience for their children help shape hopeful personalities. Through their earliest bonding experiences, children can recognize love, security, and hope. Simultaneously, if God is perceived as a reliable caregiver for their providers, children will find through them God's eternal hope and become hopeful as well. As part of their general experience, they develop confidence that the universe itself is ultimately trustworthy. There can be a growing, positive reciprocity between children and the world. On the other hand, when there is not reliable attachment and caregiving in childhood, they will have trouble trusting others and God. Hoping for a bright relational future or promising outcomes in difficult circumstances will be a struggle.

According to psychologists Warren Brown and Brad Strawn, research indicates that caregivers' responses to their infants generally lead to four attachment styles in children:

---

3. See Brown and Strawn, *Physical Nature*.

Secure attachment results from consistent parent availability and reliability. Children with secure attachment can depend on parental responsiveness.

Anxious attachment results from inconsistent parental responsiveness and produces anxiety or uncertainty in children, since they do not know when they are going to be disappointed.

Avoidant attachment results from such inconsistent, erratic, or irregular parenting that children have an expectation of disappointment. Based on their early experiences in relationships, they may become distrustful and avoid closeness with others.

Disorganized attachment, also called nonattachment, results from chaotic or abusive parenting and may lead to significant mental illness. Children with disorganized attachment are confused and unpredictable in relationships.

These attachment styles, along with other patterns related to relationships and personality, typically endure into adulthood.[4]

Children learn empathy by being shown empathy. When children are shown empathy by a caregiver, they can recognize that person as separate and yet someone who has feelings, thoughts, and relational perspectives similar to their own. Children who experience secure attachments with empathetic caregivers will have more adaptive, flexible personalities; better regulate positive and negative emotions; explore multiple perspectives more easily; and become more resilient and hopeful. Conversely, anxiously attached children have a more difficult time separating their perspectives and emotions from those of others, and will have less flexible, resilient, and hopeful personalities.

Can We Develop a Hopeful Personality?

In adulthood, our personalities and lives are enhanced with relationships based on love, friendship, and collaboration. The hopeful personality is one that assumes relationships are essentially beneficial and rewarding. Over time, a hopeful person learns to hope through disappointments and acts with positive anticipation. Actually, hopeful people can initiate with greater responsibility and risk than may be required of others. Social skills and

---

4. Brown and Strawn, *Physical Nature*, 59–63.

patterns of interactions that generate love, belonging, friendship, loyalty, and gratitude are employed by people with hopeful personalities.

But what if we haven't developed a hopeful personality naturally? What if we have been brought up under one of those attachment styles, described in the section above, where we were not led to hope and trust as a child? Without secure attachments, a child will experience more fear. But by patiently and gradually striving for good outcomes for ourselves and others, we can grow a hopeful personality and overcome fear.

Forming hopeful personalities, ultimately, is based in love. Our Creator is love: love that is constantly expansive, creating more life-enhancing opportunities for the expression and experience of joy. God is love within us. We are told in the New Testament that God's love casts out fear. Following God means to follow the direction of love as our ultimate reality and purpose on earth. To be consciously aware of it, to experience love in ourselves and with others, is what makes life meaningful and boosts healthy personality.[5]

But while we are born from love, fear too often is what we've learned. We may be afraid that this may not be the right relationship, or we may be afraid that it is. We may be afraid that people won't like us, or we may be afraid that they will. We may be afraid of failure, or we may be afraid of success. We may be afraid of dying young, or we may be afraid of growing old. Fear constricts personalities and makes them more defensive, shallow, rigid, and reactive. When people are in states of conflict, a preliminary consideration is the recognition and resolution of fear. In a fearful state, the fear of losing or being hurt means people's differences become a threat instead of an opportunity. When a society is fearful, we observe how the fear leads to denial, defensiveness, reactivity, hostility, and violence.

Fear may cause us to avoid honest communication with another person because we may doubt they will accept us, if they see us for who we really are. Healthy personality formation, in part, is the relinquishment or unlearning of fear and the acceptance of love back into ourselves. Taking the risk of love, instead of fear, allows us to become aware of the unworkability of certain anxious patterns of interaction and can motivate us to let them go.

---

5. Williamson, *Return to Love*, 17–26.

SECTION TWO: HOPE TRANSFORMS HUMAN PERSONHOOD AND COMMUNITY

Living In Love Instead of Fear

In every moment, we may either extend love or project fear. To return to love from fear is to return to who we really are. The unconditional love of Christ in us is the truth that sets us free because that love saves us from our own fearful thoughts.[6] In the presence of love, anxious patterns that may govern our experience in relationships can slowly be overcome.[7] This is a manifestation of a hopeful personality: that we recognize people as magnificent sacred creatures with a potential abundance of love and power to share.[8] God has created our relationships as eternal opportunities for us to love, be loved, and exercise hope. Our personalities engage in the shift from fear to love as part of God's work in us. Personality becomes more hopeful if we set our minds and hearts on how we are loved and how we can love others and ourselves. The more we experience love, the easier it becomes.

When people are in states of fear, despair, or hopelessness, they are often in relational poverty. They tend to be socially withdrawn and isolated. They may have been hurt by others in significant ways during childhood or adult years and have little trust capacity. Part of a holistically based strategy for relationally impoverished people includes making gradual initial contacts, finding ways to connect with reliable, caring people on a regular basis, and beginning a process of knowing and being known in an environment of safety and grace.

Often anxious people are afraid that they can't be attractive and are undesirable to others. Maybe one's body is somehow evaluated as unattractive. It may seem better to keep social distance and avoid feeling unliked or rejected.

One way to shift our perspective concerning outward appearances is to ask: "Who is, or are, the most beautiful people we know?" For instance, if we identify the most beautiful person in our life, then we can recognize the aspects of that person and our relationship to determine what is actually attractive. Typically, that beautiful person and our relationship have qualities such as accepting, trusting, transparent, supportive, caring, companionable, respectful, and hopeful. We like being with this person because we simply are comfortable with them and enjoy the experience. It turns out

---

6. Williamson, *Return to Love*, 42.
7. Williamson, *Return to Love*, 66.
8. Williamson, *Return to Love*, 67.

that the person's physical appearance is not a primary factor in what makes this person or relationship attractive. Beauty is in the eye of the beholder.

Finding ways to engage others regularly, often around at least one common interest or project, can create opportunity for growing friendship.

Becoming a less fearful person often begins with a willingness to risk being open with at least one caring person. This person can be familiar or a complete stranger whom we have recognized as equipped to listen, understand, support, and, perhaps, struggle with us. It had been the case in my practice that, sometimes, for acutely distraught folks, it was important for someone to live with them on a temporary basis until they became more trusting. A single caring relationship is often a key to emerging from the depths of anxious hopelessness. There is no substitute for having that kind of relationship, even if it means seeing a therapist.

Forming a Hopeful Personality through Relationships

The most profound question that anyone can ask of us is, "How are you?" Unfortunately, in our individualistic and mobile culture, we turn this question into a passing greeting without really wanting to know and respond by pure reflex. The responses of "good," "fine," or "OK" are likely reciprocated by a similar question and response. But if someone is carefully and authentically asked, "How are you?" they are given an opportunity to share their thoughts, their current emotional experience, what's happening to them spiritually, and how their body is feeling.

Relationships of trust and hope are built on authentic questions and answers, and relationships can grow as understanding and acceptance between people grows. People with hopeful personalities are willing to know others even ahead of themselves being known by others. Sometimes this requires us to be a friend in order to have friends. "How are you?" should be a meaningful question in our relationship toolbox in order to learn the current state of the other person's mind, emotions, spirit, and body. After they have spoken, we listen best by accurately summarizing the speaker's main points to the speaker's satisfaction. When people feel that someone is really seeking to understand or know them in the moment, it is much more likely that they, in turn, will reciprocate similarly.

It's good to remember that God demonstrated hopeful communication by coming to us in Christ. This divine initiation meant that Jesus Christ came into human history as the presence of God in order to know and be known by people. With compassion and empathy, Jesus left his divine world behind in order to achieve solidarity with humanity.[9] Jesus wants to know people in all their human experience and love them unconditionally. Likewise, he invites people to know and love him unconditionally. Reading the Gospels can give us an up-close look at what knowing and following Jesus is about.

In human relationships, we can engage in a similar incarnational communication by entering into the space or world of others and seeking to know them from their perspectives, on their own terms, according to what they want or hope for. Being loving involves radical acceptance and freely giving the gift of human presence with grace and compassion. People with hopeful, empathetic personalities modeled after Christ have a relentless curiosity about others' experiences and welcome opportunities to be educated by them; then we can more accurately sense our impact on them and plan our behavior accordingly. This empathy is the single most important ingredient for growing understanding and confidence in relationships. We know we are empathetic when, in our engagement with others, they understand, develop trust, and eventually seek us out.

Relationships anchored in hurt, rather than love, constrict, harden, and diminish our personalities. By rebuilding our relationships and trust through accountability and forgiveness, we can nurture hopeful personalities in ourselves and in others. All that is ultimately significant from the past is love that is given and received. To surrender the past to God's grace is to accept loving, hopeful thoughts. There isn't anything people have experienced that cannot be used to bring a better present. In sum, forgiveness releases us from past pain and facilitates loving relationships.

Life is a gift! People with hopeful personalities recognize this and are grateful. They understand that people are created by God to enjoy giving and receiving with others in a compassionate fashion. Hopeful personalities mutually address people's basic needs and use different approaches to be helpful to others. God has given us the resources, individual and social, to be well and do well. People are most effective in interacting with others if they have already established a life-giving relationship with themselves and God. Likewise, close friends may help us learn to love and care for ourselves. Through exercising personalities of hope, belonging to others is part of an abundant life.

---

9. Phil 2:5–11.

SOUL WORK: HOPEFUL PERSONALITY

When people constructively reflect on themselves and God, they can be truthful regarding their strengths and weaknesses. Because of God's grace, we can accept limitations without a sense of entitlement or failure and reflect on our judgments and patterns of interaction. Letting go of right and wrong evaluations and, instead, looking at strategies that people are using to meet their needs, moves us toward greater acceptance and compassion.

All people have needs and desires for survival, protection, meaning, autonomy, interdependence, honesty, well-being, empathy, regeneration, and a sense of transcendence.[10] We can, and should, compassionately connect to meet people's basic needs and celebrate our support for each other in community. It's been said that love isn't simply gazing into another's eyes, but each looking outward in the same direction.

Relationships with others are what we *do* as well as who we *are*. Personality involves habituated appraisals and emotions, prompting behavior that may be replicated many times daily. Perhaps the majority of our daily behavior is outside conscious awareness or complete predictability. Often, people simply don't know why they are compelled to act in certain ways, present or past, until later reflection.

We know that new experiences change peoples' thoughts and often provide a chance for behavioral change. Hope is essential in bringing about change as it motivates people to learn, explore, expand, imagine, invest in relationships, and socialize effectively in society. That's why learning to operate with a hopeful personality is so important, whether we come by it naturally or if we must work harder to achieve it. A hopeful personality leads to healthier connections with people, generating love, friendship, trust, loyalty, belonging, purpose, mutual service, meaning, and gratitude.

Our mind and its thinking can connect us to the deepest and most profound part of ourselves—our spirit. We will explore our spiritual selves next.

---

10. Prieto Jr., *Joy of Compassionate Connecting*, 275.

10

Soul Work: Hopeful Spirit

> "I have watched many people whose lives impressed me with their dignity and beauty. What is it that is so attractive in them? I think it can be summed up in the word 'expectancy.' They began each day as if it were the day of the Lord. They rejoice in it and are glad.... They look at the world with wonder and amazement.... That is what life is—walking between two mysteries of birth and death—with wonder and amazement."
>
> —R. N. Helverson

ALL OF US SEARCH for spiritual experience. Usually, spirituality has to do with some form of inner or outer success and meaningful experience. In a culture that focuses on material and function, we have been taught to strive for more. The hunger for true intimacy or connection, ultimate meaning and purpose, doesn't necessarily give us the ability to discriminate between true and false spirituality. Intimacy, for many, is whatever pursuit gives us a feeling of closeness or shared experience. In North American culture, we often associate intimacy with sensual personal acts like sexual intercourse. We may search for a "higher power" in exotic pleasures, such as extreme sports and many forms of "me-centered" meditation. Following new technologies and pursuits may feel like spiritual experience. Many churches teach that God wants us to feel good and strive to create a sense of euphoria in worship services.

The part of ourselves that is deeper than our own consciousness—the part that provides us ultimate meaning and purpose—is our spirit. Spirit is *dynamis*, that energy, power, and vitality deep within that is the source of

SOUL WORK: HOPEFUL SPIRIT

our desire to be fully alive, to be fully human.[1] When we identify our impulses to be more, know more, find more, connect more deeply with others, and find the energy and vitality of life itself, that is spirit.

All people are spiritual at their core and have ultimate concerns. This is true for atheists, Buddhists, Hindus, Jews, Christians, Muslims, agnostics, and everyone else. No matter what philosophy people live by, all share the desire to be fulfilled and at peace. Everyone searches for healthy experiences they can rely on to provide ultimate value, security, and significance. Any healthy spiritual life is life-enhancing, anchors us in the present, and helps us appreciate life's beauty now. While organized religion can be a way of avoiding authentic practice of faith in God and an intimate relationship with the divine, healthy spirituality leads us to a posture of surrender, openness, and trust in the big picture of life.[2]

What we most long for—to experience love, joy, and peace—is immediately available to us in our spirit. We are human beings on a spiritual journey, and we are spiritual beings on a human journey. We actually do not possess a spirit, but rather, we *are* spirit. All of us have a desire to live eternally and we all eventually can. It's wise to look back over our life history and identify the many experiences that have made us aware of our spirit.

Our spirit grounds us in human history and moves us to share life with all things. There is no part of our human experience, internal or external, individual or communal, that does not have a spiritual foundation. Anything that we perceive as ordinary can become extraordinary with our spiritual sensitivity.

We don't seek God as much as God seeks us. Our spirit lets us know that we are more than our thoughts and feelings and that they don't have to define our identity. In fact, it is when we know little or nothing that we may be more spiritually awake.

Authentic spiritual truth comprises what is most personal, intimate, and engaging.[3] "Knowing," in the spiritual sense, is trusting, accepting, and believing. It tells us that reality is destined for renewal and change and is ultimately good and coherent. Spirituality involves all the parts of us—body, emotions, thoughts, personality, character—and always inclines us toward

---

1. Rohr, *What the Mystics Know*, 6.

2. Rohr, *What the Mystics Know*, 74; see also Benner, *Soulful Spirituality*, 22–23 for the dimensions of life-enhancing spirituality.

3. For additional discussion of spiritual knowledge, see Willard, *Knowing Christ Today*.

wholeness. The word *spirit* comes from a Latin word, *spiritus*, meaning "breath." As we have noted, in the Genesis creation story, God breathed divine breath into people, and they became living beings.[4] God's Spirit was part of our creation from the beginning and creates our spiritual essence. When our spirit joins with God's Spirit, it generates in us a desire to experience total harmony, a sense of shalom or peacefulness.

Our spirit hungers for God's Spirit. As we are in a trusting relationship with God, we are also in relationship with God's Holy Spirit, the Spirit of Jesus. The Holy Spirit lives in us and can become bonded with our spirit. When we are in fellowship with God's Spirit, our spirit is most alive.

In God's Spirit, we are free to live in the present while simultaneously being free from immediate attachments.[5] With the Holy Spirit, our spirit may carry a deep, divine wisdom and ultimate truth about who we really are, where God is, and where we are headed. Through the Holy Spirit, the spirit of life, we are most able to understand our existence, experience life, maintain a sense of wonder, and embrace all of God's creation.

The Holy Spirit reminds us that it is not our task to adjust ourselves so that God may love us, but rather that God loves us in a fashion that moves us to be healthy and transformed.

Pastor and author Eugene Peterson suggested that Christians must discover what Scripture says about spirituality and immerse ourselves in it. We should seek wise spiritual counsel or direction from godly leaders who practice a robust faith and spiritually based friends. The saints who have been walking with God for millennia can be wise teachers.[6]

Spiritual Work

Our spirit moves us to find the parts of ourselves that are most difficult to accept, those dark places that may generate our despair and hopelessness. There is no part of ourselves in which we cannot learn to accept, love, and foster an inner harmony. What is painful or dark on the inside or outside becomes an opportunity for increased healing and wholeness. Guided by the Holy Spirit, we don't need to get rid of the unhealthy parts of ourselves or others but rather use our God-given resources to bring healing out of brokenness, right out of wrong, good out of evil, and hope out of despair.

---

4. Benner, *Soulful Spirituality*, 30; Gen 2:7.
5. Rohr, *What the Mystics Know*, 95.
6. For a brief summary of these insights, see Peterson, "Spirit Quest," 27.

Perhaps the most significant spirituality is achieved when we trustingly respond to suffering in ourselves or others.

It is our experience of darkness that brings us opportunity and capability to find light. Touching on her own experiences, Episcopal priest Barbara Brown Taylor said in an interview in *Time*, "I have learned things in the dark that I could never have learned in the light. Real life starts in the dark. Whether it is the seed planted in the ground, a baby in the womb, or Jesus in the tomb, it starts in the dark. I need darkness as much as I need light."[7]

Our connection to God is immediately a connection with all that is. Flowing from God's creation, everything that exists is unified in the resurrected Christ.[8] We can have a unity with everything in creation, because all life is held together in Christ. This solidarity with all of life means that there are no divisions created by people that cannot be overcome and transformed into loving, just, peaceful relations.[9] Those things that have been separated in us or others are brought together in God's Spirit. Our body is connected with our soul, our emotions and spirit are connected to our mind, the masculine is connected to the feminine, people are connected to community, and humans are connected to the divine.[10] There is a place in this universe for us to live well and contribute to the wellness of everyone and everything.

To reach a state of shalom, we must let go of attitudes that generate separation from others. For example, if we are driven for success by accumulating wealth, the result will be that we acquire possessions others need more. If we believe that we are entitled, privileged, or always right, we will generate relationships of implicit bias, disparity, hierarchy, control, and self-righteousness. If we strive to achieve power over others, we will create microaggressions, conflict, and even violence. However, it is God's Spirit that moves us to let go of the demand for success, privilege, or power over others, so that there can be a unity and healthy integration of the neglected parts of ourselves, others, and the community.[11]

Christian psychologist and spiritual guide David Benner, in his book *Spirituality and the Awakening Self*, wrote that a spiritually based

---

7. Taylor, "Let There Be Night," 39.
8. Col 1:15–17.
9. Gal 3:28; Eph 2:13–22.
10. Rohr, *What the Mystics Know*, 57.
11. Rohr, *What the Mystics Know*, 42.

organization of our consciousness involves our willingness rather than willfulness, faith and trust instead of fear and caution, surrender rather than attempts to control, and a desire to be awakened rather than living habitually. Spirit-led people say *yes* to life, to love, to others, and to the world, all in a hopeful manner.[12]

When we pray, which is one of the primary expressions of our spirit, we open our whole self so that we can connect all the parts of us with God. Prayer moves us beyond our conscious mind and involves our bodies, emotions, personality, and character. In prayerful meditation, we don't try to control our many ongoing thoughts. Our mind may be distractible and our thoughts roaming. For instance, we can't predict with certainty what thoughts will come to us even an hour from now. It's better to allow our thoughts to roam and bring them into conversation with God. Our most profound praying involves simply being completely with ourselves and with God. We want to release everything to the Lord and define ourselves not by what we are attached to but by to whom we are attached.[13] We are participating in the very life of God, the source of our life. Prayer is about our changing, not God changing. C. S. Lewis wrote, in his *Letters to Malcolm*, that our initial foundational prayer should be: "May it be the real I that speaks. May it be the real Thou that I speak to."[14]

In prayer, we move from our mind to our senses and to a more immediate and direct contact with reality. It's the present moment that can facilitate knowing our truth and it is the only place where we can truly meet God. Benner continues,

> Prayer is an opening of the totality of self so that we might encounter God in the totality of our being. This is why holistic prayer includes not just the conscious mind (works and thoughts) but also our bodies, emotions, imagination, unconscious, and much more . . . Prayer is much more than praying. Prayer can be our whole life, just as our whole life can be a prayer. But if it is to become this, we must learn prayer as being, not simply prayer as doing. It [contemplation] recognizes that the essence of prayer is an encounter of being with Being. It is, we could say, a knowing of our being-in-Being. It is standing naked before ultimate reality in the reality of our own being . . . Without regular times of such stillness, we will remain caught up in our psychospiritual

---

12 Benner, *Spirituality and the Awakening Self*, 156.
13. Rohr, *What the Mystics Know*, 164.
14. Rohr, *What the Mystics Know*, 168.

self-improvement projects and our growth will have little transformational potential.[15]

My Own Spiritual Journey

When I became a committed Christian, during my junior year at the University of Washington, I was experiencing a personal emptiness and anxiety. I had planned on attending law school and was active in resistance to the Vietnam War. Living in a fraternity house, there were plenty of parties, dating, pleasurable experiences, and of course, alcohol and marijuana. After living in a fraternity house for two years, I found it difficult to be comfortable with who I was and had little sense of inner peace or satisfying love. Though I was almost entirely focused on achieving success and using external stimulation and rewards to feel good, I still wanted to feel more whole, instead of simply pursuing pleasure-making activities. Working hard academically, socially, and politically was not fulfilling enough.

Somehow, I connected with a staff member of Campus Crusade for Christ and began conversations that inspired me to join a men's group at the university. I witnessed a quality of life I had scarcely imagined. They had a living relationship with God, experienced joy, and felt a passionate zeal for life. I was taught and mentored by these young men and came to believe that God was working through them to let me see a deeper and more complete reality.

Eventually, I made a commitment to Jesus Christ and sought an intimate personal relationship with him. Slowly, I began to feel more secure and peaceful on the inside. My interests began to change. Over time, I realized I had been missing a whole dynamic, spiritual life that I could no longer do without. Prayer became vital, essential as I conversed with the Lord regularly and trusted that God was going to shape my life going forward. I began reading and studying the Bible, found a new interest in understanding the New Testament, and wanted to learn what I could about Jesus and the Christian life.

Given that my academic life at the university encouraged me to cultivate an inquiring, analytical mentality, I began to devour a number of books that discussed the reasonableness of Christian faith. I could not practice a spiritual life that did not make sense or that, in any way, sacrificed my

---

15. Rohr, *What the Mystics Know*, 163–64.

own intellect. Among other things, I read several books dealing with the historicity of Jesus and his resurrection.

I was a member of this Christian men's group for over a year. During that time, we shared and prayed together, and I realized the value of people caring for me and my spiritual life. My plans of going to law school slowly fell away. I wanted my life to count, and I knew that the meaning and purpose of my life, my security and joy, was something I wanted to cultivate for myself and others. My peers in the men's group encouraged me to go to graduate school and study Christian thought. If I was going to give my life to Jesus Christ and ask other people to do the same, I wanted to know all I could about the dimensions of Christian faith.

Near the end of my senior year, with the Vietnam War and military draft fully underway, I was required to take a day-long military physical in preparation for deployment to support the war. After my physical, the sergeant discovered in my medical record that I had spring hay fever, which could become more serious and perhaps include asthma in the Vietnamese climate. I was deferred and never had been more grateful for my allergies, as they saved me from entering a war in which I didn't want to fight.

With this blessing of time and freedom of choice, I decided to take two years and, as a graduate student, study the ins and outs of my Christian faith. Never had I studied so hard! I focused on the New Testament, systematic theology, apologetics, Christian discipleship, and spiritual life. After making a personal commitment to Christ, studying Christian thought, and practicing new, rewarding spiritual disciplines, my orientation to myself, God, people, economics, culture, and politics continued to be enhanced and enlarged in ways I could not have anticipated. I became a much more hopeful person and my outlook toward relationships and life's purpose significantly expanded.

Eventually, I grew interested in psychology, sociology, and clinical ministry, largely because of my experience in that group of compassionate Christian men at the University of Washington. Committed to living the life of God's kingdom and sharing that with others in the larger community, it became important to integrate my spiritual life with all the other elements constituting who I was. If Jesus Christ is Lord, then he must be Lord of all of who I am. If he is not Lord of all, then he is not Lord at all!

With my interest in social and political life, I wanted to understand how I could share in the community in a way that embodied what I knew to be true about the nature of God's peace, love, and justice. All these things led me, over time, to the work I have done in counseling, investing in community, resistance to nuclear weapons, advocacy for the poor, social justice, and ecological responsibility. As I look back, I see more and more that it was my spiritual journey, more than anything else, that led me to the place I am and the person I've become.

Assessing Our Spiritual Journey

To cultivate a hopeful spirit, we may begin assessing our spiritual journey by looking back at any time when we felt more at peace with ourselves, others, or God. Have we ever felt a deep sense of being loved unconditionally or experienced a deep acceptance of ourselves or others? Can we remember times when we felt a deep connection to life in general? Perhaps we can recall a time when we observed a baby being born. Maybe we were on a hike in the mountains and recognized the beauty and majesty surrounding us. Surviving a trauma or human tragedy may have generated in us a sense that there is more to us than what we have been living. Maybe we were simply sitting next to a burning white candle and reflecting in a way that made us feel the intimate presence of Christ.

How do we recognize and pursue an authentic and vital spiritual life? There are counterfeit spirits operating in our world, and there are distortions of spirituality virtually everywhere. We want "the real deal."

David Benner reminds us that a distorted spiritual path can lead to

> an escape from a robust commitment to reality, the repression or dissociation of sexuality, disconnection from the emotions, alienation from the body, and increasing distance from one's unconscious depths. Too easily, spiritual practices lead to increasing identification with those of one's own religious tribe and an ever-weakening sense of solidarity with all humankind. Too easily, spirituality involves a narcissistic me and God relationship that insulates us from, rather than sensitizing us to, the problems of our world. Too easily, it is associated with a focus on beliefs rather than on being. Too easily, it directs us away from life rather than toward a genuinely deeper, fuller, and more vital life.[16]

How will we recognize a wrong spiritual path? If our spirit is not leading us toward a deeper love of God, life, our self, and others, then

---

16. Benner, *Spirituality and the Awakening Self*, 4.

we must question its authenticity. Let's look at some key criteria of God's authentic work in our lives.

God is the Life-Giver and Sustainer. All reality has its source in God. God is personal, loving, and always on the side of our health and growth. God is the deepest level of our joy, wonder, strivings, and longings. God is the deepest dimension of both the challenges and the gifts that present themselves to us. We are loved, not because we are performing well, but because God is good.

Where the action in our life is, God is most present and active. God wants life for us. The human project is God's project. Life is God's gift and God's purpose in giving it is for our enjoyment and relationship. Whenever healing, liberation, justice, and growth are taking place, God's purposes are being realized. Jesus' resurrection is an uprising against all that oppresses, limits, and causes pain. The life of Jesus is the best model of God's purpose and activity in the world.

A Christian response to suffering is to resist and try to overcome it. Suffering is an evil, not good. When we must suffer, God works with us to bring whatever meaning and good that can be experienced out of the suffering. Specifically, depression, anxiety, hopelessness, broken relationships, and loneliness are evils, and we should seek to challenge and overcome them, through faith, hope, and utilizing the best resources.

People's lives are basically oriented toward the good. God wants what we want: namely, he wants our life to be lived as fully as possible. In the depths of ourselves, where we come in contact with who we truly are, we can find God at work.

Jesus' resurrection is the key to interpreting our experience. God works within death to bring life. Jesus' faithful life is the central model for how we can live, die, and rise again. Deaths of relationships, projects, or groups contain the very opportunities for new life for those trusting God.

It is love we are made for: love for others and love for ourselves. Love is the genesis and meaning of our life, and we are most happy and fulfilled in the giving and receiving of love. Nothing else will do, personally or socially. God's love is an event of healthy interaction and justice where everyone involved is being elevated.

God works with us both in the light and the darkness, in life and in death. As Jesus chose to follow the spirit into the desert wilderness, so we can, with discernment, move into our own darkness and deserts. It is important for us to experience our darkness with discernment and hope.

God is both at the center of our spirit and completely transcendent. We can connect with God's Spirit deep inside ourselves, and we can equally connect with God's Spirit looking beyond ourselves. God is in our relationships as the life-giving source that confirms, confronts, celebrates, and underlies all interdependence, cooperation, receptivity, vulnerability, and affection.

God's power in us is the capacity to be both self-directed and receptive. God's power is the ability to influence another without compromising their personhood and to absorb the influence of another without losing one's self. It is the ability to allow for difference or diversity without feeling defensive or insecure. Power shared is power enhanced.

God is the author of all true surrender and integration. Both totalitarian control and alienation, inside or outside, are resisted by God's Spirit. Working with what we hate most inside and outside is probably a key to better self-awareness and healing. The poor parts of us and the poor parts of society are typically routes for God to lead all of us to be more insightful, empathetic, and reconciled. We come to God through our limitations, and our reception of imperfections allows for more perfection in us.

God has made us to be part of community, such that unhealthy societies or groups limit our growth while healthy societies or groups promote it. Attempting individual change in an unhealthy society is like trying to put on makeup in a steam room: temporary, frustrating, and often for naught.[17] Unhealthy societies can make good people part of evil dynamics. Healthy societies can lead dysfunctional people to more constructive behavior. In God's work, individual change and social change are interrelated.[18]

Pursuing a Hopeful Spirit

In the Christian tradition, there have been varying contemplative practices to help people more accurately and authentically find their true selves in God. I have found these practices helpful and hopeful, and I'm particularly inspired by German theologian Dorothee Sölle's four-step contemplative practice, in addition to the work of spiritual psychologists such as Gerald May and John Finch.

Sölle suggests that we begin our contemplative practice in a state of *amazement*. We behold the world as God intended it to be and we recognize how very good it all is. It's the state of wonder that we see in our children's exuberance. In this amazement, we are freed from the routines, customs, and convictions that reinforce business as usual. Touched by the Spirit of life, it is our deep gratitude and appreciation for what is that moves us to be open to what might be. Gifted with life and hope, our wonderment moves us beyond the ordinary and the trivial. Recognition of the flaws in all of us and our world that generate darkness and despair is part of our beholding existence. We are in a state of receiving life, listening, being still, contemplating, and meditatively praying.

Purgation involves us emptying ourselves and letting go of all things that keep us from our true self and God. In the contrite, repentant moment, we discharge all the props and crutches that have blocked us from our own vital reality, including patterns of consumption and pleasure-seeking. We remove all avoidance patterns and weaknesses that have permitted us to escape true vulnerability and willingly engage our inner darkness. In this is a world of relinquishment and defenselessness. We let go of all requests or demands on our parents or other caregivers to make up for their failings. The knee-jerk customs and norms of our culture diminish in significance. As we become more and more empty, we mourn the impact of

---

17. See Rohr, *What the Mystics Know*.
18. Adapted from Hart, "Counseling's Spiritual Dimension."

principalities and powers on ourselves, our common humanity, and our planet. We experience emptiness in order to find our true "hunger and thirst."[19] Letting go of all false gods and hopes, we radically accept and surrender ourselves and our reality.

Illumination is a phase in which we open ourselves to learning anew who we really are and aligning ourselves with who God really is. Feelings are present without overpowering us. Our darkness lessens as we affirm our true self as creatures dependent on a loving God. We can feel deeply attuned to all the parts of ourselves, experientially and viscerally.[20] In this phase, we learn to forgive others and ourselves, and take responsibility for our joy and peace. God's grace is needed because we have often not been true or faithful to ourselves and others or God. We learn to love ourselves as God loves us, knowing God in ourselves and knowing ourselves in God. A contemplative agenda includes the recognition of our place in community, insight into our interconnectedness with all things in Christ, and a perception of Christ in all things.

Unification is the culminating stage in which we discover that, through our primary relationship with our spirit and God, we can be in unity with all that is. As we take care of ourselves and our relationships, there is more potential for everyone's health and abundance. We can freely find our mission in the world because we don't need to be externally rewarded or base our success on results. Love's reward is being cherished by God. In each moment and incident, there is a desire to be focused, concentrated, and consecrated.

By trusting that God will be faithful and help us cultivate life, we practice an unfettered lifestyle of honesty, dignity, compassion, reverence, peacemaking, community, responsibility, justice, and simplicity. Beyond personal self-realization, we find our mission to overcome and resist all that degrades and assaults life. Though we would rather avoid it, we are not afraid to suffer, and we accept that there is a longing in us that will never be completely satisfied until our resurrection. Our ongoing awareness is that we are alive and sojourning with Christ.[21]

19. Matt 5:6.
20. Ps 111:10.
21. For more detail on this contemplative practice, see the work of Gerald May and John Finch discussed in Sölle, *Silent Cry*, 89–93.

When I struggle, my thoughts and emotions slide into anxiety. I tend to fret about my day, my relationships, my work, my presence in the world, or the future. What is most helpful to me, when I struggle, is the experience of turning my attachments, relationships, projects, and future plans over to God. I have found that to experience freedom from the demands I place on myself requires me to, as Bonhoeffer said, "come and die with Jesus."[22] Full freedom to be in the present requires detachment from the present. To let go of all things, to die to all my attachments in life, I name all of my principal concerns, responsibilities, relationships, and everything I care about and, one by one, simply let them go. I "die" to these things. As I experience this relinquishment, I begin to feel free. I don't have to hang on to anyone or anything. If I actually die today, so be it.

Freedom in letting everything go helps me sleep better at night. During the day, this freedom provides a more flexible approach toward my investments. I approach the events of my day with a sense of basic acceptance, allowing what is to be. Attempts to control, compete, or demand give way to a state of accepting and freely receiving the opportunities I have. I believe that this is apostle Paul's wisdom when he says, "I am crucified with Christ so that it is no longer I who live but Christ lives in me."[23]

There is such a peace in this state of detachment, where I can simply exist and do what I can when I can without ultimate demand and pressure. I then welcome my day to unfold with a deeper sense of inner calm and joy. My spirit is not only at rest, it is hopeful.

For me, a healthy spirituality takes me into my history with an attitude of gratitude. I recall former proximate hopes, any clear memories that feel lively, enriching, graceful, healing, educational, inspiring, loving, joyful, and godly. Multitudes of examples can meet these descriptors. Doing this spiritual discipline provides me with a foundation for deep appreciation, amazement, and joy.

Along with a thank-you to the past, I want to look forward with a *yes* toward my future with God in the new creation, the new heavens and earth, the new Jerusalem. I desire to live with an anticipation of this bright future and can visualize the culmination of everything in life that seems beautiful and good. Confidence in God's future includes so much: teeming life, splendor, exuberance, abundance, victory, unlimited joy, love in all and for all, harmony, complete health and wellness, universal just and

---

22. Bonhoeffer, *Cost of Discipleship*, 44.
23. Gal 2:20.

peaceful community, and a fully restored creation. Natural life can be pictured thriving with unlimited beauty, flourishing people in relationships, all the saints and hosts of heaven, ancestors and loved ones, and God, the source of it all, being "all in all."

My goal is to recognize that this picture of God's future is my true citizenship and that I'm in the world but not of the world. I want to image my future vividly, as the personal divine reference point, so that I can see it, smell it, taste it, touch it, and hear it.

Imagination can bring a more immediate knowing and relishing in the current moment. I can picture myself with that certain destiny while having an initial experience of that reality now. Spiritually based, destiny-congruent behavior is a daily project.

11

Soul Work: Hopeful Character

> "I have come to a place in experience where, in every sense of the word, I have surrendered myself to our Creator because literally there was no one else. . . . I have been shown in darkness, light, have learned that even in prison, one can be free. I am grateful. I have come to see that there is good in every situation, sometimes we just have to look for it."
>
> —Kayla Mueller, executed in captivity by ISIS in Iraq

We can understand hopeful character as our internal, moral structure that is revealed by our long-term patterns of valuing elements in our life. Character is based in the kinds of ethical thoughts, feelings, and tendencies we habitually act from, and it helps us predict how people will act in the future. Character gives us a moral consistency so we don't have to endlessly recreate our own moral compass. It is the continuity of our purpose and valuing behavior that shows our lives have been made more than we could acknowledge at any one time.

Christian character is not as concerned with simple decisions and choices, but more with the kind of people we are prior to all choices. We are people of a particular social location, a particular mission, a particular future. Too often, aspects of our character are underdeveloped and may be fragmented with unreconciled priorities. We frequently engage in self-deception in which we can rationalize, avoid, deny, and even be dishonest with ourselves, others, and God. Many people attempt on their own to improve their character and many attempts at self-invention or improvement fail without an overall strategy.

If not centered spiritually, our character may become mired in duplicity. I believe the strongest human character is one that is following God's design and acts daily on this hope. Character develops when we trust God fully, knowing that God has redeemed us all and will always work in our circumstances to bring us to a better place.[1]

Through the Scriptures, we understand that though we are capable of being devious, God is greater and knows all things.[2] Because we can repent and are forgiven and loved, we are free to lay aside every encumbrance and every personal excuse and run with endurance the race that is set before us, fixing our eyes on Jesus.[3]

Jesus has shown us how to live in single-minded pursuit of God's will, even to the point of death. The apostle Paul wrote that he, too, pressed toward the call of God in Christ Jesus.[4] It is important that we cultivate a master image of One who, "for the joy set before him . . . endured the cross, scorning its shame," and is now with God.[5]

Christian Character in Historical Perspective

Christian character arises from a particular understanding of history. Though we are deeply embedded in human history, we have discovered that historical progress is not linear. We cannot plot on a line where we are in relationship to the beginning or the end of history.

The progress of history is marked by our participation in the work of Jesus in the world, not by a chain of cause and effect. History's end goal is the coming of God in Christ. It is a gift to us, and we do not control when or how we will receive it. We know what gives history meaning, and we know where it is headed—toward God's kingdom with the new heaven and earth—but we cannot ourselves give meaning to history, nor can we manipulate history toward its destiny. Our hope is grounded in God's power to provide meaning to our existence and complete our future. As we discussed earlier, our hopeful view of today is generated by our anticipation of God's tomorrow.

---

1. Rom 5:5; 8:28.
2. Jer 17:9; 1 John 3:20.
3. Heb 12:1–2.
4. Phil 3:13–14.
5. Heb 12:2.

SECTION TWO: HOPE TRANSFORMS HUMAN PERSONHOOD AND COMMUNITY

So, we are historical people on a journey. Knowing our destiny, though we haven't yet arrived, moves us to be peaceful and hopeful. We can be patient because, ultimately, God is bringing healing and justice. Since our being and our future are given by God, we who hope in Christ have no need to protect ourselves through violent resistance or strive through selfish ambition. We can endure suffering and find the meaning that comes from God.[6]

Character is relational just as hope and personality are relational. We are shaped by the relationships surrounding us and by the history and context of those relationships. The Bible gives us many examples of people who were steadfast in the face of adversity, and, by remembering them, we become part of the historical narrative that generates power to prevail in our circumstances. God has created a peoplehood capable of sustaining the character of Christ.

This hope we have in Christ—"Christian hope"—is for the entire universe, not just humanity. We see this most clearly expressed in Paul's letter to the Romans:

> For the creation waits with eager longing for the revealing of the children of God; for the creation was subjected to futility, not of its own will but by the will of the one who subjected it, in hope that the creation itself will be set free from its bondage to decay and will obtain the freedom of the glory of the children of God. We know that the whole creation has been groaning in labor pains until now; and not only the creation, but we ourselves, who have the first fruits of the Spirit, groan inwardly while we wait for adoption, the redemption of our bodies. For by hope we were saved. Now hope that is seen is not hope. For who hopes for what is seen? But if we hope for what we do not see, we wait for it with patience.[7]

Christ is also described as the mediator of all living things.[8] The first Jesus followers saw Christ in all things and all things in Christ.[9] As we read in 2 Peter 3:13, peace and unity with nature will happen through the resurrected Christ on God's earth. Similarly, Dietrich Bonhoeffer

---

6. Wilson, *Gospel Virtues*, 111; Hauerwas, "On Developing Hopeful Virtues," 337.
7. Rom 8:19–25.
8. 1 Cor 8:6.
9. Col 1:15–17.

maintained: "Only the one who loves God and the earth in one breath, can hope for the kingdom of God."[10]

When we have a picture of the coming future of all things in Christ, we will care for the creation because (a) God loves it and sent Jesus to redeem it, (b) our very life comes from it, and (c) the Spirit of Jesus goes with us each day. We and the rest of the created order may groan together as we wait, pray, and hope for this consummation. We are able to wait because the future reconciliation of all things has already begun, and we are a part of it.

Character Formation and Friendship

As with our understanding of personality, our reflection on Christian character should move us to seek out other Christians, sharing life through fellowship, play, celebrations, work, ministry, prayer, and study. We cannot develop a well-formed character outside the company of others. Healthy friendships can satisfy our desire for closeness and connection over time and we can share life with mutuality and reciprocity. In the context of character-building friendship, we can practice values such as compassion and magnanimity. Our long-term friends help us know our true character and, sometimes, they see us better than we see ourselves. Good friends are generous and thoughtful, see beyond themselves and share life for each other's benefit. Our closest friends may not necessarily be like us in many ways, and we should celebrate those differences: they offer us an unfolding adventure of stimulation to be more than what we've been. Close friendship brings likeness and difference together.[11]

Living with long-term friendships may develop our capacity to trust and be trustworthy. As we are able to confide in others and share confidences, our character can grow. All of us want to know and be known completely, without fear of judgment. Our best friends allow us to share our deepest fears, disappointments, failures, and places of shame. True friendship is a shared vulnerability of sacred trust where our deepest parts are known with emotional and spiritual sensitivity and safety.[12]

True friendship teaches us how to love because it asks us to share time, sacrifices, patience, forgiveness, solidarity, adversity, and loyalty. Long-term friendships help us overcome our self-deceptions, insecurities,

---

10. Quoted in Moltmann, "Resurrection of Christ," 148.
11. Wadell, *Becoming Friends*, 55–65.
12. See Wadell, *Becoming Friends*.

or felt inadequacy. They teach us more about ourselves and our values than we can learn on our own and help us stay committed to our most important goals and projects. When we learn lessons of goodness and virtue and faithfully live our deeply held values, we become people of integrity, the goal of character.[13]

In ongoing, character-building friendships, we routinely reflect on our values and inquire about what we might be missing. A quality friend has a vision of our wellness and completeness, helping us strengthen our relationship to God and ourselves. We are far better off facing the challenges and adversities of life with our closest friends, cultivating hope and hopeful character together.

My character formation has been significantly enhanced by a long-term relationship with my friend Al. For over thirty years, Al has shared much of the faith and vision of life that I am describing. As a medical doctor, he pursued a mission of service in the community, especially to those whom he treated as a physician. Believing that God called him to care for the poor and most sick, he chose to practice medicine with what was our area's most underserved and health-challenged population—the Puyallup Tribe of Indians. Instead of living in a comfortable middle- or upper-class neighborhood, where many well-paid physicians reside, he decided, along with his wife, Shari, to live in one of the poorest neighborhoods of Tacoma, Washington.

Here, in an environment of poverty, higher crime, and instability, Al and Shari raised six children. Al's children were sent to underfunded public schools, and he and Shari added to their education with music lessons, academic instruction, and the establishment of a neighborhood basketball team. Shari taught in a poor, urban middle school and focused on developing capable, curious minds, challenging the racial achievement gap, enhancing student self-esteem and prosocial behavior. With Al and Shari's support, their children excelled academically, musically, and athletically, forming a brass band and leading their high school basketball team to two state championships. The family became involved in an urban Lutheran church that itself has a strong mission in the local community.

A few years ago, with his encouragement, Al and I took a trip to Europe in order to visit important healing places, including the Chartres Cathedral, Lourdes, Assisi, and Rome. Each of these sites holds spiritual significance for us and we prayerfully experienced their edifying environments.

---

13. Wadell, *Becoming Friends*, 67–76.

Al has continued his medical work with the Puyallup Tribe of Indians for more than thirty years and, partly in response to my illness, advocated for a new cancer treatment facility, the Puyallup Tribe's Salish Integrative Cancer Care Center.

For about twenty-five years, we have met regularly for breakfast at the same restaurant with the same waitress, usually at the same table! Our conversations have been full of grace, support, challenge, and information. Al's friendship embodies virtues of personal commitment, prayer, service, social justice, spiritual nurture, and hope. Ultimately, his personal character has reinforced my hope, resiliency, and determination to live well.

How Character Develops

Healthy long-term friendships are one of many internal and external contributions to our character. Psychologist Lawrence Kohlberg, who made significant contributions in the twentieth century to the study of moral judgment, believed that we develop our moral selves when confronted with challenges or moral dilemmas that may require a more adequate understanding and reasoning than what we've used previously.[14] In general, he maintained people progress morally from (a) youthful compliance with the external control of caregivers, to (b) self-understanding and obedience when caregivers are away, and finally to (c) self-directed moral behavior. Kohlberg proposed that most important values and character traits are those universally good for everyone. Universal values that take into account peoples' ultimate good are supported across cultures and inspire people to think and act for their common humanity.

As part of his research, Kohlberg conceptualized six stages of moral—and aspects of character—development. Each stage moves the moral compass forward from a self-centered preoccupation with individual needs to an others-directed attention to human thriving for all.

Kohlberg's Stages of Moral Development

Level 1	Preconventional	Stage 1	Obedience & Punishment	Avoid getting in trouble
		Stage 2	Individualism & Exchange	What's in it for me? (less pain, more pleasure)

14. See Gonzalez-BeHass and Willems, *Theories in Educational Psychology*, 139–72.

Kohlberg's Stages of Moral Development

Level 2	Conventional	Stage 3	Good Boy / Good Girl	Makes me look good, gains approval of others
		Stage 4	Law & Order	Because that's the rule / it's the law
Level 3	Postconventional	Stage 5	Social Contract	For the common good & the welfare of others
		Stage 6	Universal Ethical Principles	Personal integrity, no matter the price

From the above diagram, we note the fifth and sixth stages, characterized as post-conventional morality: social contract orientation and universal ethical principles. In the fifth stage, the values or traditions we seek to follow display our character. Our rights and the rights of others are being protected. In the sixth stage, we become aware of internally based values or principles transcending any immediate context, for which we may sacrifice.

But not all social psychologists agree with his approach. Carol Gilligan argued that Kohlberg's stages focus too heavily on a male orientation toward justice rather than a female orientation toward care, undervaluing women's empathy-based ethics and relational responsibility. Other critiques of his work have noted the missing moral impact of diversity, including race, and some have argued that moral and character development should include a vision of our ultimate concerns with a trust in God's present action. If Kohlberg's stages—and our ranking of them—are imperfect, he does offer us a partial way of understanding character development important for community life.

It is important to recognize that transcendent vision and values need to be incorporated in group decision-making for the most just and democratic process possible. We all form perspective and make daily decisions involving our priorities. When our daily priorities line up with deeply held, life-enhancing convictions over time, it is likely our character is moving in a hopeful way.

SOUL WORK: HOPEFUL CHARACTER

Strengthening Hopeful Character

How do we intentionally evolve character? Beginning with ourselves, it is important we survey the central values that currently contribute to our character. As we look back over our lives, we may ask: When have we exhibited values such as compassion, reverence, responsibility, respect, accountability, service, justice, forgiveness, hospitality, commitment, truthfulness, or discipline? When have we felt internal strength or fortitude? During prior crises or challenges, what character disposition showed forth?

How about today? What perspective or convictions do we embody regardless of others' opinions?

Consider people widely respected as models of great character. Which of their qualities are outstanding? On our wall in the family dining room, we have pictures of Christian character whom my wife and I admire. We have looked, each day, at the faces of Rigoberta Menchu, Nelson Mandela, Martin Luther King Jr., Sojourner Truth, Oscar Romero, Charles Finney, Frances Willard, Dag Hammarskjöld, Marie Corrigan, Dorothy Day, Thomas Merton, Dietrich Bonhoeffer, Francis of Assisi, Susan B. Anthony, and Cecily Saunders. It was important for our children to be exposed to people with exemplary lives. Though each of these people had their imperfections or flaws, they embodied, often in inspiring fashion, wonderful, hopeful, Christlike qualities that contributed to their flourishing and perseverance through adversity.

It's helpful for us to study people whose character we admire and wish to emulate, by listing their specific qualities.

It can take emergency situations for many of us to discover or rediscover some of our own values. Imagine with me, if you will, a rather hopeless individual—we'll call him John—who tended to be fairly solitary and lacked confidence in engaging other people or traveling far from home. If John were confronted with a real human emergency, such as seeing a child being hit by a car in front of his house, he would likely—as would anyone, hopefully—put aside any limitations he felt and attend to that child. Perhaps that child would need to be taken to the doctor or an emergency room. Without access to an ambulance, our rather secluded, hopeless individual would likely pack that child into the car and speed off to the closest emergency room. Arriving at the emergency room, John would stay with the child until the child's parents could be notified and arrive. He may not know these people, but his humanitarian response would have been driven by his character and specific values such as compassion, responsibility, and service. Without the challenge, John may not have recognized just how important those particular convictions were or have had the opportunity to act on them.

If we find ourselves in challenging or stressful situations, what motivates us to act for ourselves or others? When we are reflecting on our action or inaction, can we imagine different scenarios like the one above, clarifying what convictions we really live by? Perhaps we can enlist others who may perceive our character differently to share their observations.

Another route toward discovering our values involves exploring what generates passion or healthy emotional arousal in us. When we examine aspects of ourselves, others, or the community at large that we either really like or strongly dislike, we are experiencing values that we either have or wish we had. What new values would we like to incorporate in our character? What existing values would we like to strengthen?

Values are cultivated when we are exposed to situations where human life is being challenged, diminished, abused, disabled, or neglected. When our daughters were in their grade-school years, we decided they should be introduced to human need in a fashion that would help build social awareness and compassion. Every month for many years, my daughters served dinner to individuals in our community who were experiencing food insecurity or homelessness. That exposure to human need and serving others had profound impact on both of them.

Fast forward to 2020. Our older daughter continues to do passionate social work with homeless people in our area. Our younger daughter, who is an educator, has intentionally taught at two of the poorest, most diverse schools in the North Puget Sound Region. Both developed values of compassion, responsibility, and service in a very organic manner. Most of us will grow values as we have opportunity to give to others who are unable to give back.

We can also clarify our mission and values by visualizing a future projection. Let's imagine that we're now in our mid-eighties, visiting our doctor for an annual physical. Though we have been in reasonably good health, our physician informs us of both bad and good news. The bad news is that we have an illness that is going to end our life as we know it, beginning in about six months. The good news is that, in the next six months, we are free without any restrictions to do what we want, with whom we want, where we want, how we want, and for whatever reasons we want. The doctor says to us, "Go, live well, enjoying all you want to experience in the next six months." The doctor advises us to return in six months and promises to help us prepare for our mortality. She reminds us that it would be a good idea if, during those six months of freedom, we do what we can to prepare for our death.

We leave the doctor's office and immediately are faced with important questions about how we will live the next six months. What do we want to do? What do we want to experience? With whom do we want to spend time? Where do we want to go? What do we want to learn about ourselves or others? What do we need to experience or reflect on with others that will help us face our mortality with hope? Who do we want to be with when we are dying? What do we want to say to them and what do we want to hear from them?

Our imaginary eighty-year-old self, who has wisely lived those last six months ahead of returning to the doctor, may have good counsel for us currently. What advice would this experienced person have for us today? What would our future person encourage us to do or not do? How would we be encouraged to spend our time? What values would be most important to live at this time?

No one lives out their values all the time in every way. Our goal is to be proactive, incorporating and experiencing the mission and convictions most important to us on a regular basis. When we are following our heart, living from the inside out, we are a person of integrity. In the end, integrity is the goal of a hopeful character.

Living the Hopefulness of Christ

As we've explored, character can develop in despair and suffering. Challenge brings us opportunity to identify with Christ and his future coming. Suffering may point us toward Jesus' action in our world.

The apostle Paul said that endurance in suffering is what turns our fate into destiny.[15] This is true of any affliction or adversity we may encounter. We endure suffering because, through our resurrected, crucified Christ, we have been given enduring power over death and all forms of subjugation that rely on the power of death. We can have confidence that, though our enemies may even kill us, they cannot determine the meaning of our death.

---

15. Stanley Hauerwas has written more persuasively about the theology and ethics of Christian character than anyone I know. See, for example, " On Developing Hopeful Virtues."

SECTION TWO: HOPE TRANSFORMS HUMAN PERSONHOOD AND COMMUNITY

The power of our character allows us to endure the face of oppression because we refuse to let our oppressors define our victimization. Suffering can be endured, in part, because no matter what may be done to us, we know that those who would try to determine the meaning of our life by threatening our death have themselves already decisively lost.

When we endure suffering, we discover that God has given us a character capable of sustaining a hope that does not disappoint. Hopeful people have enduring courage and contextualize their pain as part of the larger story of God's sacrificial redemptive movement. By nature, we all have proximate hopes for our temporal affairs. While those hopes are important, our human strength is not necessarily sufficient to sustain hope in adversity, unless we are led beyond provisional hopes to a lasting hope in God.

An example of hopeful suffering comes from Etty Hillesum, a young Jewish Dutch woman who was eventually deported to Auschwitz. She kept a diary as she awaited her inevitable deportation. She wrote:

> When you have an interior life, it doesn't matter which side of the prison fence you're on . . . I have already died a thousand deaths in a thousand concentration camps. I know about everything and am no longer appalled by the latest reports. In one way or another I know it all. And yet I find life beautiful and meaningful. From minute to minute . . .
>
> The few big things that matter in life are what we have to keep in mind; the rest can be quietly abandoned. And you can find these few big things anywhere, you have to keep rediscovering them in yourself so that you can be renewed. And in spite of everything you always end up with the same conviction: life is good after all . . . The realms of the soul and the spirit are so spacious and unending that this little bit of physical discomfort and suffering really doesn't matter all that much. I do not feel I have been robbed of my freedom; essentially no one can do me any harm at all.[16]

This outstanding example of character and faith illustrates our capacity to be well with ourselves and God in the face of major persecution.

As we have seen, the values coming from being recipients of God's love are of a different kind than "natural" values. The person whose life is lived in hope and peace with God simply does not understand the world the same way as the person who is unaware of God. They inhabit different stories and, ultimately, different interpretations of life. When we are attuned to Christ, we feel the most harmony with who we are and can directly face reality.

---

16. Quoted in Lenoir, *Happiness*, 97, 179.

SOUL WORK: HOPEFUL CHARACTER

Daily life praxis is identified with God's reign and our time oriented by God's future. Character is shaped by spiritual disciplines such as solitude, fasting, worship, and service. These disciplines cultivate enduring dispositional skills and values that cannot easily be compromised.

In Galatians 5:22–23, we read of character traits such as love, joy, peace, patience, kindness, goodness, faithfulness, gentleness, and self-control, also known as the "fruit of the spirit." These values are determined by our commitment to Jesus and the presence of his Spirit in us, not a set of abstract dogmas. Our character evolves, not only as an improvement of what we have been, but as a transformation of who we are. In Christ, we are becoming new persons who live by hope: "Therefore, if anyone is in Christ, he is a new creation; old things have passed away; behold, all things have become new."[17]

The hope we have been given through Christ makes possible the re-positioning of our lives in a new history, a new journey, that is not possible without his life, death, and resurrection. Jesus fills us with his Spirit and, as we allow him, lives out his life and love through us.

We recall words from the apostle Paul: "I have been crucified with Christ; it is no longer I who live, but Christ lives in me; and the life which I now live in the flesh I live by faith in the Son of God, who loved me and gave himself for me."[18] It is Jesus who forgives us, transforms us, and empowers us to step forward in cultivating our character. Jesus' life in us, not our own strength, determines the course of our journey, our character, and our destiny. From that, we gain hope!

---

17. 2 Cor 5:17 (NKJV).
18. Gal 2:20.

12

Building Hopeful Community

"It is the responsibility of caring others to do hope with us."

—Kaethe Weingarten

THE CAPITALISTIC MARKET ECONOMY in which we live threatens to completely define our cultural identity. In this environment, people are valued as units of production and the selling price is the means of value. Advertisers tell us we need more, need to change, and need commercial help. A consumer mentality creates the illusion that "success" is purchasing and utilizing goods and services. Our temptation to receive institutionally defined care is too often based on the concept of commodification: take a human concern, define it as a problem, and then market an advertised solution.[1]

Christian covenantal community resists and contrasts culturally defined notions of scarcity and dependency.[2] Our true freedom and hope come not simply through our individual efforts or goals but in being joined to God's historical movement of salvation. Jesus provides us a story of how God saves people and ultimately saves the world. God, not nations, is the future of the world. We understand ourselves and others as part of a grand story that begins with creation and ends with new creation. It is a narrative that stretches from the beginning of time to the end of time, from an age that ends in death to an age that ends in life.

In the Gospel of John, the Greek word for "world" describes the attempt by people to live as if their lives are their own and under their own control. It suggests that security comes through the power of the nation, military might, or other human enterprise. In Jesus, the "world" has been

---

1. McKnight and Block, *Abundant Community*.
2. See Block et al., *Other Kingdom*; and McKnight and Block, *Abundant Community*.

redirected and the new creation has begun. God is witnessed most clearly through people called to follow Jesus together in a visible community displaying Jesus' victory over all competing authorities. Being transformed according to the world's true future, we become better people following Jesus together. It's a blessing to live God's truthful story in a world that often lives as if there is no God.

God's way of saving us, of giving us hope, is social, countercultural, and communal.[3] German theologian Dietrich Bonhoeffer maintained that Christianity is the only religion for which the concept of community is essentially inseparable. We are called to a shared life that is the principal locus of God's presence and future. God creates community, sharing the fellowship of life by socializing us to be a certain kind of people with a particular vision of human existence. It is in community with others that we can often learn how to see what God sees and do what God does. When we rightly see the world from God's perspective, we can confidently act in the world. In a faithful, intentional Christian community, we can find a radical political alternative in which people refuse to let the politics of deceit and death determine their lives. These communities may practice a nonviolent presence and courage that makes little sense to the world.

The Trinitarian relationships of God, Jesus, and the Holy Spirit involve an open community in which we can all participate. God, Jesus, and the Holy Spirit relate to each other interconnectedly, providing us with a pattern for our own community. All living things live in one another and with one another, from one another and for one another. We are all participants in an interdependent ecological community of God's creation. Bringing the entire creation, all of life, together in culminating community is the Holy Spirit's work.

Life in God's Spirit resists all that diminishes or assaults people. Where the Spirit is, there is freedom.[4] As we are faced with forces that bring death, the principalities and powers of our age, we cry out for the Holy Spirit who sustains the entire creation. Through God's Spirit and the community the Spirit builds, we can deepen our experience of life and our existence can become more joyful.

In the Trinity we find motherhood and fatherhood, sisterhood and brotherhood. Along with God as Creator and Jesus as Redeemer, the Holy

---

3. See Hauerwas and Willimon, *Resident Aliens* for a good description of Christian community in North American culture.

4. Col 3:17.

Spirit includes femininity, comfort, and motherly love. Theologian Jürgen Moltmann wrote, "God comes to us in Jesus as the brother next to us. We come to face him as the Abba father of Jesus, and we live out of our mother, the Holy Spirit."[5]

This feminine conception of the Spirit is repeated in the New Testament. In the Gospel of John, Jesus teaches that the Spirit will comfort his followers and guide them as a mother comforts her children.[6] It is the Spirit that brings new birth to the followers of Jesus.[7] Believers are children of the motherly Holy Spirit. It is said God's Spirit facilitated Jesus' mother's pregnancy. Our recognition of femininity central to God's image leads us to a resistance of patriarchy and a just human community of sisters and brothers in Christ.

Franciscan friar and spirituality author Richard Rohr, in his *Divine Dance*, helps us clarify certain aspects of God's Trinitarian community. Our Creator's agenda is the deepest possible communion and fellowship with every creature on earth. God is the life force of everything, between each and every object in all of life, flowing through everything since the beginning of creation. This "whirling cosmic dance" is a threesome of flow, radical relatedness, and perfect communion. The divine dance of relentless affection is inherently moving, dynamic, and generative. Change is integral to God, because God is love and love is constantly transcending itself toward greater union. As three in one and one in three, the Trinity is unity in diversity and diversity in unity.[8]

In our human experience, three or more people are needed for intentional community. What often inhibits us from this divine dance is fear, doubt, or personal alienation. When we have resources and people, and we stop this divine flow through us, with us, and in us, we fall into what traditionally is called sin. Sin is the state of being closed down, shut off, blocked, isolating, and thus resisting the eternal life-flow of which we were designed to be a part. Sin, in general, keeps us from intentional community and accepting our deep interconnectedness with humanity and the earth.[9]

---

5. Bauckham, *Theology of Jürgen Moltmann*, 170.
6. John 14:26.
7. John 3:3–6.
8. Rohr, *Divine Dance*, 39, 56, 142–50.
9. Rohr, *Divine Dance*, 56.

People of the Covenant

In order to deal with a flawed and often rebellious world, God chose Abraham and Sarah to begin what would eventually be a peoplehood for God's never-ending project to redeem all people.[10] Living as strangers in a foreign land, Abraham and Sarah trusted God for their future.[11]

Abraham and Sarah's descendants became covenantal, uniting in allegiance to their God.[12] In Exodus 19:5–6, God said: "Now if you obey me fully and keep my covenant, then out of all nations you will be my treasured possession. Although the whole earth is mine, you will be for me a kingdom of priests and a holy nation." God was working through these folks to create a new group alternative not depending on props of coercive power and the influence of surrounding theocracies.[13]

The most important covenantal event in early biblical history happened at Sinai, where escaped Hebrew slaves from Egypt were called into a community following the proclamation of the Ten Commandments. God wanted the covenant community to embody divine life: "See, I set before you today life and property, death, and destruction. For I command you today to love the Lord your God, to walk in his ways and to keep his commands, decrees and laws . . . Now choose life, so that you and your children may live."[14]

God intended Hebrew tribal units, as covenantal communities, to be a principal focus of God's action in the world. Each tribal group operated with considerable autonomy, sometimes cooperating with other tribes and sometimes not. As we observed, what God willed for people, and what covenantal relationship was meant to promote, is best characterized in the concept of shalom: people experiencing together a salvation of wholeness, harmony, peace, justice, and freedom in intentional community. In God's peoplehood, each tribe shared the symbols, language, norms, values, rituals, laws, and confession that allowed them to withstand the influence of surrounding groups. These communities were meant to be a stronghold of human kindness, worship, and social integrity.

---

10. Gen 12:1–3.
11. Heb 11:9.
12. Josh 24:24.
13. Yoder, "Exodus," 29.
14. Deut 30:15, 19.

SECTION TWO: HOPE TRANSFORMS HUMAN PERSONHOOD AND COMMUNITY

Life in the New Covenant

Jesus announced the beginning of God's new age and new covenant, the kingdom of God.[15] Jesus did not take time to write or create a theological system, but instead invested himself in creating a new peoplehood, a new kind of human family. As the bearer of the new covenant, Jesus' countercultural community would function as an outpost for God's kingdom, carving out its distinctive life in the midst of the values, assumptions, and structures of an age passing away.[16]

A hopeful community anticipates the future of God and shows the world a picture of its true identity. It exists as a preview of human possibility, a model of what God has wanted all along. The ultimate unity and commonness of human destiny was inaugurated in Jesus' community.

One theologian summarizes the new social reality that Jesus created thus:

> When he called his society together, Jesus gave its members a new way of life to live. He gave them a new way to deal with offenders—by forgiving them. He gave them a new way to deal with violence—by suffering. He gave them a new way to deal with money—by sharing it. He gave them a new way to deal with problems of leadership—by drawing upon the gift of every member, even the most humble. He gave them a new way to deal with the corrupt society—by building a new order, not smashing the old. He gave them a new pattern of relationships between man and woman, between parent and child, between master and slave, in which was made concrete a radical new vision of what it means to be a human person. He gave them a new attitude toward the state and toward the enemy nation.[17]

When God raised Jesus from death, the divine plan for the destiny of all people was clarified and inaugurated. The future of the world was decided with Jesus' resurrection, such that people's current attitude toward him was hopeful for their personal destiny. Covenantal life was anchored in Jesus. Because he was present in the community through the Holy Spirit, the reality of God's future was part of the community's experience.[18] The Holy Spirit

---

15. Mark 1:14–15; Heb 8:8–13.
16. Yoder, "Exodus," 29.
17. Yoder, *Original Revolution*, 29.
18. Moltmann, *Church in the Power of the Spirit*, 293.

is the power of the resurrection, the power of creation and new creation.[19] Calling into being that which is not, making the godless righteous, and raising the dead is the work of God's Spirit. The Spirit is the reviving presence of eternal life in the midst of the history of death.[20]

For the first community of Jesus' followers, God's Spirit created a transparent common life, gave charismatic gifts, transformed economics, inspired shared action, catalyzed evangelism, and engendered social solidarity. In its worship and common life, the earliest Jerusalem community became an essential feature of the gospel proclamation. Writing in his Acts of the Apostles, Luke explained, "All who believed were together and had all things in common; they would sell their possessions and goods and distribute the proceeds to all, as any had need. Day by day, as they spent much time together in the temple, they broke bread at home and ate their food with glad and generous hearts, praising God and having the goodwill of all the people. And day by day the Lord added to their number those who were being saved."[21]

So, early Spirit-led followers of Jesus garnered hope from the resurrection of the crucified Christ and journeyed in light of the cross of the risen Christ. This community of the Way, and others that followed, centered themselves in the worship of Jesus, whose Spirit was really in and among them, doing his ministry.[22] In their worship, early disciples remembered to whom they belonged and whom they served.

The apostle Paul argued that to be justified and saved before God, to share in Christ's death and resurrection, removed any basis for personal barriers, hierarchies, privileges, or unequal status among Jesus' followers. This social life put everyone on the same footing: Jew and Greek, male and female, rich and poor, slave and free.[23] As biblical scholar Markus Barth argued, God's saving action established that

> Justification is a community-building event: sharing in the death and resurrection of Jesus Christ is the means of justification: only in Christ's death and resurrection is the new person created from at least two, a Jew and a Greek, a man and a woman, a slave and

---

19. Rom 8:11; 4:17.

20. 1 Cor 15:45; Moltmann, *Church in the Power of the Spirit*, 293.

21. Acts 2:44–47.

22. In fact, the reality that the resurrected Jesus was with them and would bring a future consummation that resembled a messianic banquet led to great joy (Acts 2:46).

23. Gal 3:28.

a free man. . . . The new person is present in actuality where two previously alien and hostile people came together before God. Justification in Christ is thus not an individual miracle happening to this person or that person, which each may seek or possess for himself, but rather is God's grace joining together this person and that person, of the near and far . . . It is a social event.[24]

Paul believed followers of Jesus would be so impacted by awareness of Christ that the fellowship would literally be called the "body of Christ."[25] Christians were to be members one of another and recognize each sister or brother in Christ as a basic part of one spiritual family. Becoming involved in a group of followers of Jesus was like becoming part of a new humanity that anticipated the reconciliation of the entire cosmos. This hopeful community of the future may reflect a social life that, by its very existence and its lifestyle, threatens and predicts the eventual overthrow of all death-dealing human dynamics.

Our first family is our intentional community of sisters and brothers in Christ.[26] Intentional Christian community today begins with the calling together of Jesus' followers giving witness to God's kingdom in the power of the Holy Spirit. The community is prophetic through its common life that gives witness before the world to God's promised future. It is a priestly fellowship, interceding for others and witnessing the liberating presence of Christ. It is a kingly people participating in the divine rule.[27] It is a messianic people finding its destiny through the workings of the risen Christ.[28]

Professor James W. Jones summarized the social power of the body of Christ, a communal entity of hope filled with the Spirit:

> If the church can give the world an example of *koinonia,* it will do more toward healing the problems of society than by any program it might undertake. From this taste of community, economists and political scientists might mine a new economics and politics of community, which would overcome the dilemmas represented by capitalism or socialism, anarchy or totalitarianism. In contributing thus to the healing of the world, the church would also heal itself. Living in community would teach people a balance between individual experience and corporate responsibility. 'He who would

24. Quoted in Ross, "Journey in Egypt," 22–23.
25. Gal 1:22; 4:19.
26. Mark 3:31–35.
27. Rev 1:5; 5:10; 20:6.
28. Moltmann, *Church in the Power of the Spirit,* 301.

gain his life must lose it' is part of the paradox of community. In *koinonia*, the individual's needs are fulfilled and they become themselves without loss of any of their personal integrity. Yet they are also pointed beyond selfishness to their brothers and sisters and they are freed from their hang ups in order to love others."[29]

Our communal life is shaped by the character of our God. God is the one who showed us how to love enemies; reconcile all people; create the earth for everyone to share; demonstrate a special concern for the poor, the hungry, and the persecuted; display that this world can crucify innocent people; and take initiative in redeeming and saving humanity. This is the common life worth living for and dying for. Followers of Jesus today face the truth of challenging social realities, from global pandemics to global warming or global nuclear annihilation, with resurrection faith in the One who has made heaven and earth.

Intentional Relationships in God's Community

One historian observed this early Christian community practice:

> Every one of them who has anything gives ungrudgingly to the one who has nothing. If they see a traveling stranger, they bring him under their roof. They rejoice over him as over a real brother, for they do not call one another brothers after the flesh, but they know they are brothers in the Spirit and in God. If they hear that one of them is imprisoned or oppressed for the sake of Christ, they take care of all his needs. If possible, they set him free. If anyone among them is poor or comes into want while they themselves have nothing to spare, they fast two or three days for him. In this way they can supply any poor man with the food he needs.[30]

Small countercultural Christian groups often similarly organized during the early Protestant era. Jörg Tucher's testimony in 1526 reveals an orientation toward God, hope, and community:

> They prayed a prayer together, that God might strengthen them to be able to carry the cross patiently. After that they interpreted the Scriptures according to each one's spiritual understanding, that they do nothing against God and act in love toward their neighbors, give enemies food, drink, and love them, etc. In short, that

29. Jones, *Spirit and the World*, 66.
30. Claiborne and Campolo, *Red Letter Revolution*, 19.

SECTION TWO: HOPE TRANSFORMS HUMAN PERSONHOOD AND COMMUNITY

all things should be held in common and each one should do their work, and if someone were needy, then they should share some of the common good with the needy.[31]

Followers of Jesus today come together in intentional community to discern how to understand and practice both personal and public discipleship. Most movements of significant social change develop out of various intentional communities at the grassroots level. Because of the unusual learning ability of the human brain, relationships can shape healthy personal growth and change. In turn, community relationships of secure attachment allow for more personal flexibility, adaptability, and reliability. Intentional Christian relationships create the basis for personal expansion, enhanced spirituality, and more complete sharing with others. Together, Christians can imitate the godly behavior surrounding them and grow in their desire to love and serve. Fidelity among God's people is formed by being part of a community to whom we are accountable and whose life is sustained by a God who models faithfulness for us.

Finding or starting an intentional Christian community is often very challenging. We cannot expect the institutional church to bestow community on us. It's up to us! Our individualistic culture and the belief of absolute rights to private property are difficult to overcome. We may search for potential community from a larger church of hundreds or a small handful of people. There may be a small variety of existing groups or churches we can investigate and explore. Our community-building God can be trusted to go with us on the search to find other appropriate followers of Jesus to share a hopeful life. We can trust that God will guide us as we actively ask, seek, and knock.

We can use these eight key group characteristics to discern intentional Christian communities:

1. **Spiritual Authenticity.** Do we recognize evidence of God working in the group under biblical authority? Is there an interplay of Christ-centered belief and action, faith and works?

2. **Liability.** Is there a sense of mutual responsibility where community members are protective, supportive, and loving to each other? Can the "we" be as strong as the "I?"

---

31. Snyder, *Following in the Footsteps of Christ*, 123.

3. **Accessibility.** Are the relationships allowing people to be available to each other as needed? Is there a growing sense of group stability and sufficiency?

4. **Accountability.** Based in God's grace and unconditional love, are the relationships open to discernment, confession, guidance, admonishment, or discipline? In potential relational conflicts, does the group have a well-defined strategy for processing differences and bringing healing or reconciliation?

5. **Servant Leadership.** Does the group practice a trusting servant leadership, following the example of Jesus, where everyone's talents, gifts, and resources are discerned, cultivated, and employed for the benefit of the group? Are community members open to sharing, where appropriate, childcare, caring for vulnerable people, housing, transportation, education, recreation, gardening, tools, and other resources?

6. **Collaboration.** Is the community in dialogue and cooperating with other intentional Christian communities close by and around the world in order to bring healing, social justice, and reconciliation beyond itself? Jesus acts through Spirit-led collaboration and ministry in the worldwide "body of Christ."

7. **Transparency.** Are people's possessions or wealth handled with transparency and appropriately deployed based on discerning the legitimate needs of others?

8. **Courage.** Since following Jesus is costly discipleship, are community members willing to face uncertainty, limitations, and losses? Is the group able to collectively sacrifice and grieve?

Developing a "covenant group" can be a helpful way to form intentional community. Whenever three or more people join together to explore covenantal commitment, with Christ at the center, they can confidently pray for discernment and a vision for their life together. In this growing, interconnected sacred space, people live by God's grace and develop a sense of being at home and safe with one another in secure attachments. With an emerging covenant group, people share the gifts of God in ministry with each other and experience interdependence. Balancing internal care with external service, the group avoids both emotional enmeshment and fragmenting disengagement. Spiritual disciplines can be practiced as people commit to encouraging, supporting, engaging in accountability, and praying for one another. It is in the company of compassionate others that we learn from God new thoughts and behaviors that are faithful, loving, cooperative, truthful, and forgiving.

In a nonanxious presence for each other, people are moved to accept parts of themselves and others that previously were avoided or denied. Since everyone is saved by grace the same way, there is no need for judgmentalism, and people can communicate with each other honestly and transparently. Anger and hurt can be accepted and constructively processed as people learn to resolve differences together. Healing happens when people understand each other, practice a loving conflict resolution, and forgive.

Alice Calhoun describes, in general, four stages of typical group development:

1. **Forming.** The group comes together and decides its purpose, content, and structure, and defines its covenant.

2. **Storming.** The group eventually struggles with differences and conflict, with control issues emerging.

3. **Norming.** The group constructively finds its way through struggle and conflict and turns its focus on members' shared gifts for the long haul.

4. **Transforming.** The group witnesses the fruit of its collective practice and continues to grow in trust, accountability, and vision. Unity is achieved as different people belong to, and experience oneness in, Christ.[32]

A blessing of Christian community is the opportunity for large- or small-community worship. Though styles may vary, we all seek to express our praise and thanks to God and experience togetherness in Christ.

Participating together in the real world that God is bringing, we learn the divine stories and practices that are often different from our own and which are, therefore, full of hope. Group worship connects us with our one true love, our first love, and our last love, and it helps us remember to whom we belong. It celebrates the victory of Jesus with both exuberance and contemplation.[33]

Through intercession, praying to God for specific people and situations, we acknowledge the current world is not fully redeemed and, at the same time, recognize God is even now at work in the world through

---

32. See Calhoun, *Spiritual Disciplines Handbook*, 173.
33. See Wadell, *Becoming Friends*, 16.

the power of the Holy Spirit. We pray for the discernment we need living our way into God's future, knowing God has given us everything we need in Christ Jesus. Since all our gifts and possessions come from God and God sustains our being, all of who we are and have is to be celebrated and shared. Together, we practice resurrection hope.

13

Healing Broken Community: Addressing Homelessness

> "The Spirit of the Lord is upon me, because he has anointed me to bring good news to the poor. He has sent me to proclaim release to the captives and recovery of sight to the blind, to let the oppressed go free, to proclaim the year of the Lord's favor."
>
> —Jesus, Luke 4:18–19

THERE IS NO GENUINE hope that is not intended for everyone to share. If hope is not shared, it gradually ceases to be hopeful. Everyone has a stake in developing hope, because lighting a spark of hope when you're surrounded by despair can be just as difficult as finding a needle in a haystack. Hopeful groups and communities can thrive just like hopeful individuals thrive. We all hope better when we are in communities of hope, and communities of hope do better when the individuals that comprise them are hopeful.

An entire society cannot be hopeful unless its weakest parts move from despair to hope. Just as we want to generate hope in the poor parts of ourselves, so too should we seek to bring hope in the poor parts of our community. The poorest, most vulnerable parts of our society deserve and require as much investment from us as we invest in ourselves and our loved ones. Hope may be infectious, but despair is every bit as contagious. This reality requires our diligence and attention to the places in our community where despair abounds and hope is scarce. Personally, my desire to share and cultivate hope in community has led me to focus on advocacy and change for people without shelter and housing.

Regardless of the reasons behind homelessness, those without shelter and housing live in a constant state of acute distress or trauma, and I believe no social group in our society is more vulnerable, at risk, persecuted, traumatized, and treated as subhuman than those who find themselves "homeless." In most places, to be homeless is to be illegitimate, outcast, and often illegal.

In my hometown of Puyallup, Washington, a city and surrounding suburbs with a population of about 70,000, it has been illegal by city statute to be homeless—there is no private or public place to safely and legitimately sleep. Instead, tents and other makeshift shelters are used in and around the city: on the banks of the Puyallup River, in brushy, wooded areas, inside vacant buildings, in cars parked randomly around town, and in commercial parking lots. Regrettably, public restrooms have been closed most nights, resulting in folks without housing relieving themselves outside. Homeless men and women are continually vulnerable to verbal abuse, shame, ridicule, harassment, assault, rape, and theft.

Other than during the five coldest months of the year, when our local churches have offered a nightly shelter program for the past seventeen years, adult homeless people have been offered no overnight hospitality in the city, and little recognition of their dignity, equality, or human rights. Often, the de facto message to people without shelter is *You don't belong here. You don't fit. There is no place for you. Go away.*

Understanding Our Neighbors without Housing

Stereotypically, people experiencing homelessness are characterized as nuisances, vagabonds, trespassers, purveyors of indecency, unclean, contaminating, threatening, mental deviants, drunks, drug addicts, panhandlers that disrupt businesses, lazy, or sexually deviant. They are customarily set apart from society through this descriptive language and are regularly subject to criminalization.

People without shelter often have illnesses that go untreated unless they can get past the dread of emergency rooms. Ahead of the COVID-19 pandemic, homeless folks in general got sick at more than three times the rate of the housed population, remained sick longer, and were three to four times more likely to die prematurely than the general population.[1] During the first six months of 2020, individuals who were homeless and infected

---

1. See National Coalition for the Homeless, "Health Care and Homelessness," para. 9.

with COVID-19 were significantly more likely to be hospitalized, require critical care, and die from the virus.[2]

Families that become homeless tend to share certain characteristics: they have extremely low incomes, tend to have young children and be headed by a younger parent figure, lack strong social networks, and often have a history of housing instability. Losing a home disrupts virtually every aspect of family life, damaging the physical and emotional health of family members, interfering with children's education, maturation, and sometimes resulting in the separation of family members.

The disproportionate effects of homelessness on children are striking: the average age of child homelessness in the United States is estimated to be about twelve years. Homeless children are twice as likely to experience hunger and four times as likely to experience developmental delays.[3] They are often sent to school with instructions from their parents to lie about their living situation and are usually considerably behind in school performance. Only 77 percent of children without shelter attend school regularly, and they are nine times more likely to repeat a grade, four times more likely to drop out of school, and three times more likely to be placed in special education programs than their housed peers.[4]

To cope with the many challenges homeless people face, many members of the homeless community use drugs and alcohol. Even those who did not previously struggle with psychiatric issues will often develop emotional problems related to the many traumatic stressors of a life without permanent shelter. Sometimes they must rely on people who often resent them or treat them suspiciously. Survival, from one day to the next, is the priority. In summary, our neighbors without shelter live in varieties of emergency states. This is subhuman existence.

The words, phrases, and images we use to describe people without shelter are tools in reinforcing the systems and policies that marginalize them. It's been said that "people who are homeless lack that 'special something' that makes us fully human." This statement—and many others like it—are representative of a process called dehumanization. Dehumanization means that we consider some people to be lesser beings, because

---

2. Cullane, "Estimated Emergency," 2.

3. See National Coalition for the Homeless, "Homeless Families with Children," para. 12.

4. National Coalition for the Homeless, "Education of Homeless Children and Youth," para. 2.

they don't look, act, live, or think like "regular" people. Dehumanized people are objectified and depersonalized, living a cruel form of life—life without hope in this world.

An example correcting the above misperceptions regarding people without shelter is a recent study from Vancouver, British Columbia, where fifty people ages nineteen to sixty-four were given $7,500 for one year to freely use. A control group of sixty-five people was followed separately and contrasted with those who received the cash. These folks, who had been homeless for at least six months, were not struggling with serious substance abuse or mental health issues. At year's end, folks who received the cash typically moved into stable housing, spent 52 percent of their money on food and rent, 15 percent on other items such as medications and bills, and 16 percent on clothes and transportation. The majority achieved food security and their spending on alcohol, cigarettes, and drugs decreased on average by 39 percent. Remarkably, the average participant retained $1,000 at the end of twelve months! The report indicated the cost to maintain survival services for a typical homeless person on the street was $55,000 annually. This one-year cash allotment saved the local shelter system approximately $8,100 per person by freeing up shelter space.[5]

When people without shelter are treated humanely and are not struggling with serious drug, alcohol, or mental health issues, we have reason to believe, based on this small sample, that people will respond to a public cash allotment with constructive decision-making and save taxpayer dollars.

The Issue of Empathy

It is empathy with the experience of people who find themselves homeless that often energizes us to advocate for social policy change. When we don't visualize ourselves in their shoes, when our empathy is lost or missing, the biblical description of this condition is a "hardening of heart." Sometimes, hearts are hardened and empathy blocked because of complicity toward the plight of the poor. When push comes to shove, many of us just don't want to change our lifestyle or do anything for them that makes us uncomfortable. Sadly, it often feels easier to harden one's heart, hang on to one's social position, and every now and then make contributions to charitable organizations, than to stand up, protest, and advocate for change. If we don't do anything, our personal status quo remains, as does homelessness.

5. See "Global First Direct Cash Transfer Study," para. 1.

As we have seen, sometimes our hearts become hardened because people without shelter are rendered, in our mind's eye, as lesser human beings and are, therefore, undeserving of our empathy and service. We might blame people who are homeless for their own plight: "She got herself into this mess." "I guess that's just what happens to addicts." "Some of them don't want help." "Their choices make it impossible for them to change." "They're just living off the system." "They've never worked a day in their lives." We negatively stereotype the lives and experiences of folks without housing to justify our indifference. Perhaps our hearts are hardened with the belief that some greater good will happen if present policies are continued. We could reason that some people simply have to suffer because a community has many other priorities affecting many more people. Often hearts are hardened when people lack necessary information or adequate social analysis, skewing the situational injustices contributing to homelessness. Or, maybe this social analysis is deemed flawed or a hoax! Often, we don't understand or believe that God's heart is actually in solidarity with these people.

If we can find empathy for our despairing neighbors without shelter, then we can have some confidence that hope is possible for everyone. If hope is not possible for everyone, then we cannot be confident that it will always be there for us. Social hope is either a human requirement for all or it is selective and, ultimately, elitist. The injustice of hope reserved for some would be a contradiction of God's loving intention for all individuals and groups who bear God's image.

What can we learn from God's revelation about this humanitarian crisis?

Homelessness and Hope in the Old Testament

In the Old Testament's creation narratives, God established an earthly home out of pure, holy, ecstatic, life-giving joy. God's earth is to be home for everyone, a place of stability, security, love, welcome, affiliation, and belonging. Humans are charged to care for all creatures and earthly inhabitants, including the vulnerable, marginalized, and homeless.[6] The biblical presumption is that the earth is bountiful enough for everyone's need, not everyone's greed.

In *The Sacredness of Human Life*, David Gushee wrote,

---

6. Deut 10:17–19.

HEALING BROKEN COMMUNITY: ADDRESSING HOMELESSNESS

> Human life is sacred; this means that God has consecrated each and every human being—without exception and in all circumstances—as a unique, incalculably precious being of elevated status and dignity. God has declared and demonstrated the sacred worth of human beings and will hold us accountable for responding appropriately. Such a response begins by adopting a posture of reverence and by accepting responsibility for the sacred gift that is a human life. It includes offering due respect and care to each human being that we encounter. It extends to an obligation to protect human life from wanted destruction, desecration, or the violation of human rights. A full embrace of the sacredness of human life leads to a full-hearted commitment to foster human flourishing.[7]

The term "human dignity" is a modest secularization of "sacredness" emerging from Greco-Roman culture.

In Hebrew, Greek, and later translations of the Bible, the poor are characterized in diverse terms that convey, at least in part, the diversity of experiences of poverty and homelessness in the ancient world. Hebrew words for the poor and homeless described people who were wrongfully impoverished or dispossessed, beggars, deprived peasants, and those who were so destitute that they had to depend on others to survive. In biblical times, the low economic status of the poor was considered a direct result of disaster, sickness, or oppression. The well-being of widows, sojourners, and the fatherless, those most in need of hope, was seriously endangered in many periods of ancient Israel. Treating them justly, the Bible tells us, was to deliver them from danger and imitate God. In Psalm 82:3–4, we read, "Give justice to the weak and the orphan; maintain the rights of the lowly and the destitute. Rescue the weak and the needy; deliver them from the hand of the wicked."

The connection between community justice on one hand, and the fate of widows, orphans, foreigners, the homeless, and the impoverished on the other, is clear throughout Scripture. Moses instructed Israel to institute a judicial system that would uphold justice and protect those who were systematically treated unjustly, for it was the downtrodden who had God's heart. The "downtrodden"—another typical biblical reference for the poor—lived with the consequences of injustice, and the conditions in which they lived needed to be corrected as a moral imperative. Special social legislation such as the sabbatical and jubilee years was established to prevent chronic injustice, poverty, and homelessness, stop concentrated land ownership or monopolies, and allow people to periodically regain

---

7. See Gushee, *Sacredness of Human Life*, 32.

lost land or housing (Lev 25). There are examples of strong admonishment when this legislation wasn't followed (see Neh 5).

Although the Bible speaks over 1,000 times about justice, it does not give a strict definition or theory of justice. Rather, it was presumed that readers would know well enough what justice is. "Justice, and only justice, you shall follow," wrote Moses.[8] Amos proclaimed that Hebrew worship services were of no benefit unless "justice is rolling down like water and righteousness like an ever-flowing stream."[9] In the same vein, Isaiah 61 tells us, "I, the Lord, love justice." The motivation for doing justice was the recognition that God's people have all been saved and liberated by God, and their own injustices have been righted by a forgiving God.

During his exile, the prophet Isaiah wrote extensively on justice. He argued that domineering powers are evil and use wicked devices and false words to prevent justice, even when the plea of the needy is justified. The government was working directly against God's will, for God intended that people live in a peaceful habitation, secure dwellings, and in quiet resting places. God directs people to establish justice, to abolish oppression and fear.[10] Isaiah believed God will prevail over every pretentious, arrogant, self-sufficient, and exploitive power. When injustices are sanctioned by governmental authority, Isaiah cries out: "Woe to those who make iniquitous decrees, who write oppressive statutes, to turn aside the needy from justice and to rob the poor of my people of their right, that widows may be your spoil, and that you may make the orphans your prey!"[11]

Unjust housing practices were a particular concern of Isaiah's. He said, "Destruction is certain for those who buy a property when others have no place to live."[12] The prophet announced that homes of the rich would stand deserted, the owners dead or gone. Additionally, said Isaiah, God wanted people to fast in a way that loosened the bonds of wickedness, let the oppressed go free, and broke every yoke. He said that God's fast is for people to share bread with the hungry and bring the homeless poor into their homes.[13]

---

8. Deut 16:20.
9. Amos 5:22–23; Isa 58.
10. Isa 54:14; 26:2–10.
11. Isa 10:1–2.
12. Isa 5:7–9.
13. Isa 58:3–7.

In chapter 65, Isaiah envisions a city where housing issues are addressed for all people: in this city, there is no gentrification, people live in what they build, there are no absentee landlords, and there is no housing speculation. Generally, the prophets understood God's ancient property regulation to mean that one person would have one house that stood on one allotment of land. Every family would have equality of economic opportunity so that everyone could have resources to earn a living, provide food, clothing, and housing, and be respected participants in the community. God wanted justice, not mere charity.[14]

Homelessness and Hope in the New Testament

Isaiah was Jesus' favorite Old Testament prophet. In his inaugural address in Luke, Jesus announced, from Isaiah 61, good news to the poor, liberty to those who were oppressed, and release to the captives.[15] Jesus believed that God's coming kingdom included the jubilee mandate.

Despite facing ridicule and outrage from the Jewish elite and imperial Roman rulers, Jesus sided with poor peasants who were often in perpetual debt. He confronted the authorities forty times in the Gospels, exposing them for seizing widows' houses,[16] instituting oppressive tax schemes, turning the temple into a corrupt enterprise, and missing the weightier aspects of the law. For instance, in Mark 12, Jesus resisted Caesar's tribute tax, which he knew to be oppressive to the poor and idolatrous for faithful Jews. He held up a denarius, an idolatrous Roman coin with Caesar's divine inscription, and told the Pharisees and Herodians to "Give back to Caesar what is Caesar's and to God what is God's."[17] And what is not God's? God, not Caesar, is Lord.

Jesus singled out the rich and the powerful who controlled most of the resources, leaving the poor often without enough to meet their basic needs. The poor sometimes lacked even a plot of land on which to grow food or construct a house. Restoring the outcasts, the excluded, the gentiles, the exiles, and the refugees to his new community was central to the mission of God's kingdom. In Luke 6:24, Jesus announces "woe to you who are rich,"

---

14. See Shook, *Making Housing Happen*, 34. This resource is beneficial in clarifying how the prophetic tradition can inform housing policies.
15. Luke 4:18–22.
16. Matt 23.
17. Mark 12:13–17.

SECTION TWO: HOPE TRANSFORMS HUMAN PERSONHOOD AND COMMUNITY

those who have wrongfully gained their wealth by not sharing resources with the poor or by complicity with injustice.[18] Jesus told stories of dire consequences for rich people blindly walking by beggars or building bigger barns for themselves when poor people were hungry and homeless.[19] The rich were called to give their nonessential possessions to the poor, and Zacchaeus was held up as an example of repentance when he gave half his income to the needy.[20] The rich would have difficulty entering God's regime,[21] while the good Samaritan had God's favor.[22]

Different from most of our translations, but in line with Plato in *The Republic*, the Greek New Testament actually uses the same word for justice and righteousness. In the Sermon on the Mount,[23] Jesus displayed God's mission of doing justice in these statements: "Blessed are those who are persecuted for the sake of justice, for theirs is the kingdom of heaven." "Blessed are those who are persecuted in the cause of right." "Blessed are those who hunger and thirst for justice, for they shall be satisfied." "Seek first your heavenly Father's kingdom and his justice, and all these things shall be yours as well." Jesus' listeners would automatically have connected God's kingdom with the doing of justice and the righting of injustice.

Jesus displayed the truth of human life's sacred worth through his teaching that the degrading of the life of the lowest human being ultimately degrades Jesus himself.[24] He said "I was hungry and you gave me food, I was thirsty and you gave me something to drink, I was a stranger and you welcomed me, I was naked and you gave me clothing, I was sick and you took care of me, I was in prison and you visited me . . . Truly I tell you, just as you did it to the least of these who are members of my family, you did it to me."[25] The resacralizing of human life, including people who are homeless and dehumanized, is finally a project that anticipates God's final consummation of all sacred life.[26]

---

18. Luke 6:24–25; Mark 10:17–27.
19. Luke 16:19–31; 12:13–21.
20. Luke 18:18–28; 19:1–10.
21. Luke 18:25.
22. Luke 20:25–37.
23. Matt 5–7.
24. Matt 25:31–46.
25. Matt 25:35–37, 40.
26. Gushee, *Sacredness of Human Life*, 415–23.

Jesus' death for our sins cannot be separated from what he stood for, how he lived, those he chose to get close to, and what he valued. He was crucified because of his relentless identification with the messianic hopes of people on the margins of society, his refusal to embrace the status quo, and his confrontations with the corrupt temple system that contributed to oppression of the poor.

The earliest followers of Jesus practiced a radical sharing among themselves, having all things in common. Land and houses could be sold, and the proceeds distributed to the needy.[27] The apostle Paul spent considerable time raising money for those in Jerusalem who were destitute, and he argued it was a requirement of fundamental economic balance in the body of Christ.[28]

In summary, the Bible clearly and repeatedly teaches there is godly hope for poor and homeless people. God is at work in history uplifting the poor and casting down the rich who got that way by oppressing or neglecting the poor.[29] At pivotal points of revelation history, God acted to free the poor. In the book of Exodus, divine power was used to free oppressed slaves and end economic oppression. During the monarchy, God prophetically acted against God's own people when they became oppressors. The explosive message of the prophets was that God destroyed Israel, both the Northern Kingdom and the Southern Kingdom, in part because of their mistreatment of the poor.[30] At the supreme moment of redemptive history, when God took on human flesh, Jesus' vision and mission included liberating the poor and the oppressed.[31]

A Homeless God

After looking at God's passion for poor and homeless people in Scripture, we can reflect on our images of God's engagement with our own world. Dietrich Bonhoeffer recognized that the Christ event depicted in the Scriptures is about God's apparent powerlessness in our world.[32] From birth to death, Jesus was largely dependent on the hospitality of others.

27. Acts 2:43–47; 4:33–37.
28. 2 Cor 8:13–15.
29. Luke 1:46–55.
30. Amos 6:4, 7; Isa 10:1–3; Mic 2:2; Jer 5:26–29.
31. Luke 4:18–22. For further detail, see Sider, *Rich Christians*.
32. Noted in Dicken, "Homeless God."

Bonhoeffer also wrote that God in Christ was edged out of the world and on to the cross. God was in Christ on the cross, reconciling the world to God's own self, says Paul.[33] Jesus, in his Father/Son relationship, found God absent on the cross and was godforsaken and fatherless. God the Father, in this dynamic, experienced a radical grief of sonlessness, was weak and displaced. God in Christ is crucified. Bonhoeffer suggests that this is the way, the only way, in which God can be with us and help us in our struggles to keep hope alive. It is not by an intrusive divine omnipotence that God helps us, but rather through faithful accompaniment, sacrifice, and suffering.

We may experience God's absence. We would all like a powerful, intervening God to take care of us, but it is the suffering of God and God's solidarity with us in our weakness that encourages us to fully develop and take responsibility for our lives. The apostle Paul said, "God chooses what is foolish in the world to shame the wise; God chooses what is weak in the world to shame the strong."[34] Yes, God has chosen the weak of the world—those most vulnerable—to accomplish God's purposes.

If we extend this idea, it can be said that we have a homeless God and that our homeless God generates hope for those without shelter as well as for ourselves. God is in the unwashed person with terrible body odor and tattered clothes who panhandles for food. God lives in the bushes and under bridges and in the corners of supermarket parking lots, and God is in an incarnate bonded state with those who suffer.[35]

Is it not true that Jesus, as God incarnate, found his place among the homeless and had no place to lay his head? Because God assumes life among the poorest of the poor, we can conclude that God is omnipresent for everyone. Human darkness is immediately understood, for God is supremely attentive, carries the depth of our affliction, and shares our emotional struggle.[36]

God's omnipresence in the darkest, most despairing corners of our world shows there is no greater presence that can be conceived anywhere in our community. It is this divine presence that generates new possibilities for all in our common life. When we look at poor and homeless folks, we can know that God is there in solidarity with them.

---

33. 2 Cor 5:18–19.
34. 1 Cor 1:27.
35. Matt 25:31–46; see also Dicken, "Homeless God."
36. Dicken, "Homeless God," 151.

God does not typically take away human suffering as much as share it with us and give us the strength to move through and beyond it. The psalmist has said: "If I make my bed in hell, you are there."[37] Theologian Thomas Dicken describes God as the One who lies down with nullity and insignificance, who clings steadfastly with the nothings of the world, the lowly bodies and those whose humanness is assaulted.[38] God is the quintessential homeless One.

Our awareness of this homeless One can be difficult. Like looking through a glass darkly, God's presence, both to the homeless advocate and the person who is homeless, may be fleeting, confusing, painful, and dim. Our God is linked both to the homeless advocate who struggles to achieve solidarity with the destitute, and the homeless person struggling to receive help. God's liberating movement comes from the resurrection victory of Jesus and allows both the homeless advocate and the homeless person an inexplicable joy in the face of suffering. To experience God's presence in this relational way is to be met with a divine grace that generates hope, levels the playing field for advocate and victim, joins people together, and sets people on a path toward empowerment, justice, and housing. This is the God of hope for people without shelter and their community.[39]

Responding to God's Mission

If we are called by God to do something about homelessness, then it is morally impermissible for us not to. Although most of us are not in moral control of the humanitarian crisis in our cities, we can be moral listeners, open to recognizing the worth of others and the claims that such recognition places on us.[40]

Many cities require that homeless adults show good citizenship, respect, decency, and cooperation while, at the same time, our homeless neighbors are relegated by city policy to live in the bushes, at the river, in dilapidated buildings, or on darkened streets in parked cars. Ultimately, these regulations are supremely unwelcoming, disrespectful, and delegitimizing. How can we ask our homeless neighbors, who are degraded daily, to respect and contribute to the welfare of a community that degrades them? Does not Jesus' Golden

---

37. Ps 139:8.
38. Dicken, "Homeless God."
39. Shook, *Making Housing Happen*, 28–41; see also Sider, *Rich Christians*.
40. See Wolterstorff, *Justice*, 130–44.

Rule apply here? Is not a city to treat its homeless neighbors as the city demands those citizens behave toward the city? Elaborating on Jesus' teaching, before we look at the sliver in the eyes of these economically destitute people, we should find the log in the eye of the community. From Jesus' teaching in Matthew 25 and elsewhere, we can hear him say to a city: "When you, by legal decree, send homeless people to live in the bushes, riverbank, rundown buildings, and cars on dark streets, you are doing it to me."

The reality of "geographic moral sensitivity" means that we best become empathetic, civilly and morally responsive to shelterless neighbors when the presence of their need faces us consistently. How many of us would turn away a hungry homeless person at our door on a cold winter night? Would we send a homeless child back outside after inviting her in for a meal? How about her parents? Imagine a homeless person sleeping at our front door nightly. How would it change our perspective and our behavior? Would it change our purchases or monthly budget? Would it change our approach to local housing policy? Might we get politically or socially involved if homeless people were sleeping in our yard? What if we positioned ourselves so we encounter and engage our most vulnerable neighbors regularly?

Mahatma Gandhi has this advice for our social and economic decision-making:

> Recall the face of the poorest and weakest person whom you may have seen, and ask yourself if this decision you are considering is going to be of any use to him or her. Will this person gain anything by it? Will it restore him or her to a control over his or her own life and destiny? Will it lead to freedom for the hungry and poor? Then you will find your doubts and yourself melt away.[41]

I was given an opportunity to view the health of our society through the eyes of the poor in my engagements with people without shelter. I recall at least four individuals who were suffering from cancer, as I have been, and who were suffering largely without appropriate medical care. Not having medical insurance or appropriate access to medical help left these folks with a lack of treatment options and a poor prognosis. They join about 68,000 US citizens who die yearly because healthcare is unaffordable.[42] I found it painfully distressing that I, as a privileged, housed, middle-class white male, had access to excellent medical care while other

---

41. See Gandhi, *Mahatma Gandhi*, 65.
42. Lemon, "Medicare for All Would Save."

people were left largely to die from cancer without ever receiving similar access to quality services.

These experiences gave me a disturbing perspective on how our society places value only on the lives and well-being of some of its citizens and can look the other way when people without social status or resources are suffering and dying. The COVID-19 pandemic has generated a dismal picture of a country unable to secure such a basic human right as healthcare for all its citizens. Often, I have thought that I have no right to accumulate medical resources for myself when others are left sick and dying. Should I die in solidarity with them? What would Jesus do?

Economic Injustice as Sin

In 2018, more than 38 million Americans lived in poverty.[43] For the average American family,[44] this amounted to less than $21,000 a year.[45] Since the 1960s, the poverty rate has fluctuated between 30 and 50 million people each year, and at least half of all people in poverty in the United States are on the verge of homelessness at any given time. When the poverty rate goes up, so too does the number of homeless people. While the longer-term effects of COVID-19 are frighteningly unclear, we know that at least 1.6 million people in the United States became homeless during the great recession.[46] COVID-19's effect in local communities may dramatically increase the number of people without shelter.[47]

Christian people have a reference point in their social analysis of poverty and economic inequality. They have the theological capability of naming these social realities as *sin*. The Bible suggests at least two perspectives on inequality. First, the biblical principle of justice demands that each person and family have access to productive resources so that, if they act responsibly, they can earn a decent living and be dignified members of society. Whenever the extremes of wealth and poverty make it difficult or prevent some people from having access to adequate productive resources, then that inequality is unjust, sinful, and must be corrected. And second, if, in our broken world, one group of people acquires excessive and dominating economic or political

---

43. See Semega et al., "Income and Poverty 2018," para. 9.
44. See Duffin, "Average Number of People," para. 2.
45. See Semega et al., "Income and Poverty 2018," para. 18.
46. Stasha, "State of Homelessness in the US—2022," para. 35.
47. Moses, "COVID-19 and the State of Homelessness," para. 6.

power, we are shown through historical accounts that they will almost always use it for their own selfish advantage. As Lord Acton said long ago, "Power corrupts, and absolute power corrupts absolutely."[48]

When North American economic inequality today is greater than at any time since the Great Depression, that's a problem.[49] When the richest 10 percent of the top 1 percent of the population have more income than the poorest 120 million combined, that's a problem.[50] When more than half of all increase in income in the United States goes to the richest 1 percent, that's a problem.[51] When, in the last three decades, the average annual personal income of the richest 1 percent has jumped by $700,000, while the average North American has actually lost economic power, that's a problem.[52] When three billionaires own enough wealth as the poorest 50 percent of the entire population and pay a lower tax rate than most workers, that's a problem.[53] When 50 percent of the US population lives paycheck to paycheck, with the average worker making $35 less each week than forty-seven years ago, after adjusting for inflation, that's a problem.[54] When child poverty in the US is higher than in most wealthy countries, that's a problem.[55]

For black, indigenous, and people of color (BIPOC), major wealth disparity in the United States contributes to homelessness. Wealth injustice stems from a history of stolen land, genocide, slavery, evolving segregation, redlining, and housing and employment discrimination. At the personal level, daily microaggressions, including verbal and behavioral implicit biases, generate and perpetuate injustices in public spaces, healthcare, and the criminal justice system. That's a problem.[56]

But why is economic inequality so problematic? If we believe what the Bible says about God's concern for the poor and homeless, if we believe what the Bible says about justice, then we must denounce the gross inequality of opportunity and income in our country today as blatantly sinful.[57]

48. See Sider, "Economic Inequality," para. 5.
49. Sanders, "Bernie Sanders Urges Supporters," 0:34–0:41.
50. Sider, "Economic Inequality," para. 9.
51. Sider, "Economic Inequality," para. 10.
52. Sider, "Economic Inequality," para. 12.
53. Sanders, "Bernie Sanders Urges Supporters," 0:42–0:49.
54. Friedman, "78% of Americans," para. 1.
55. Kearney, "Child Poverty in the U.S.," para. 1.
56. See Parnell, "Knowledge Is Dangerous," para. 12.
57. Sider, "Economic Inequality," para. 18.

We must prioritize enacting public policies and developing effective programs that care for and empower poor people. Our lawmakers should focus on appropriate and effective taxation and spending so poor people have the opportunity to receive vastly expanded economic opportunity.

It is beyond our scope to identify what all this means, but there are always ways to give a hand to responsible people who, for whatever reason, need help. Hope for our neighbors who are homeless rests with their initiative *and* with the initiatives brought about by public and private partnerships that change social policy and bring about social justice.

The Relationship of Charity and Justice

Most of our Christian volunteer efforts around homelessness in my hometown of Puyallup—and others as well—generally center around charity. Charity calls forth a generous response from individuals and addresses basic survival needs homeless people struggle with. With cultural emphasis on individualism and diminished social responsibility, North Americans tend to emphasize charity over justice.

To love one's neighbor means to recognize and respect their sacredness and innate worth, seeking to enhance their well-being. Charity is a duty to God to treat someone well, even if they've lost their rights to equal treatment or never had them in the first place.

An outwardly hopeful, fully flourishing life is a life of benevolence. It is a life of mutual generosity, not just mutual respect for human rights. It feels good to give food, clothes, or a cot for someone to sleep on. Charity is far more rewarding, on a day-to-day basis, I believe, than the work of justice. While charity motivates us to care for the well-being of others, justice motivates us to right the wrongs that damage others.

Charity can lull compassionate people into a kind of complacency in which "managing" homelessness is all they know to do. When we provide food, clothing, tents, or find enough beds, we may lose sight of the fundamental work that should be done to end homelessness. Through charity, we can normalize destitution and maintain the unequal relationship between the haves and have-nots. We lose an appropriate sense of moral outrage regarding concrete circumstances of inhumanity and begin to accept the very structural dynamics that produce poverty and homelessness in the first place. Charity may act as a kind of moral safety net that reduces our own discomfort and guilt when we see visible signs of peoples' destitution. When we are providing direct services to people without shelter, our time and energy is consumed such that the work of justice advocacy never takes priority. Charity can give the subtle impression that, if we just distribute enough food, or create enough bed space, then we will have solved the problem.

Charity often presumes that private groups and individuals are mainly responsible for finding solutions to societal injustices. Yet, it's been estimated that if we asked religious organizations to cover the costs of just welfare for families, disability payments for the poor, and food stamps, every single church, synagogue, mosque, temple, or other religious congregation would be required to add more than $300,000 a year to its expenditures. Similarly, nongovernmental organizations would need their contributions to increase sevenfold to cover the costs of only those three governmental programs.[58]

There is a simple parable that illustrates the distinction between charitable practices and social change. It goes like this: In a small village by a river, a villager is fishing and sees a cooing baby float by in a basket. She wades into the river and rescues the infant. She brings the baby back to the village, feeds it, and finds a family to care for the child.

The next day, two villagers are down by the river washing clothes when they see two baskets with babies float by. The two men set aside their laundry to run alongside the water and intercept the baskets. That night, the village meets to discuss the problem of caring for the infants. Two families step forward and volunteer to raise the children. A committee is formed to set up around-the-clock vigilance at the riverbank.

Within a few days, the villagers have rescued over twenty babies. They form several committees to care for the children, find them homes, monitor the riverbank, and develop improved nets and tools for intercepting floating baskets.

At a tense village meeting, one young woman stands up and proposes that the community form an expedition to travel upriver and determine why the children are ending up in the water. Several of the elders dismiss her idea, pointing out that they cannot spare any people because of the enormous work involved in intercepting children and caring for them. So, weeks go by, and the flow of infants and baskets continues unabated.

In this parable, the traditional charity response is to fund the urgent services in the village to care for children. Traditional charity might even

58. Hilfiker, "Limits of Charity."

contribute to improved research and technology for intercepting babies, including new nets. No one can dismiss the immediate and compassionate need to do this. At the same time, a social justice strategist like the young woman in our parable would take an expedition upstream to find and address the source of the problem. This may involve resistance and sacrifice.

Charity needs justice if homelessness is to be resolved—not just in my own hometown, but in all of our cities—because justice is more than just philanthropy. Philanthropy is commendable, as Martin Luther King Jr. said, but it must not cause the philanthropist to overlook the circumstances of economic injustice that make philanthropy necessary.[59] Justice requires concerted communal action to transform institutional policies, societal law, and unjust economic situations.

Homelessness is the inevitable result of the structures of our society—economic, governmental, social, and religious—that provide the foundation for inequality. Sadly, poverty is built into these systems. Nonlivable wages, unemployment or underemployment, inadequate unemployment benefits, lack of healthcare access, and scarce affordable housing are all factors in generating poverty and homelessness. While the work of charity is critically important, only our governments can guarantee rights and create or oversee programs that assure everyone adequate access to what they need. The biblical concept of justice focuses on the rights of individuals, families, communities, and creation. It analyzes social situations or social structures and works for long-term social change.

Hope for homeless citizens finally is realistic only when courageous, determined people in all sectors of a community are willing to take more urgent steps, buttressed by spiritual and moral conviction, to act in solidarity with the poorest of the poor.

Hopeful Action

We can all ask ourselves: How can we move beyond our charity to justice? Is our community compassionate and just? Where justice is served, hope abounds.

Concepts of justice and human rights are based on the hope of human flourishing. We all hope for a life that goes well, where we can enjoy good things and the right kinds of relationships. When a homeless person is wronged—when people do not relate to the person justly—that person's

---

59. See Collins and Wright, *Moral Measure*, 181–83.

life is not going well even if he or she may be leading it well. People who are disrespectful to folks without shelter are also not living well. When we practice justice, we live a hopeful life and assist others' hopefulness as well. It is love that leads to the practice of charity and justice because it is God's love for the needy and the wronged, that motivates our action.

Though God's hope is for each person, that hope is best lived in community. But that community can't end with our immediate network of friends and neighbors. Instead, the world changes for us when we recognize and embrace the truth that hope is available for *all*. And, as we experience the hope of God poured out in our own hearts, we are to extend it to others—even and especially "the least of these."

―――― Section Three ――――

Hope Gives Us a New Horizon

14

In How We Seek Healing

"Healing is the strange act of the power of life being present in the midst of the power of death, or more simply and directly, healing consists in human life making contact with human life and finding together the gift of new possibility strangely given."

—Walter Brueggemann

During my life with pancreatic cancer, I've been blessed by many people who have prayed for me. Often, prayers are for me to win the battle, triumph over cancer, or somehow escape its deadly reality. I have been assured, at times, that God will heal me—after all, Jesus healed people, didn't he? Some praying for me invoke passages from James 5, describing how God will work: "The prayer of faith will save the sick, and the Lord will raise them up; and anyone who has committed sins will be forgiven."[1] Some well-intentioned people believe it's right that I should be healed. After all, it's right that I should be healed because I'm a Christian, I help people, and there is much good left for me to do on this earth. God wants to do what is right and is able to do it, right?

We know that healings happen through a variety of medical treatments or apart from them. When healing and other good things happen, God gets the credit and praise. Too often, though, God does not get credit when things go "wrong," and we may conclude that God did not answer our prayer. Our praise may turn to blame. It's sometimes hard to know what God's perspective might be.

We tend to have a selective appreciation for God's healing work. Maybe God doesn't want us healed, or maybe God can't heal us, or maybe God's

---

1. Jas 5:13–18.

healing would disrupt a plan for greater good. God's wisdom and choices are confusing to us, because we cannot see what God sees, know what God knows, or do what God does. Theologian Stanley Hauerwas reminds us that sickness challenges a most cherished presupposition that we are, or at least can be, in control of our existence.[2] It forces us to recognize that we and the medical establishment are not God.

Healing can be described in diverse ways. Stephen Parsons offers one example in *The Challenge of Christian Healing*. He defines healing as

> a capacity in an individual or group to change for the good the course of a disease in another, whether physical or psychological in nature. This capacity to heal is variously regarded as a psychic or spiritual gift and appears to involve the tapping of energies which so far are beyond the realm of conventional science to explain. Healing may also sometimes be understood as the calling forth of an individual's own self-healing powers by some as yet little understood psychic communication between healer and patient.[3]

Christians usually believe the source of all healing is God. The Holy Spirit uses our natural processes—mind, nerves, and hormonal systems that govern all cells—to accomplish healing. Dr. Paul Brand, a renowned Christian surgeon, describes his understanding of healing and prayer:

> God primarily works through the mind to summon up resources of healing in a person's body. Any healing observation should note the design features that are built into the human body as it attempts to heal. . . . Those who pray for the sick and suffering should first praise God for the remarkable agents of healing designed into the body, and then ask that God's special grace give the suffering person the ability to use those resources to their fullest advantage. . . . The prayers of fellow Christians can offer real, tangible help by setting into motion the intrinsic powers of healing in a person controlled by God. This approach does not contradict natural laws; rather, it fully employs the design features built into the human body.[4]

After reviewing 250 studies documenting the possible healing effects of religious practice, Dr. Larry Dossey, a respected physician, concluded, "Not to employ prayer with my patients was the equivalent of deliberately

---

2. Hauerwas, *Naming the Silences*, 62.
3. Quoted in Swartley, *Health, Healing and the Church's Mission*, 62.
4. Quoted in Yancey, *Prayer*, 254.

withholding a potent drug or surgical procedure" and "will one day constitute medical malpractice."[5] In turn, author Philip Yancey reminds us that people who are at peace and who have loving support, including the support they gain from prayer, heal better as they draw on the resources of body, mind, and spirit.[6] Prayer is a substantial asset in how we deal with any kind of adversity.

Measuring the Power of Prayer

When we feel our prayers for healing have gone unanswered, we often begin to question our prayers and our relationship with God. We might wonder: If I pray for someone's healing and he or she is not completely physically healed—let's say, for example, he or she dies—was my prayer mistaken? Was it not "powerful and effective?" Was God not listening to me?

Empirical research regarding the healing effects of prayer for disease involves attempting to use scientific methods to answer deeply personal questions. Although reconciling spiritual experience and scientific data is ultimately impossible, both qualitative and quantitative data has yielded some interesting and perhaps helpful information.[7] Here is some recent data collected from these studies:

- Roughly 84 percent of North Americans believe that praying for healing improves the patient's chances of recovery.
- Eighty percent of North Americans believe that miracles happen today, and more than half of all doctors report observing recovery in their patients that defy medical explanation.
- People who regularly attend worship services are said to have a 25 percent reduction in their mortality rate compared to those who do not regularly attend worship.
- In one study, using prayer and music lowered death rates by 30 percent compared to control groups.
- Two or three out of every thousand people with cancer will experience a "spontaneous remission" that is apparently unrelated to treatment.[8]

5. Quoted in Linn et al., *Simple Ways*, 2.
6. Yancey, *Prayer*, 254.
7. See, for instance, Kalb, "Faith and Healing," 44, 46, and 54.
8. Yancey, *Prayer*, 257.

- More than half of the medical schools in the United States now offer courses in spirituality and medicine.

But just as prayer, joy, and hope can be important tools in healing, bad health outcomes can also be generated by certain beliefs about prayer. For example, if patients believe that God protects them from disease or that their illness was some kind of divine punishment, their health outcomes may diminish. People who believe that God is not answering their prayer, for whatever reason, have a tendency toward self-reproach, despair, and physical deterioration.

When thinking about healing prayer, we should focus on recovery that depends on the mobilization of our own God-given mechanisms of resistance to disease. Remember that some of the earliest ancient societies had successful healers, even though medical interventions generally offered little effective therapy.

The Healing Ministries of Jesus and the Early Church

The Christian creation story reminds us that human beings are Adam, *adamah,* made from the ground, and are thus frail, mortal creatures.[9] We are dust and we will return to dust.[10] Human health must involve our embeddedness with God's earth and how we relate to it. Since we are so connected to the earth, we must accept our mortality. We are reminded in Psalms 39 and 103 how fleeting our life is. At the same time, humanity is made in God's image to reflect God in the world. Though we are a flawed humanity,[11] Jesus helps us to significantly restore a divine partnership and carry out stewardship over all the earth.[12]

Though Jesus healed numbers of Palestinians, there were far more he did not heal. When Jesus healed the paralyzed man by the pool of Bethsaida, there is no mention of all the other disabled persons lying around the same pool who were not healed. Jesus was not attempting to reverse the laws of nature or of human anatomy and physiology. Indeed, it was not his task to heal all sickness; rather, Jesus' healings came to manifest the presence of God's kingdom inaugurated through his ministry. His miracles

9. Gen 2:7.
10. Gen 3:19.
11. Gen 3.
12. Eph 4:20–24.

were indicators of what life in God's coming creation will be, a creation teeming with unrestricted life.

The kingdom of God, God's reign, was enacted by Jesus on many fronts, from his teaching and preaching to his prophetic actions, exorcisms, and healings. Jesus' miracles are perhaps best understood as "intermittent acts of compassion."[13] He never promised to take care of all human need, suffering, violence, or poverty, nor was he able to: Jesus could not do many great things among the people because of peoples' unbelief.[14] Biblical scholar Walter Wink summarizes Jesus' healings and exorcisms as "not simply patches on a body destined for death regardless; they are manifestations of God's reign now, an in-breaking of eternity into time, a revelation of God's merciful nature, a promise of the restitution of all things in the heart of the loving Author of the universe."[15]

The leaders of the early church experienced occasional healings, usually in teachable moments. Many of these pillars of faith struggled with great adversity without experiencing healing for themselves. The apostle Paul prayed for healing and, instead, God responded that God's grace would be sufficient, and Paul's weakness would become his strength. Paul refers to friends such as Epaphroditus, Trophimus, and Timothy, all of whom had serious unhealed illnesses. Paul, James, Peter, and many other leading apostles were tortured and executed. They were not protected. These folks prayed, not so much for God to change circumstances, but for the courage and strength to withstand their adversity and joyfully bear the sufferings of Christ.[16]

Christians know that healing is complete only when the struggling creation is made complete.[17] God conquers disease and death in the manner of Jesus' cross and resurrection. In the end, our physical healing will be complete at the point of our resurrection from death.[18]

God's desire is shalom for all people. Shalom includes a person's physical, emotional, and mental well-being and wholeness. Ultimately, it may be impossible for a person to be healed in an unhealthy community.[19]

13. Witherington, "God Wants to Heal Us," 62.
14. Mark 6:5–6.
15. Wink, *Engaging the Powers,* 144.
16 Yancey, *Prayer,* 264.
17. Rom 8.
18. 1 Cor 15:42–49.
19. Mark 6:4–6.

When some people are deprived of healthcare, the community of shalom is threatened. Jesus' healing ministry demonstrated God's heart to restore the whole person, a priority that was carried on by his disciples as they established early intentional communities. Though Roman authorities provided its poorest citizens with grain, followers of Jesus took initiative in caring for the hungry, the dying, and the sick.

Christians and Prayer for Healing Today

We're all tempted to misrepresent God and engage in false hope for healing born out of our anger, fear, or despair. Our grief can be painful, and we may look for relief that skews our image of God. We may pray in a fashion that confuses God's sovereignty and love. Sometimes our prayers are simply unrighteous, like slave owners praying for slavery to be upheld or soldiers praying to kill instead of being killed. When we pray for what we desire, it's important to recognize that our prayers can be misdirected. It's always helpful to ask if our petition is something we should want and should be asking God for. We can recall Paul, in Romans 8:26, rightfully claiming, "We do not know how to pray."

Our petitions to the Lord are best if they are framed in a confessional and humble approach. Confession can include our sometimes lack of discernment about what is actually best for us. In our humility, we are still called to pray for healing and to recognize God's desire for human health and wellness.

My approach to healing prayer includes the psychological concept of differentiation, which means that we can develop our inner spiritual, mental, and emotional resources so that we can be in relationship to God in a reflective rather than a reactive manner. As the second section discussed at length, our goal is to develop a sense of inner sufficiency based in a well-functioning primary relationship with God and the six parts of ourselves. We can be in possession of ourselves and remain closer to who we are and who God is than we are to any other person or group or disease. This contributes to how we pray for healing.

If we are well nurtured from our two primary relationships, then we can approach physical illnesses with a settled, sufficient inner self. We have a desire to be healed, to defeat life-threatening disease, but we do not demand or require our healing from God. Rather, we pray for healing with confidence that serves to protect our God-given life without being in a state of anxious reactivity to the diseases or illnesses we face. We are always closer, once again, to God and ourselves, than we are to the disease. Our inner sufficiency is not based on our healing and we embody it in life and in death. We will be healed sooner or later, because God wants to heal us more than we could ever desire healing for ourselves. Our healing will come in God's time.

God's creative and transforming power is at work in many communities and people, and with each person we can discover stories of human courage and divine grace. Wholeness from healing, or freedom with physical challenges to live life with purpose and fulfilment, is exemplified by Marva Dawn in her book *Being Well When We're Ill: Wholeness and Hope in Spite of Infirmity*.

So, how can we find wholeness and freedom? Here are ten helpful suggestions for living with illness:

1. Accept all the strange sensations connected with the illness. Do not fight them.
2. Talk about the illness. If it's cancer, call it cancer. We can't make life normal again by trying to hide what is wrong.
3. Accept death as a part of life. It is!
4. Waste no time on "what might have been" or "if only."
5. Consider each day as another day of life, a gift from God to be enjoyed as fully as possible.
6. Realize that life is never going to be perfect. It wasn't before, and it won't be now.
7. Learn to live with the illness and accept dying from it. We are all dying in some manner.
8. Set new goals; realize our limitations. Sometimes the current elements of life become the most enjoyable.
9. Put our friends and relatives at ease. If we don't want pity, don't ask for it. If we know that we are going to die, encourage candid conversations that allow everyone to share their thoughts and feelings over time.
10. Discuss any confusing or unresolved issues with our family and friends. Include the children if possible. After all, our difficulties include others.[20]

20. Adapted from a similar list written by Kelly, *Make Today Count*.

Although health is certainly an important part of the experience of being human, author Willard Swartley confirms that "health as such is not the chief goal and purpose of life. Health or healthcare cannot become our idol. While we value health and laud universal healthcare access, we must recognize also that health is a gift, not something money can buy."[21]

Many people uncomfortable with serious or terminal illness use clichés when addressing the reality of disease and other life struggles. But for someone facing adversity and disease, what do these well-intentioned comments really achieve?[22] Here, I share with you a selection of the many clichés I've heard over the past ten years, and what these comments actually mean to me as a person facing cancer.

"I'm praying for you." While it's great that people pray for me, it is important for me to know that they are first and foremost praying for my courage, strength, discernment, and peacefulness, recognizing that the eradication of the disease is not as important as the manner in which I live with the disease. I want to be a more faithful and complete person, whether or not I'm healed in a certain timeframe. At times, it's more important for caring, supportive people to demonstrate their concern with actions that display mercy, rather than a promise to pray for me.

"Everything happens for a reason." This implies that God directs all things and we are little more than puppets with no free will. While God can bring good out of any evil, God does not bring evil. We may not be able to comprehend the reasons for tragedy.

"God never gives us more than we can handle." God wills our health and wellness and works with us in dealing with disease or adversity. Disease is part of the flawed creation in which we live. In extreme situations, the challenge may indeed feel overwhelming.

"But for the grace of God, there go I." This cliché is typically offered by people who are not struggling with disease or other adversities. Apparently,

---

21. Swartley, *Health, Healing and the Church's Mission*, 124.

22. See Sandlin, "10 Things You Can't Say"; Piatt, "Ten Clichés"; Piatt, "Ten More Clichés"; Piatt, "Nine (Final) Christian Clichés"; Piatt, "Five New Christian Clichés"; Mattson, "Seven Lies"; and Patton, "8 Sayings."

those with adversity or disease do not have God's grace or, at least, not in the same fashion as those who are not being challenged. Does God pick and choose to whom grace is given, or is grace available for all?

"I must be living right." The assumption, then, is that those who are struggling with disease must not have been living right. How would someone know with certainty what "living right" means? It implies a spiritual superiority and immediately blames the victim for some inadequacy that is being punished by the disease. For someone living with a serious illness, this comment may be particularly unhelpful to hear.

"It gets better." Yes, eventually, it will get better. But it may get worse before it gets better. Christians are called to work through challenges in relationship with God. As was true for Jesus' disciples, we may die before any physical healing occurs.

"Don't worry. God's in charge." If God were truly in charge, I wouldn't be suffering pancreatic cancer. It's good not to worry, but let's not hold God responsible for the disease or its outcome. Jesus was realistic about the power of evil in our world.[23] God is in a battle with the principalities and powers that generate human suffering and disease.[24] We do know that God will bring full healing for the entire creation without intrusively pushing an agenda.

"Just call me if you need anything." Because those who are sick are often the least likely to know what they need, much less how to ask for it, this offer (however sincere in intention) can come across as a glib dismissal, ironically creating distance instead of offering authentic connection. When someone is suffering from serious illness, an incarnational listener moves toward the sick person in a state of solidarity against the disease, on the side of the person's health, instead of appearing to toss the ball into the sufferer's court. It's important for the sick person to know and experience a fellowship of suffering initiated by those with compassion. If we truly want to support someone who is sick, suffering, or hopeless, we must reach out

---

23. John 14:30.
24. Eph 6:12.

and be active in our support and solidarity. In general, suffering disease generates desire in us for human connection.

"We should always be happy." While happiness is a good thing, there are times when a truthful reality check shows that there is more lament than happiness. Even Jesus wasn't always happy. Sometimes we must face sorrow, loss, or sadness knowing that happiness is hard to come by. It may be really difficult for us to endure and understand the challenge.

So, how can we pray? Following are some suggestions for prayer that can help us achieve a more authentic experience with God and each other.

It's best if we pray from a global kingdom perspective. We know that to "seek first the kingdom of God" is universal and unhampered by national borders, linguistic divides, or cultural differences. We pray with countless Christians and non-Christians worldwide for our physical needs. Tens of thousands of people, many Christians, pray in poor countries simply that God would bring them daily bread so their malnourished children can live. And yet we know that some 17,000 children die each day simply for lack of adequate nutrition.[25] Where is God? Why doesn't God provide help for children who are suffering and starving and dying every day? God loves all the children of the world and those who have faith like children are examples for Jesus. Yet children die today.

A global perspective, however, helps us understand what God sees in the entire human family. It helps us recognize that—as much as God would like to heal every child's disease—violence, environmental pollution, and distributive food injustices are real; God does not violate human freedom and responsibility by intrusively acting to correct our systemic failures. From a strictly human perspective, there are many people, I'm sure, who need healing more than I do.

Some North American Christians, wedded to a corporate capitalistic economic system, tend to expect, based on their relative affluence, that God brings them health, wealth, and happiness. Yet when Mother Teresa saw thousands of hungry, dying people on the streets of Calcutta, India, she did not pray for their health insurance, medical care, or expect their physical healing. She simply provided her compassionate presence and touch. There

---

25. UNICEF, "Levels and Trends," 2.

was no divine healing intervention other than what was most important: God was intimately there in suffering solidarity with the dying in her presence and would ultimately prevail over dying and death. Rather than pleading for healing, we may remember that we are praying to the same God who loves as Mother Teresa loved. A more profound healing may actually come when we place our healing in a global perspective.

We must honor the paradox of Christian discipleship. Jesus called his followers to "take up the cross" and follow him.[26] Those who share their life, relinquish their life, and lose their life for Jesus' sake will receive it. Authentic healing prayer begins with letting go and surrendering to our loving Creator and Redeemer. We start by letting God be God and facing adversity in a state of acceptance and truth. Healing can come through the process of "letting go," whereby we enter a state of deep rest, resonance, and peace that alters even our biochemical ecology.

We need to recognize that God loves us *through* our suffering and disease. Jesus taught us how to live with problems and he faced death when there was no other divine option. He, who did great acts in the name of God's inaugurated kingdom, also suffered an awful death in faithfulness and hope. Through his atoning sacrifice on the cross, Jesus bore our disabilities and sicknesses. Can we believe that he is with us as we live with our disease, and suffers it in solidarity with us? Our suffering may generate meaningful deepening faith in us and those accompanying us. The apostle Paul wrote he was "always carrying in the body the death of Jesus, so that the life of Jesus may also be made visible in our bodies. For while we live, we are always being given up to death for Jesus' sake, so that the life of Jesus may be made visible in our mortal flesh."[27]

God works against all disease. Indeed, anything that strikes against the health and wellness of this creation is against God and is part of the "principalities and powers." We know that God wants our healing and hopeful dying because God is ever creating life and restoring what the "powers" seek to destroy.

---

26. Mark 8:34–35.
27. 2 Cor 4:10–11.

God wants us healed more than we do, even before we pray. Can we believe that God is closer to us than the disease that may be assaulting our body and grieves it more than we do? Though we are called to pray for healing, there is no need for us to beg God when God wants our healing more than we do. We pray to be aligned with God's perspective on our disease.[28]

Can we believe that resurrection often comes through suffering and not in spite of it? In our experience, the cross often precedes resurrection. Christian baptism is a sign to us that new creation often proceeds out of death. As we have noted previously, the apostle Paul desired to know Christ, the power of his resurrection, and sharing his sufferings by becoming like him in his death.[29]

In our prayer for healing, we should also pray for our enemies and those who oppose us. As Dietrich Bonhoeffer writes, "We are taking their distress and poverty, their guilt and perdition upon ourselves, and pleading to God for them. We are doing vicariously for them what they cannot do for themselves."[30]

Our healing prayer requests are offered, hopefully, as part of a community bearing the disease with us. It is the intentional community of Christ that God often uses to support and guide us through suffering and disease. We are not intended to be alone and can be part of a body that gives us saints, models for living, and caring each day as we "walk the walk."[31] Our friendships and communities of faith, from Bible studies and prayer groups to congregations and synods, may share and bear our burdens. We want to celebrate together, if we can, the victory of God!

Our biggest enemy is fear itself. "Be not afraid" was a prominent message with Jesus. Self-defeating fear is a tool of those demonic forces that attempt to limit and disable us in order to stop or distort our prayer, extinguish our hopeful imagination, introduce false hopes, tempt us to avoid and escape, and generally diminish and immobilize all of life. Perhaps the greatest

---

28. For a more scientific assessment of the healing power of faith covering many cultural and religious expressions, see Vance, "Mind over Matter."
29. Eph 3:10.
30. Quoted in Foster, *Prayer*, 224.
31. See 1 Cor 12.

miracle and asset in our living with disease and discovering healing is the overcoming of fear. Do we need to be afraid?

When facing the prospect of life-threatening disease, prayer may include the reality that dying is also a ministry opportunity. The faithful relinquishment of our life is itself a sign to others that the powers of death are being defeated. Our true power often comes through vulnerability and weakness. A tragedy may open us to share God's heart and true presence. My living with cancer and resurrection faith has been meaningful and hopeful at times to numbers of friends, family, and clients.

There is something evocative in stepping out against all that generates death. When we can relinquish our false hopes and live in light of our true hope, we know that elements of the life-giving power that raised Jesus are with us as well. My prayer for the healing of my cancer must face the reality that much cancer itself is a result of unfaithful humanity polluting God's creation. Is God going to heal my cancer if humanity does not stop releasing cancer-causing pollutants into our environment? To pray to be healed from cancer is to immediately be called to creation care and environmental action regarding climate change and the policies and practices that enable humans to pollute and destroy our earthly home.

Thanking God for resurrection, we ask the Lord for strength and discernment to protect all life and thereby witness to God's new creation.

The most important ingredient in healing is love. Writer and retired pediatric surgeon Bernie Siegel said, "I am convinced that unconditional love is the most powerful known stimulant of the immune system. If I told patients to raise their blood levels of immune globulins or killer T cells, no one would know how. But if I can teach them to love themselves and others fully, the same changes happen automatically. The truth is: love heals."[32] All healing love ultimately is a gift from our compassionate Creator.

Prayer and healing are not about analyzing how much faith is enough. Even a small amount of faith, no more than Jesus' example of a tiny mustard seed, is enough faith in God and God's ability to act on behalf of us and others. Healing faith is a question of quality rather than quantity. Even

---

32. Quoted in Linn et al., *Simple Ways*, 63.

a small, simple, heartfelt prayer can change our reality on the inside and outside.[33]

We recognize that our doubts are normal and that we can experience both sorrow and joy simultaneously. If we are approaching the end of our life and our rational capacity is deteriorating, we know that God will hear the prayer of our hearts whether we can speak or not.

When we pray for healing for ourselves, those close to us, or for those suffering in our world, we may consider reciting this prayer:

> God, you are our creator and we are your creatures: human, earthly, and mortal. We know that all life is a loving gift from you and that we live by your grace. When we are sick in body, mind, or spirit, we look to you for our faith, hope, and healing. Help us approach our suffering with relentless security in you and confidence in your future. You will go with us, sharing our living and our dying, resurrecting us through the power of Jesus' triumph over death. We ask to align ourselves—our bodies, emotions, spirit, mind, and relations—with your design for our lives and this world. Help us to be in solidarity with others in their struggles and suffering as well as our own and to remember that all our sufferings are Christ's and Christ's sufferings are ours. We ask for your discernment, strength, resilience, grace, and hope as we navigate suffering and disease. Help us realize your intimate presence and commitment to live and suffer in solidarity with us every day on this earth. You will guide us forward and create all things new. We are grateful for your presence and ultimate healing!

We will take a look at how God engages our suffering in the next chapter.

---

33. Luke 17:5–10.

15

In How We Endure Suffering

"We are afflicted in every way, but not crushed; perplexed, but not driven to despair; persecuted, but not forsaken; struck down, but not destroyed; always carrying in the body the death of Jesus, so that the life of Jesus may also be made visible in our bodies. For while we live, we are always being given up to death for Jesus sake, so that the life of Jesus may be made visible in our mortal flesh. So death is at work in us, but life in you."

—The apostle Paul, 2 Corinthians 4:8–12

In my work as a psychotherapist, I regularly encountered people who questioned God's goodness and love. They would ask me, "What did I do to deserve this? Am I being punished? Why did my child die? Why did my husband leave me? Why is it so hard to make a living? Why are hundreds of millions of people hungry on this planet? Why is there a pandemic? Where is God? Does God really care?" Many very honest and good people reject Christianity because they *do* care for people who suffer, and they *don't* believe God does.

Does God care when we suffer? Yes. Does God interrupt our suffering in the ways we'd like? No, God doesn't. Even Jesus encountered this paradox. He was a human like us, who knew evil and who was tempted as we are to ask questions about God's righteousness and care. Jesus' desperate cry, "My God, My God why have you forsaken me?"[1] is the central

---

1. In Matthew 27:46, Jesus cries, "*Eli, Eli, lema sabachthani?*" in Aramaic. In most translations of the Bible into English, both the transliterated phrase—words written using our alphabet but preserving the original pronunciation—and the translated phrase appear.

place where we can identify the love of God for ourselves and all others who are struggling. The dying cry of Jesus teaches us about the very nature of God—how God relates to us, our future, and imparts hope to us in the midst of our (and others') suffering.

In Jesus' day, there was nothing more irreligious than a crucifixion. The crucifixion of rebels or slaves, for Romans, was the most degrading kind of punishment. In fact, it was regarded as an offense against good manners to speak of this hideous death in the presence of decent people. For the Jews, to die on a cross meant nothing less than to be cursed and rejected by God.[2]

Golgotha, the site of Christ's crucifixion, was a forsaken place. People did not typically travel near the crucifixion site unless an infamous person was being executed. Only those with the deepest loyalties or strongest stomachs could stand to watch the inhuman torture and slaughter. The cross symbolized death, destruction, pain, suffering, humiliation, contradiction, scandal, total alienation, futility, and abandonment. To be crucified was to be godless, cursed, broken, and forced out from this world. Here is where Jesus hung.

Jesus' suffering and humiliation came as a result of his obedience to God. He was faithful and did the right things. He was a good man. He invited everyone to be part of his community; he healed many who suffered and taught people to live a different way.

And they rejected him.

Alone on the cross, he was in a state of conflict with the world and no one understood. Out of control, helpless, and defenseless, Jesus suffered a violent death. He absorbed the evil and pain of this world and forgave his executioners.

But this is not enough for our understanding of the cross. Many people suffer difficult lives and horrible deaths and sometimes people even suffer for others. Why is Jesus' death so special? What sets his experience apart?

What *is* unique about Jesus is that he died without God. He cried, "My God, My God! Why have you forsaken me?" and nothing happened. Just more suffering, more pain, and no escape. At the climactic end of his life, this person who had performed miracles, cast out demons, and taught with great authority was broken, powerless, and alone. The God with whom he had practiced a oneness unique among people, the Father of the kingdom he so faithfully represented, left him abandoned on the cross. The one who was

---

2. Deut 21:33; Gal 3:13.

called Son experienced on the cross a radical fatherlessness. To know his God was so close and yet so far was the worst torment imaginable.

At stake on the cross was Jesus' own theology: his own relationship to God, and his understanding of what God is like. In quoting Psalm 22, Jesus was not only questioning, "Why have you, my father, rejected me," but also, "Why have you rejected our ministry, our words, our actions, our kingdom?" In effect, Jesus cried out, "My God, why have you forsaken yourself and what you have done in my life?"

The dying cry of our godforsaken leader shows us the ugliest imaginable tragedy—brutal death, alone and abandoned by God. The triumph of the power of evil in this world is amazing! We all know something of it, but Jesus experienced it all, alone.

A Victory for Us

Christians view the cross from the reality and vantage point of Jesus' resurrection. We know that, in the end, Jesus was raised from death and reunited with his Father. What he lived and stood for was divinely validated after his execution. The suffering servant who had gone around Palestine preaching and healing in the name of God became the One who was preached about as the prime liberating act of that great God. Jesus became *Christos*, the Messiah, and the new age of righteousness in the Holy Spirit began.

In raising Jesus from death, God displayed publicly that executioners do not triumph over their victims, that injustice and pain will not be the final word, that faithfulness to God's kingdom *is* the truly good life, that love triumphs over hate. With that in mind, we must consider the dying cry of Christ from God's perspective, as well.

What was God doing while Jesus was being tortured on the cross? It is a question that millions ask about their own situations of pain. The apostle Paul answered this with the radical notion that God was *in* Christ reconciling the world to himself.[3] God did not abandon Jesus—God was crucified with him. God the Father suffered a radical sonlessness and the infinite grief, abandonment, and misery of experiencing death at the hands of evil.

In the cross event, God absorbs evil and swallows it up. God's outrage against all that corrupts the creation is turned against God's own self in the person of his son. God suffers in Christ to be the crucified God of all who feel lost, weak, hopeless, and afraid. This God knows the agony of pain,

---

3. 2 Cor 6:19.

oppression, and death. This God truly loves. God was on the cross for us so that we might live. Jesus died for this God even before he died for us.

It is the cross experience that displays God's nature and relationship to our broken and suffering world. Jürgen Moltmann insightfully states: "God is not greater than he is in this humiliation, God is not more glorious than he is in this self-surrender. God is not more powerful than he is in this helplessness. God is not more divine than he is in this humanity."[4]

Picture a scene described by Elie Wiesel at Auschwitz-Birkenau, the most notorious of the Nazi concentration camps and the site of "evidence of this inhumane, cruel and methodical effort to deny human dignity [. . .] one of the greatest crimes ever perpetrated against humanity."[5] Young Elie was among more than a million inmates who were eventually housed at Auschwitz-Birkenau. In front of the prison camp, the Nazis had just hanged two Jewish men and a child. While the two men died quickly, the child's agony drew on.

The innocent child struggled, gasping and gagging, as the noose tightened around his neck. As they were forced to watch, a person asked Wiesel, "Where is God? How can God allow this evil?" Any God that would allow the torture of a child, if God could do anything about it, would be demonic. Wiesel recognized that God was there hanging with that boy on the gallows, just as he had borne the cross with Jesus and walked beside so many others in their trials and suffering. For our loving, redeeming Creator to be anywhere else is impossible.

That is where our God is today for those who suffer. In the history of the cross, even the terror of Auschwitz is taken up into the grief of the Father, the death of the Son, and the transforming power of the Spirit. The cross experience of Jesus and his subsequent resurrection means the worst evils of this world are overcome and transformed by God. It is possible now to accept all of life with the knowledge that we can endure our crosses and be part of the sacrificial power of God.

The love of God begins and ends at the cross where Jesus hung for each of us. To those who suffer today, who are treated unjustly, who starve, who live in brokenness and fear, who cry out like Jesus did to his father, "Why have you forsaken me?" we can only point to the creative work of a passionate, suffering God. God has once and for all time displayed an

---

4. Moltmann, *Crucified God*, 205.

5. UNESCO World Heritage Convention, "Auschwitz Birkenau," para. 6. The account following is from this source.

ability to identify with the worst of this world and transform our injustice and suffering into something new and beautiful. We can consider ourselves, in all our frailty and weakness, to be beautiful and good because we are loved by this God.

The only God we want is one who is completely involved in the tragedies, pain, and grief of human experience. To live is to love and to love is to suffer, but to suffer like Jesus in obedient faith is the way to wholeness and ultimate victory. While Christ experienced pain and death in godforsakenness, we can know that God is deeply involved in our personal lives and is leading us to a place where there is lasting peace.

Suffering in Our Own Context

God joins with all of us in our suffering. God has been with me on long, grueling days of chemotherapy treatments as I coped with its side effects, and through the motionlessness of radiation treatment. I share my story of suffering and solidarity and hope so that you may reflect on your own.

When I was first anticipating receiving chemotherapy through my newly inserted port, I had some anticipatory anxiety and dread. I'd heard from some that chemotherapy was more than just a little difficult. It could produce energy loss, nausea, weakness, loss of appetite, and many typical flu-like symptoms. Chemotherapy is, after all, a toxic, systemic treatment. It attacks fast-growing cancer cells, but also fast-growing cells that are part of our hair, stomach lining, fingernails, mouth, skin, and other areas of our body. It's a shotgun approach to treating malignancy.

As a side note, I know that slowly but surely chemotherapy is giving way to more humane, easier, and more effective cancer treatments. I expect, in the next decade, that chemotherapy will be considered by most an antiquated and rather barbaric treatment for cancer. The developing new cancer treatments include immunotherapies that help our immune system successfully target and defeat growing or spreading malignant cells. Imagine simply getting a couple of shots that would stop cancer from spreading! These new treatments, the results of human innovation, persistence, and hope, are exciting.

But back to my story. The combination chemotherapy regimens that I received took as long as seven or eight hours to administer, considering all the preparation ahead of the actual infusion and then consecutive infusions of up to four different chemotherapies. During the infusions, my face would become pale and I felt weak and dazed. As I sat there, I began to picture Jesus Christ sitting next to me in his own chemo chair and, in solidarity with me, receiving my chemo in himself as well. This divine sharing of chemotherapy gave me a peace and confidence that helped me sustain, find resiliency, and be hopeful.

I have been through a number of these chemotherapy regimens for ten years. With the help of an innovative oncologist, the combinations of chemotherapy with metronomic dosing—though difficult at times—have been tolerable and largely successful at controlling this lethal disease. It's been a breathtaking act of love that Jesus would actually sit next to me and take chemo treatment in his own self! He shared this solidarity, presence, strength, and calm with me, over and over again.

At one point, I had to do twenty-eight days of intense radiation therapy around my surgical site. It was a sophisticated engineering of laser beams being targeted to the pancreas while bending around organs and tissue that should not be radiated. This very delicate, precise procedure required me to be motionless on a table to the degree that I was not permitted to even cough or sneeze during the treatment. With my body strapped in and lying on my back, face up, looking at this overarching machine, I could feel closer to the Lord than to the radiation. In solidarity with me, I could know he was receiving my radiation into his own self. Fortunately, this comforting presence allowed me to completely surrender and relax, knowing there was a way to tolerate this intervention with Jesus Christ sharing it with me. Fortunately, I had no noticeable side effects during this month-long therapy.

So, I experienced God in my treatment. I was given an approach to my treatment that, however challenging, allowed for my ability to better tolerate the physical assault. As I write this, I am no longer treating this pancreatic cancer with chemotherapy or radiation. After ten years, my body can no longer tolerate the toxicity and my death will come before long. I want to die in a state of gratitude and compassion for my body.

Just as God suffered human tragedy on the cross in what felt like the triumph of evil, so we too experience suffering during which we may question the righteousness of God. But through the cross of the risen Christ, we learn that the loving Source of the universe is, in fact, actually here with us, sacrificially experiencing our pain. We can know, then, that there is ongoing hope for us not only in God's future, but even during dark and agonizing moments. In the deepest places of our heart, we may experience God's abiding reality and divine companionship and can suffer hopefully.

IN HOW WE ENDURE SUFFERING

It's important for us not only to live in hope, but to die in hope as well. The next chapter explores this culminating event.

16

In How We Face Death and Dying

> "Like all virtues, hope requires practice to develop. Preparation for hopeful death should therefore begin well before dying; ideally by young adulthood. . . . The best way to enable 'a hopeful dying' is by 'a hopeful living.'"
>
> —David Elliot

Most people struggle with imagining the end of their life. In the face of such unknowns, we can easily operate with significant misconceptions about our future and God's future for us. It is the work of hope to stimulate our imagination so that we may be inspired to think beyond what is and have a clarity about what is coming from God.

At different points in my life, I have reflected on my inevitable death. When I was young, I was taught the customary bedtime prayer, "Now I lay me down to sleep. I pray the Lord my soul to keep. If I should die before I wake, I pray the Lord my soul to take. All this I ask for Jesus' sake, Amen." I listened to many sermons that had to do with sin, death, heaven, and hell. Death was scary and, in many ways, so was God. But I certainly wasn't ready to die then, because I had things to do. When I was twelve, I recall asking God to not take my life until I had a chance to be married and have sex!

In early graduate school, I wrote an extensive paper on helping people who were dying. Among other things, this paper allowed me to come to terms with my own fears: when I finished it, my anxiety about death and dying receded and I invested in living my life. Along the way, I did an internship as a chaplain on a hospital oncology unit. This gave me my first direct exposure to dying people and helped me, once again, develop more acceptance of my mortality.

Watching my grandparents die was difficult. All of them were in nursing homes and became less and less self-directed and more and more institutionalized. Their lives extended far beyond what we would consider quality living. I naturally disliked nursing home environments and decided that a nursing home was the last place I wanted to die.

When I discovered at age sixty-two that I had pancreatic cancer, I was forced to review and expand my understanding of my own mortality. "Dying" moved from what happened to others to what was happening to me, and my many abstract reflections quickly shifted to very practical and pragmatic considerations. I really was going to die and, perhaps, fairly soon.

Facing our death is a prime test of resurrection faith. Many religious people who say they have a general hope for eternal life will, nevertheless, nervously struggle to prevent their death. Often, people feel a sense of desperation and hang onto this life at virtually any cost. What people confess regarding their future with God is contradicted by a practical atheism that focuses almost entirely on maintaining life today. While people may believe that the best is yet to come, at the practical level that belief is often not a factor when people are making decisions regarding the end of their life. Why is this?

How we perceive death plays a crucial role in our worldview. Death is not only an event in life; it is *the* event—all of our attitudes toward life are also attitudes about our mortality. We experience death with our entire life, and we experience life with our final death. Just as a good book has a final chapter that develops or adds meaning to the book's earlier chapters, so the way we picture the end of our current existence determines much of the meaning and significance of our earlier years.

Confronting Our Fear of Death

One of the paradoxes of our human condition is this: we all know physical life will end and, at the same time, we find facing the prospect of dying difficult. So, we avoid it, because not thinking about it is so much easier than accepting it. North American culture, in particular, tends to avoid or deny death. Many imagine death as a universal negative that repudiates and nullifies life's objectives. Death is an inverted image of life, hope, vitality, youth, and progress. When our society emphasizes future progress, the prospect of no future at all is disconcerting.

When we are afraid of dying, we live with more anxious apprehension, our world shrinks, and we lose confidence and trust in ourselves, God, and others. While we all possess a natural survival instinct and want to preserve the treasure of our life, fear imposes on us an unhealthy demand for control and certainty, and it prevents us from feeling relaxed, free, and fully alive. Our worries are something that we often create, and they can be a source of great subjective suffering. Doing life and healing involve the overcoming of self-defeating fear on a regular basis, as does death.

Contemporary North American popular culture often seems negatively obsessed with death: the existence of our certain death tells us that life is fragile and ending. This death seems to have the final word over life. After all, we all die, do we not? Evil is real, and sooner or later, it is experienced by everyone. Death is fearful. We fear the end of the world, the collapse of moral society, the meaninglessness of human existence, our painful demise, the loss of all that we have invested in, and distance from God. Humans enact death more than any other creature. We systematically kill each other, destroy our life-giving environment, and propagate deadly diseases. What we consider to be normal is actually life permeated by the reality of death.

In "For the Time Being," poet W. H. Auden captures the human struggle with death in an Advent prayer petitioning for the miracle of God saving our human body: "We who must die demand a miracle. How could the eternal do a temporal act, the infinite become a finite fact? Nothing can save us that is possible: we who must die demand a miracle."[1] Many people presume that it would be better to live forever. After all, if life is good, then surely having a longer one is better. Theologian Gilbert Meilaender suggests that the notion of eternal life on earth would not be a cure-all, even if it were possible.[2] He suggests that living on and on, forever, would become rather boring. We'd live a life of longing for all that we had lost, rather than a life of hope for all we have to gain.

Meilaender draws an analogy to eating a full-course dinner. However good and pleasurable a full-course meal may be, it would slowly lose its appeal if we continued to eat the same courses over and over. The meal has a sequence of courses, just as life has a series of stages, and the meal's

---

1. Quoted in Verhey, *Christian Art of Dying*, 9.
2. Meilaender, *Should We Live Forever?*, 39–73.

enjoyment requires that we pass through these different courses and complete the meal without overeating. No meal, however sumptuous, can delight us forever in the way it once did.

Our life stories are most understandable when there's an end. Without an end, it's harder to find significance at every step or every season along life's journey. Our lives have a narrative trajectory. They go somewhere and create their place in a comprehensive story that can make sense. A story that moves toward no ending would only meander with fragments along the way. Desperately trying to cling indefinitely to our physical life when we are approaching its end threatens to distract us from what gives our life its meaning and beauty.

Part of a complete life is letting go: of our control, our power, our plans, our earthly future. We create the next generations, and we must inevitably give way to them as they pave their own path into the future. If we try to live forever, even if our bodies would last, we would be seeking to be like God instead of recognizing the limited people we are. In many ways, our limits are our strengths, because a life lived with limits can be a life full of virtues and wisdom.

The bioethicist Daniel Callahan suggests that the proper goal of medicine for those who have already lived out a natural lifespan ought to be the relief of suffering rather than the extension of life. Why is it that our doctors cannot write "old age" on death certificates?[3]

Life has mystery from birth to death. When a mother is giving birth for the first time, she hopes everything will be okay. During delivery, she goes through a memorable natural physical process involving inevitable uncertainty, losing control, vulnerability, and a certain amount of pain and anxiety, yet she looks forward to a great reward. Likewise, when we are dying, we surrender to a memorable but natural physical process of inevitable uncertainty, loss of control, vulnerability, and a certain amount of pain and anxiety, yet we hopefully look forward to a great reward. Life may be just one big breathing exercise—we come into this world with an inhale, and we leave this world with an exhale. In and out.

When people are born, we celebrate the arrival of a new life with such rituals as showers, naming, baptism, and dedications. Death and the journey into it is the most sacred part of our lifecycle after birth, because it is a time in which we touch the deepest dimensions of our existence. Yet we often avoid comprehensive planning for dying and death.

3. Meilaender, *Should We Live Forever?*, 33, 10, 11, respectively.

Author Wendell Berry believes there is no more profound lesson older people can teach the young than how to receive the gift of death. In the 1972 essay "Discipline of Hope," Berry writes,

> Concepts of renewal are always accompanied by concepts of loss or death; in order for renewal to take place, the old must not be forgotten but relinquished; in order to become what we may be, we must cease to be as we are; in order to have life we must lose it. Our language bears abundant testimony to these deaths; the year's death that precedes spring; the burial of the seed before germination; . . . the spiritual death that must precede rebirth; the death of the body that must precede resurrection."[4]

At every point during the lifecycle, we find that we must let go in order to move forward. Every letting go means some form of dying. While we are living, we are dying.

Hopeful Aging

Physical aging is the accumulation of damage to DNA and other molecules. Our bodies can slow the aging process by repairing some of this damage, but, in the end, it's too much for our bodies to fix. Gravity wins. We eventually die.

The process of aging is natural and actually healthy for human beings.[5] Healthy aging recognizes that losses lead to gains and physical deterioration can lead to increased inner freedom and new perspectives. In aging, we can clarify what is most important to us, pace ourselves according to our limits, clarify the people that we want to be, and gain wisdom. Though our earthly time diminishes, our understanding of ourselves and the world can expand. Our sense of wonder and surprise may grow. Important values like simplicity, delight, and empathy for others may develop as we age. We can focus on what is real and enjoy the utter goodness of life.

Contemplation in aging allows us to be thoroughly stimulated in the present and value existence itself. Growing old provides for solitude, prayer, and the opportunity to ponder what it means to be part of God's creation. When we focus more on "being" than on "doing," we can lighten up and

---

4. Quoted in Hauerwas et al., *Growing Old in Christ*, 164.
5. Fischer, *Winter Grace*, 8, 197.

laugh more, transcending life's struggles. Life is easier when it doesn't center on demands or pressure.

In aging, we have opportunity to see a fuller panorama of life. In *On the Brink of Everything*, published when author Parker Palmer was seventy-nine, he wrote about aging:

> I needed that tedium and inspiration, the anger and the love, the anguish and the joy. I see how it all belongs. Even those days of despair when the darkness overwhelmed me. Calamities I once lamented now appear as strong threads of the larger weave, without which the fabric of my life would be less resilient. Moments of fulfillment I failed to relish in my impatience to get onto the next thing now appear as times to be recalled and savored. And I've doubled down on my gratitude for those who've helped me along with love, affirmation, hard questions, daunting challenges, compassion and forgiveness.[6]

When we age, we can learn to live closer to our heart, and fall madly in love with life. Palmer writes that we don't say in our last breath, "I'm so glad for the self-centered, self-serving and self-protective life I've lived." Instead, Palmer observes, "In aging we can learn again how little we know and how easy it is to fail. We can learn to value ignorance as much as knowledge and failure as much as success. We stand on the brink of everything when we grow old."[7]

Being old, Palmer says, is "just another word for nothing left to lose, a time of life to take bigger risks on behalf of the common good. We can offer our self to the world—our energies, gifts, experience with real generosity. In aging we can be raising hell on behalf of whatever we care about: freedom's just another word for not needing to count the cost."[8]

A Christian Perspective on Death and Dying

In dying, as in living, we are surrounded not only by issues and problems, but also by a sense of mystery. It's common for people to call the ultimate mystery "God." Theologian Allen Verhey suggests that mystery evokes among us a sense of dependence upon some dimly known but reliable order and may generate a sense of gratitude for the "givenness" of life and

---

6. Palmer, *On the Brink*, 2.
7. Palmer, *On the Brink*, 45.
8. Palmer, *On the Brink*, 25.

death.⁹ Mystery establishes a hopeful sense of new possibilities and also a sad sense of a tragic flaw that runs through our lives and through our world. It instills a keen sense of responsibility to that which sustains the order, gives the gifts, judges the flaws, and promises hope.

For Christians, theologian William J. Abraham writes, death can be seen as an intrusion into God's good creation, a major assault on the good and therefore an enemy. In choosing to live, we naturally struggle against death even though we know that death is part of our human experience. The harsh reality of death and its immediate effects of loss and obliteration often make it the last enemy in our life to face.¹⁰

Death may seem like abandonment and separation from God. God has always wanted to save us from this fear of death. But God cannot save us without an uprising against death itself, along with our fears of death. The divine tactic—the invasive weapon that has the power of life over death—is resurrection. Resurrection is life in the face of death, life in spite of death, life after death, life that breaks the power of death. The resurrection of Jesus is God's end-time invasion against death with immediate real-time effects. What Jesus has already done guarantees what's going to happen in our future and can impact what happens today.¹¹

Our God is in the business of raising the dead, of raising all dying entities in creation. We know this because God raised Jesus of Nazareth to show us that a life that transcends death exists for each of us. The resurrection of Jesus is God's insurgency of life over death, consuming the living dead, infusing life in an age that is going to pass away. Resurrection says that God is at war with fearful death and God always wins. It is revolutionary because it touches every aspect of our life, every dimension of life threatened by death. We are partners and collaborators in God's mission, on God's side, as God's reign of resurrection assaults our death-dreading world.¹²

Rather than dying being the work of medical providers, those who are Christian should recognize that the principal story that shapes our entire life cycle, including our death, involves the life, death, and resurrection of Jesus Christ. The death of Jesus should be the beginning point for how we understand death. In general, his life was marked by death at almost every turn.

9. Verhey, *Christian Art of Dying*, 64.
10. Abraham, *Among the Ashes*, 89.
11. Blount, *Invasion of the Dead*, 91.
12. Blount, *Invasion of the Dead*, 91.

In Jesus' day, typical Palestinian life expectancy reached twenty-five to twenty-eight years, with half of newborns dying in their first year.[13] There were no hospitals, clinics, life-support equipment, insurance companies, nursing homes, or therapeutic drugs. Jesus would naturally have expected to die at an early age by today's standards. Aside from the short Palestinian lifespan, Jesus recognized that he was headed for an abrupt, undeserved death by torturous crucifixion.

Aging is not a principal focus in the New Testament.[14] For Jesus, who lived no more than thirty-six years with his terminal prognosis, the mission and purpose of God's kingdom was the most important aspect of his life. Because of his death and resurrection, many early followers of Jesus felt free to surrender and sacrifice their lives when necessary. Faithful martyrs are examples in displaying that "they did not cling to life even in the face of death."[15] Followers of Jesus want, as Paul said, "to know Christ and the power of his resurrection and the sharing of his sufferings, becoming like him in his death."[16]

To allay some early Christian concerns about dying and death, the apostle Paul wrote, "We do not want you to be uninformed, brothers and sisters, about those who have died, so that you may not grieve as others do who have no hope. For since we believe that Jesus died and rose again, even so, through Jesus, God will bring with him those who have died . . . Therefore encourage one another with these words."[17] In Hebrews 2:14–15, believers are reminded that, "Since, therefore, the children share flesh and blood, Jesus himself likewise shared the same things, so that through death he might destroy the one who has the power of death, that is, the devil, and free those who all their lives were held in slavery by the fear of death." As Jesus followers, we are not to fear death, but rather to understand that he has counteracted its threat, overcome its power, defeated its sting, and thwarted it through his resurrection.

---

13. Craddock et al., *Speaking of Dying*, 57.
14. See Hays and Hays, "Christian Practice of Growing Old," 3–18.
15. Rev 12:11.
16. Phil 3:10.
17. 1 Thess 4:13–14, 18.

SECTION THREE: HOPE GIVES US A NEW HORIZON

Learning to Let Go

Jesus called his disciples to lose their self-absorbed life for his sake, claiming that letting go and laying down one's life is the way of true freedom and gaining what is most important. Renouncing oneself and "taking up the cross" meant, in Jesus' day, to relinquish one's kinship group and join the followers of Jesus. It was an exhortation to remain faithful to Jesus, the reign of God, and Jesus' followers in the face of persecution and death by religious and political authorities. Jesus was simply preparing his followers for tragedy.

We are protected from self-absorption and a kind of egocentric anxiety with this radical call to let go of our earthly securities and trust the God who makes all things new. If we try to hang on to our life, dying will be more difficult. Dying can be the ultimate act of letting go. We may prepare ourselves for dying by maintaining a healthy detachment from all earthly things that give us a false sense of independence and control.

It is a paradox that impending death helps us clarify what we value and, at the same time, what we must let go of. Everything we have loved is to be relinquished. There is a huge grief in dying when we realize we are saying goodbye to all we have known, invested in, treasured, and found meaning in. However, letting go of our past experiences and attachments makes room for tomorrow's surprises. When we possess nothing, we can feel most free to receive. Life is truly a gift and, in dying, we surrender that gift back to our Creator. Dying is surrender to our creaturehood, the earth, and God's embrace.

For Christians, life comes through death and is not separate from it. In dying, we take our whole selves, everything we have become, and know that completion and freedom awaits us. Hopeful dying often involves strength in the midst of frailty, perseverance in the midst of brokenness, love despite pain and suffering, faith and engagement with life at the edge of death. If we anticipate our death, it can often be something we *do*, not just something that happens to us. In death, we will discover our true selves.[18]

Because the Christian church has often tended to outsource the management of dying to institutions such as hospitals and nursing homes, we need a new appreciation for the work of Christian hope in dying. Only with hope in a power greater than our own can we live life as freely as we have received it. Followers of Jesus are supposed to be a community of people

---

18. See Fischer, *Winter Grace*, 197.

who have learned that their deaths are not an unmitigated disaster. Significantly, Christian people are called to serve one another in a fashion that is as important as their own existence. Maybe preventing our own death with extreme measures or prolonging it with the most expensive procedures is not as responsible or godly if it means that the weakest members of our community don't get the healthcare resources they need. Perhaps, in line with Christian faith, we may choose a social responsibility that uses only medical procedures that should be available to all. Rather than be simply about us, our death is part of life in a larger community.

Preparing for Death

Followers of Jesus who have lived by faith, patience, and hope, and have practiced the spiritual disciplines, are best equipped to face death and live with mortality. Preparation for a hopeful death should be a lifelong project. We are bound together, as Christian people, in a universal story that provides something worth dying for and living for. Facing death allows us to remember that we are not our own creators and we should not take our lives for granted. Being part of God's life transforms aging time from threat to gift, from *chronos* to *kairos.*

Cultivating hopeful attitudes is an important asset for dying. Hope allows people facing death to bear the sadness of letting go and the grief of loss without being overcome by it. From our understanding of hope, we recognize that hope is an anticipation of the future that transforms our present reality (chapter 4). In Luke's Gospel, when the old man, Simeon, is ready to die, he "departs in peace" because he has glimpsed God's salvation for the whole world. What was yet to come for Simeon is greater than what had been. Hope makes possible the end of Simeon's earthly life without it being the end of God's story. Followers of Jesus can look beyond the culmination of their own lives to the redemption of the entire creation.

Erasmus, in his treatise "Preparing for Death," reminded us that preparation for death must be practiced through our whole life, and the spark of faith must be continually fanned so that it grows and gains strength.[19] The stronger our faith, accompanied by love and hope, the more diminished our fear.

However different we are from each other, we were all born powerless, we all die powerless, and the little differences we live in between

---

19. Verhey, *Christian Art of Dying,* 255.

dwindle in the light of this enormous truth. We all die poor and share the fragility of our human existence together. Can we prepare to die in such a way that others can continue to live, strengthened by the Spirit of our life? We are so concerned about what we do, yet we forget that we are most likely remembered by who we were. We all die in a *being* state and our *doings* should result in being at peace in our dying.

Facing our death reminds us that we are radically dependent creatures on a God who created the cosmos out of chaos, light out of darkness, life out of dirt.[20] As the apostle Paul said, "We do not live to ourselves, and we do not die to ourselves. If we live, we live to the Lord, and if we die, we die to the Lord; so then, whether we live or whether we die, we are the Lord's."[21]

Christian sacraments help our preparation for dying. In baptism, we experience dying as creatures of God and are raised to a new life in Christ. In his Epistle to the Romans, Paul writes: "Do you not know that all of us who have been baptized into Christ Jesus were baptized into his death? Therefore we have been buried with him by baptism into death, so that, just as Christ was raised from the dead by the glory of the Father, so we too might walk in newness of life."[22] So, followers of Jesus in baptism are liberated from the fear of death by dying spiritually before we die physically. Dying with Christ in baptism gives us the confidence that nothing in this world can interfere with God's claim on us.[23] It reminds us of that central paradox of discipleship: if we are detached from this world, we find our best life with Christ. It may be helpful to list everything we can let go of while claiming our solidarity with Christ. Baptism proclaims that death has been drawn into God's power.

Along with baptism, we are sustained in our walk with Christ by the Lord's Supper which, among other things, reminds us that we are one with the dying and resurrected Jesus. By appropriating the elements of bread and wine, Jesus' sacrificial death brings new meaning to our life and death.

At the heart of the Christian story, God wanted to share not only our life, but our death. Jesus' death is the most radical expression of God's desire to be with us. Since God wants to die with and for us, we too should prepare to die with and for each other.

---

20. Verhey, *Christian Art of Dying*, 263.
21. Rom 14:7–8.
22. Rom 6: 3, 4.
23. 2 Cor 4:8–10.

Living with Death

Dying presents us with two opportunities: first to gratefully remember, surrender, and relinquish all of our investments in people and projects; and second, to look forward in anticipation of a complete, flourishing, resurrected life.

God's final assault on all that destroys life began at the beginning of Jesus' announcement in the Gospel of Mark. He said, "The time is now, God's reign is at hand."[24] Jesus lived God's battle against principalities and powers that bring death in his relationships, his healing, his teaching, and his choice to love unconditionally. In his lifetime, he continually engaged the side of those who were struggling against the forces of death, whether social, religious, economic, physical, or political, and he continues to do so today. He embodied what God's future beyond death would look like. So, he lived justice over rote tradition, service over domination, inclusion over exclusion, forgiveness over vengeance, and healing over all forms of death. Jesus still engages the demonic, institutional, and human forces that represent death in our world.

In his goodness, grace, justice, joy, and peace, Jesus is God's weapon, assaulting the forms of death of his day and ours. As an invasive strike force of life, he was threatened early and often with the principalities of death. He encountered satanic, cosmic, and human resistance to the new regime of life he proclaimed and God promised. His torture and execution came from perceptions of him held by the ruling powers, threatened by his radical love for all; to them, he was disruptive, blasphemous, and seditious. He remained resolutely faithful to God's life and died in hope rather than in despair. Showing us what our future will be, resurrection people are called by him to continue this invasion of life in the midst of human suffering and death.

Brian Blount offers a hopeful vision of Jesus speaking to his disciples:

> I will die soon because of what I believe, because of how I have lived and how I promise to keep on living. Because in my present life I foreshadow a future whose ethics and rules and ways of living with and treating one another are completely different from the living deadness that consumes this world. What I believe and how I live are in conflict with what the powers of this world believe and how they continue to live and force others to live. If you want to follow me and my beliefs, you will be in conflict with those

24. Mark 1:15.

powers, too. You may well die, too. But I know no other way to flash God's future back into our present. I am sorry. I am so sorry. But I do not see another way. Regrettably, you, too, must take up your cross, and you must follow.[25]

In the age of resurrection's assault on death, we are to be Spirit-led agents of life and hope in our troubled age that is passing away. Participating in the liberation and transformation of our world, we are part of the assault against unjust economic relations, oppressive political relations, unjust race relations, patriarchal gender relations, hierarchical power relations, and the use of violence to maintain them.

In Jesus' resurrection uprising, against all that harms human life, we enact Jesus' leper-touching, sin-forgiving, prostitute-socializing, tax collector-befriending, unjust law-breaking, woman-empowering, all peoples-accepting, empire-challenging ministry that embodies God's future for the world to see. We live a cruciform existence knowing that Jesus' cross may be ours as well, and Jesus' resurrection has already begun to transform our lives. Our lives rupture the dynamics that bring death because Jesus' resurrection is more real than death itself. The death culture we know from the past and present, but our true identity lies in the future. Resurrection overwhelms our present with the reality of God's victory.

Jesus' followers throughout the centuries have modeled lives lived well in the midst of death's often gruesome and contagious impact. Imagine, for a moment, early followers of Jesus likely being led by the megalomaniac Roman tyrant Nero to a certain torture and death in the Roman Colosseum. Picture Jesus' followers singing praises to God and giving thanks for their opportunity to share in the sufferings of Christ! As these faithful, hopeful disciples were herded along the way, Roman citizens would gather to watch, mock, insult, and jeer. Miraculously, at certain points, a captivated Roman citizen or two, witnessing a power stronger than death, would leave the safety of their known life and step out from the side of the road to join Jesus' followers on the way to the Colosseum. The implicit evangelism that was persuasive enough to move Roman citizens to join Jesus' disciples toward a certain, gruesome death is testimony to the power of hope and is a principal reason why faith in Jesus spread throughout the region.

While destruction and death can function like cancer and infect, disfigure, or kill us, we are no longer possessed by them. Indeed, we are empowered to walk with and through death. We read and believe, "If the

25. Blount, *Invasion of the Dead*, 101.

Spirit of him who raised Jesus from the dead dwells in you, he who raised Christ from the dead will give life to your mortal bodies also through his Spirit that dwells in you."[26] We live now in the life-giving space created by Christ's powerful invasion against death.

Hopeful Dying

Just as every life is different and unique, so is every death. The story of dying may include joy, meaningful events, drama, conflict, crisis, suspense, pain, humor, anguish, sweetness, possibilities, disappointment, and loss. Our task, in many ways, is to join our unique personal stories of life and death with God's universal and timeless story. Healing will happen even when a cure is not possible.

When we live hopefully and intentionally into our dying, we may find significant rewards. Each moment, hour, or day can be meaningful, communication with friends and family can be treasured, favorite stories and memories may be shared, the practice of forgiveness in relationships can be healing, legacies can be established, and we can find a *kairotic* sense of wonder at the grandeur of life. In dying, we experience that there is something more significant to be discovered about ourselves and our relationships. When we have gratitude for these things, we can experience real joy. The end of life should be a time of meeting, wisdom, integrity, and purposeful closure.[27]

As I approach the end of my physical life, our family has begun meeting to process my dying and their part in it. We ask one another questions about our thoughts and feelings about my death, their individual experience of it, and their vision of life beyond my physical presence; we can address unresolved relational snags; and we create family images and practice anticipation of the new heaven and earth. Our goal is to achieve a balance between the major loss and grief that death generates and a wondrous expectation of our life together in God's future. Our closing conversations and goodbyes, in God's presence, mean that our grief is only temporary. Relationships are eternal for all of us.

In God's *kairotic* time, our awareness is increasingly directed toward what is immediate and present. *Kairos* frees us to be engaged in the present because we have confidence toward our future. In God's time, we are

---

26. Rom 8:11.
27. Speerstra and Anderson, *Divine Art of Dying*, 116–18.

processing our death as a part of the process of eternal life. We can have an immediate encounter with God and death at the same time. In *kairos*, our dying and the dying of Jesus are joined. Our resurrection will be joined with Jesus' resurrection.

Suffering and hope may go together. In *The Divine Art of Dying*, Karen Speerstra reflects, "Hope does not try to avoid the fears and pains of finite existence; nor is it naïve about suffering as part of living. If we divorce hope from suffering, we risk becoming victims of illusions and create images of false hope at the end of life. If we divorce suffering from hope, then we are likely to become victims of cynicism or despair and surrender hope altogether."[28] Suffering and hope are parts of our finite lives. Surrender involves allowing suffering and hope to happen from birth to death.

Death is part of creation. For some, actual death comes instantly, and for others, the final processes of death can last a week or more, as our body and brain begin to slow. Every aspect of death seems to be the antithesis of health in life: loss of feeling and circulation; weakness; shallow, labored breathing; and loss of consciousness. For some, death can be gross or unclean; after all, it may involve soiled bedclothes and sheets, flailing, nudity, confusion, rough language, screams, and tears.[29]

Pain, too, may be part of dying. How much the pain hurts and how we respond to it are due partially to our attitudes toward pain and partially to our fears and past experiences with discomfort. Pain is personal and subjective as well as simply physical. We are born with some pain and we often die with some pain. It reminds us of the contingencies of bodily life. Here modern medicine can help: management of pain should be effective.

There is sorrow and lament in dying. In the grief of dying, we may protest against God and love God at the same time. Lament involves our natural resistance to death. It may be displayed as groans too deep for words that move us toward a yearning for the redemption of our bodies.[30] Our outrage and lament at death is a sign that there are things in this world that are definitely not as they're supposed to be. We protest against the darkness in this "present evil age."[31] Our deep cries of loss and sorrow are legitimate because we do believe in a sovereign God who is good, almighty, and faithful to divine promises.

28. Speerstra and Anderson, *Divine Art of Dying*, 198.
29. Speerstra and Anderson, *Divine Art of Dying*, 241.
30. Rom 8:23, 26.
31. Gal 1:4.

We may find it difficult to hope at points in our dying or the dying of others. In these times we may have to cry out to our God, who raised Jesus Christ from death, to resurrect our own hope. Others may keep hope alive for us. Our God does not forsake the divine work in us but will stick with us until Jesus returns.[32]

As he was preparing to die, St. Ignatius said, "Take, Lord, receive all my liberty, my memory, my undertaking, my entire will. You have given all to me. Now I return it. Give me only your grace and your love. That is enough for me."[33]

At the end of our current life, the final decision may be the hardest and easiest: to trust God in Jesus Christ. We recall the apostle Paul saying, "We do not live to ourselves, and we do not die to ourselves. If we live, we live to the Lord, and if we die, we die to the Lord; so then, whether we live or whether we die, we are the Lord's."[34]

Hopeful dying, then, may be characterized this way: the person receives the mercy of God, shares it with others, possesses a lively hope of enjoying eternal life with Christ and with all the saints, and surrenders his or her life to God, praying, "Lord Jesus, receive my spirit."[35] In response, there is a loving, exuberant reception.

The Reality of Hope

I believe that hope can be the most important aspect of our understanding of reality: it is a certain way of seeing, comprehending, or foreseeing. Even people imprisoned physically, mentally, or spiritually in the worst of circumstances can achieve some inner freedom if they are able to hope. The future is open and the present amenable to change, beginning from inside us. And what empowers hope? Love for all that God has created, for the flourishing of all living things now and in God's future. When we love as God loves, we cannot help but hope.

---

32. Phil 1:6.
33. Speerstra and Anderson, *Divine Art of Dying*, 223.
34. Rom 14:7–8.
35. Acts 7:59.

Afterword

FOR READERS WHO ARE interested in the specifics of my cancer story, I have provided a summary here.

In 2010, I began to experience heartburn and acid reflux. I used a number of over-the-counter (and eventually prescription-strength) antacids with some relief. However, over several weeks, the stomach discomfort remained and began to worsen. I went through a series of medical tests, including blood draws, endoscopy, MRI, CT scan, and an ultrasound. At the time, all of the tests were negative, and nothing seemed to clarify why my stomach was so distressed. I resorted to taking an oral cocktail that included lidocaine when the pain was nearly unbearable.

One night, I awoke abruptly from my sleep and needed to use the restroom. On the way, I collapsed. I was completely limp and unable to get up. Fortunately, my daughter Greta was home, and she quickly called an ambulance. This was my first experience in an emergency vehicle.

At the emergency room, a blood test revealed there was some irregularity with my pancreas. They scheduled me for an endoscopic ultrasound ten days later, which was to be administered at a local hospital. The results shocked me (and everyone else): a mass in the pancreas. The doctor was almost apologetic and told me I would need to have the growth surgically removed as soon as possible.

I scrambled to find a surgeon with expertise who could be available on short notice. Four days later, I had a major surgery revealing the presence of pancreatic cancer. The back half of my pancreas was cut away, along with my spleen. Unfortunately, there were positive margins at the surgical site, which meant that there were cancer cells still active in the area, even though the disease had not spread to my lymph nodes.

When I spoke to the surgeon and the oncologist at the hospital, I was told that the "standard of care" for this type of pancreatic cancer would be single, traditional chemotherapy and radiation. My prognosis at that time was seven to twelve months of life. This dreadful, relentless disease was going to kill me, and there was nothing I could do. Pancreatic cancer is incurable and, as such, a literal death sentence.

Many people diagnosed with pancreatic cancer have unhealthy habits like smoking or drinking, are overweight, and are in their late sixties, seventies, or eighties. But I was a physically fit sixty-two-year old without any history of serious illness. No family history of pancreatic cancer. Why me? Why now? I couldn't believe it. For a while, I kept telling myself, "They must have just gotten it wrong...."

After nine days in the hospital, I went home in a state of disbelief. Almost instantly, major life questions emerged. What was I going to do with my counseling practice? How was I going to manage the homeless advocacy work I was involved in? Would my medical care be covered by my insurance? More importantly, how was I going to deal with relationships important to me, including family, close friends, and community partners?

People told me that pancreatic cancer, besides being a killer disease, is painful. An oncologist at another local hospital told me the disease would affect important spinal nerves, generating serious pain. The terminal prognosis, all parts of my life I faced relinquishing, and questions I had without easy answers led to three months of struggle—psychologically, spiritually, relationally, and physically. I would wake up screaming in the middle of the night, crying out "No, no, no!" I began each day facing the stark reality that there was nothing I could do to change this inner monster assaulting my body. It would be part of me until I died.

Along with the more obvious, shocking realities of life with pancreatic cancer, another major struggle emerged: the often well-meaning and conflicting treatment advice from professionals and friends. I soon realized that people tended to seek innovative and sometimes unresearched interventions for this disease. Numbers of differing recommendations were offered and I struggled to know what treatment directions to take. How do you decide, when you have a bleak prognosis, what treatments or interventions to take, especially when so many of them seem to contradict each other? At times, I entertained the idea of not doing any interventions at all, and simply letting myself die.

AFTERWORD

About six weeks after my nine-day stay in the hospital, I began seeing clients again in my counseling office. One of my clients suggested I check out an innovative research program studying the benefits of integrative care alongside the institutional standard of care model. I quickly scheduled an appointment with this integrative clinic in Seattle and was told, after my exam, about a holistic program south of Seattle involving oncology, naturopathic care, acupuncture, dietary monitoring, mind-body resources, and more. I was intrigued.

Visiting this holistic clinic was inspiring, and I committed to their treatment approach. They told me I had a much better prognosis than what I had received at two of our leading hospitals. I began treatment involving combinations of chemotherapy with metronomic dosing, naturopathic supplements, special infusions of vitamin C, interferon shots, and dietary changes that directed me away from sugar, dairy, and red meat. Dr. Nick Chen, Dr. Paul Rielly, and Dr. Erin Sweet designed and implemented my treatment. This approach has been elaborated in *Rx for Hope*, by Dr. Chen. I surrounded myself with very supportive family, friends, community advocates, and clinical ministry professionals, and continued an active spiritual life. I was so blessed to have a support system to lean on during this time wrought with confusion and fear.

For the last eleven years, I have been fortunate to find effective ways of holding off this disease. But the journey hasn't been easy. I've suffered at times. I've questioned many things. On top of it all, I was challenged with an insurance company that rejected providing benefits to me because of the holistic approach I was taking (they initially called it "investigational and experimental"). How was I going to get this promising integrative care without insurance coverage?

The insurance company was only interested in "standard of care," which promised me no more than one year of life, at best. In my frustration, I had to make aggressive appeals that drew from the advocacy of politicians, an attorney, pancreatic cancer researchers, and my treatment providers. After three appeals, my insurance company, without explanation, began to pay. I believe part of the reason they started paying was my demonstrating, in rebuttal to the insurance company's oncologist, that "standard of care" was not a satisfactory treatment for this incurable disease and my bleak prognosis.

I've been hospitalized in intensive care on two separate occasions. That I'm alive today is, for me, a beautiful and unexpected gift. I can give myself little credit for so far successfully coping with cancer, as I know more involved, challenged, courageous, and resilient cancer patients.

In terms of life expectancy, I am currently within the top 1 percent of pancreatic cancer survivors. In the last eleven years of living with pancreatic cancer, I have considered myself fortunate that my life has been extended through integrated progressive medical care, support from family and friends, stimulating work, challenging social action, disciplined diet and exercise, and, most importantly, a spiritually based transcendent hope. As I reflect now, I honestly believe I'm not afraid to die. Pancreatic cancer has gifted me with the opportunity to explore the meaning of my life, understand my definitions of success, live each day well, and anticipate the way I want my life to end. I feel basically resolved.

That being said, I'm also very aware that there are many variables in dying which I have yet to know or experience. It is certainly possible I will experience more fear and will need all of my psychospiritual and relational resources as death approaches. Fear is generally what causes some people to avoid thinking about death, or what causes others to become negatively preoccupied with death. Many people only consciously face death when death faces them, when they or someone they know is dying. I just happened to be faced squarely with my own mortality much sooner than I ever anticipated.

I am deeply grateful for the chance to prepare to die and actively communicate with my family and friends. The trauma of this disease has affected many others beyond myself and I've had the privilege of praying, weeping, strategizing, supporting, and generally keeping hope alive with them. We have become comfortable talking about death. Together, we have faced this gruesome prognosis, as well as the sense of an evil attack on my body. It has become clear that there is a spiritual battle going on, as well as a physical one. Being able to together name the enemy helped me continue appreciating and caring for my physical self. I know my body is not the source of this cancer and will work against it.

What an incredible gift our bodies are!

Editor's Note: On February 28, 2021, just a few months after completing this book, Ted Brackman died. Supported by family and friends, he lived with hope to the end.

Bibliography

Abraham, William J. *Among the Ashes*. Grand Rapids: Eerdmans, 2017.
Augsburger, David. *When Enough Is Enough*. Harrisonburg, PA: Herald, 1984.
Bauckham, Richard. *Gospel Women: Studies of the Named Women in the Gospel*. Grand Rapids: Eerdmans.
———. *The Theology of Jürgen Moltmann*. London: T. & T. Clark, 1995.
Belanger, Christopher. "Sanders: Child Poverty Is Higher in America Than Any Other Major Country." *Politifact*, July 8, 2015. https://www.politifact.com/factchecks/2015/jul/08/bernie-s/sanders-child-poverty-higher-america-any-other-maj.
Benner, David. *Soulful Spirituality: Becoming Fully Alive and Deeply Human*. Grand Rapids: Brazos, 2011.
———. *Spirituality and the Awakening Self: The Sacred Journey of Transformation*. Grand Rapids: Brazos, 2012.
Berger, Peter. *A Rumor of Angels: Modern Society and the Recovery of the Supernatural*. New York: Doubleday, 1969.
Block, Peter, et al. *An Other Kingdom: Departing the Consumer Culture*. Hoboken, NJ: Wiley & Sons, 2016.
Blount, Brian K. *Invasion of the Dead: Preaching Resurrection*. Louisville: Westminster John Knox, 2014.
Bonhoeffer, Dietrich. *The Cost of Discipleship*. London: SCM, 2001.
———. *Letters and Papers from Prison*. London: SCM, 1967.
Brown, Warren S., and Brad D. Strawn. *The Physical Nature of Christian Life: Neuroscience, Psychology and the Church*. Cambridge: Cambridge University Press, 2012.
Brueggemann, Walter. *A Gospel of Hope*. Louisville: Westminster John Knox, 2018.
Burns, David D. *Feeling Great: The Revolutionary New Treatment for Depression and Anxiety*. Eau Claire, WI: PESI, 2020.
Calhoun, Alice. *Spiritual Disciplines Handbook*. Downers Grove, IL: InterVarsity, 2015.
Carbon, Claus-Christian. "The First 100 Milliseconds of a Face." *Perceptual and Motor Skills* 113.3 (December 2011) 859–74. doi: 10.2466/07.17.22.PMS.113.6.859-874.
Carr, David M. *Holy Resilience: The Bible's Traumatic Origins*. New Haven: Yale University Press, 2014.
Chen, Nick, and David Tabatsky. *Rx for Hope: An Integrative Approach to Cancer Care*. Lanham, MD: Rowman & Littlefield, 2018.
Claiborne, Shane, and Tony Campolo. *Red Letter Revolution*. Nashville: Nelson, 2012.

BIBLIOGRAPHY

Collins, Chuck, and Mary Wright. *The Moral Measure of the Economy.* Maryknoll, NY: Orbis, 2007.

Craddock, Fred, et al. *Speaking of Dying: Recovering the Church's Voice in the Face of Death.* Grand Rapids: Brazos, 2012.

Cullane, Dennis, et al. "Estimated Emergency and Observational/Quarantine Bed Need for the US Homeless Population Related to COVID-19 Exposure by County; Projected Hospitalizations, Intensive Care Units and Mortality." *National Alliance to End Homelessness,* March 20, 2020. https://endhomelessness.org/resource/estimated-emergency-and-observational-quarantine-bed-need-for-the-us-homeless-population-related-to-covid-19-exposure-by-county-projected-hospitalizations-intensive-care-units-and-mortality/.

Davies, Katie. *Intrinsic Hope: Living Courageously in Troubled Times.* Gabriola, BC: New Society, 2018.

Dawn, Marva. *Being Well When We're Ill: Wholeness and Hope in Spite of Infirmity.* Minneapolis: Augsburg Fortress, 1999.

Dicken, Thomas M. "The Homeless God." *Journal of Religion* 91.2 (2011) 127–57.

Duffin, Erin. "Average Number of People per Family in the United States from 1960 to 2021." *Statista,* July 27, 2022. https://www.statista.com/statistics/183657/average-size-of-a-family-in-the-us/.

Eagleton, Terry. *Hope without Optimism.* Charlottesville: University of Virginia Press, 2015.

Elliot, David. "The Theological Virtue of Hope and the Art of Dying." *Studies in Christian Ethics* 29.3 (August 2016) 301–7.

Fischer, Kathleen R. *Winter Grace: Spirituality and Aging.* Nashville: Upper Room, 1998.

Forest, James. "Thomas Merton's Struggle with Peacemaking." In *Thomas Merton: Prophet in the Belly of a Paradox,* edited by Gerald Twomey, 15–54. New York: Paulist, 1978.

Forest, Jim. "Astonishing Hope." *Sojourners* 6.9 (February 1980) 24–27.

Foster, Richard. *Prayer: Finding the Heart's True Home.* San Francisco: HarperOne, 1992.

Frankl, Viktor. *Man's Search for Meaning.* Boston: Beacon, 2006.

———. *The Unconscious God.* New York: Washington Square, 1985.

Friedman, Zach. "78% of Americans Live Paycheck to Paycheck." *Forbes,* January 11, 2019. https://www.forbes.com/sites/zackfriedman/2019/01/11/live-paycheck-to-paycheck-government-shutdown/?sh=2baf8a824f10.

Gandhi, Mahatma. *Mahatma Gandhi—The Last Phase.* Ahmedabad: Navajivan, 1958.

"A Global First Direct Cash Transfer Study Shows Promising Results for People Recently Homeless." *Foundations for Social Change,* October 6, 2020. https://forsocialchange.org/oct-6-2020.

Gonzalez-BeHass, Alyssa R., and Patricia P. Willems. *Theories in Educational Psychology: Concise Guide to Meaning and Practice.* Lanham, MD: Rowman & Littlefield Education, 2013.

Gushee, David. *The Sacredness of Human Life: Why an Ancient Biblical Vision Is Key to the World's Future.* Grand Rapids: Eerdmans, 2013.

Hammarskjold, Dag. *Markings.* New York: Random House, 2006.

Hart, Tom. "Counseling's Spiritual Dimension: Nine Guiding Principles." *Journal of Pastoral Care* 43.2 (1989) 111–18.

Hauerwas, Stanley. *Naming the Silences: God, Medicine, and the Problem of Suffering.* Grand Rapids: Eerdmans, 1990.

———. "On Developing Hopeful Virtues." *Pro Ecclesia* 5.3 (1996) 334–48.

BIBLIOGRAPHY

Hauerwas, Stanley, and William Willimon. *Resident Aliens*. Nashville: Abingdon, 1989.
Hauerwas, Stanley, et al., eds. *Growing Old in Christ*. Grand Rapids: Eerdmans, 2003.
Hays, Richard B., and Judith C. Hays. "The Christian Practice of Growing Old: The Witness of Scripture." In *Growing Old in Christ*, edited by Stanley Hauerwas et al., 3–18. Grand Rapids: Eerdmans, 2003.
Hilfiker, David. "The Limits of Charity." *The Other Side* 36.5 (September/October 2000) 10–15.
Johnson, George S. *Beyond Guilt: Christian Response to Suffering*. Cambridge: Adventure, 2000.
Johnson, Lynn. "Happiness: How Positive Psychology Changes Our Lives." *PESI Digital Seminar*, 05:13:00. https://catalog.pesi.com/item/happiness-positive-psychology-lives-34221.
Jones, James W. *The Spirit and the World*. Gloucestershire, UK: Hawthorn, 1975.
Jones, Serene. *Trauma and Grace: Theology in a Ruptured World*. Louisville: Westminster John Knox, 2009.
Kalb, Claudia. "Faith and Healing." *Newsweek* (November 10, 2003) 44–56.
Kearney, Melissa. "Child Poverty in the U.S." *The Econofact Network*, February 5, 2021. https://econofact.org/child-poverty-in-the-u-s.
Kelly, Orville E. *Make Today Count*. New York: Delacorte, 1975.
Lemon, Jason. "Medicare for All Would Save $450 Billion Annually While Preventing 68,000 Deaths, New Study Shows." *Newsweek*, February 18, 2020. https://www.newsweek.com/medicare-all-would-save-450-billion-annually-while-preventing-68000-deaths-new-study-shows-1487862.
Lenoir, Frédéric. *Happiness: A Philosopher's Guide*. Brooklyn, NY: Melville, 2013.
Lewis, C. S. "They Asked for a Paper." In *Is Theology Poetry?*, 164–65. London: Geoffrey Bless, 1962.
Linn, Matthew, et al. *Simple Ways to Pray for Healing*. New York: Paulist, 1998.
Lopez, Shane. *Making Hope Happen*. New York: Atria, 2014.
Marcel, Gabriel. *Homo Viator: Introduction to the Metaphysics of Hope*. London: Gollancz, 1951.
Mattson, Stephen. "Seven Lies about Christianity—Which Christians Believe." *Sojourners*, December 3, 2013. https://sojo.net/articles/seven-lies-about-christianity-which-christians-believe.
McKnight, John, and Peter Block. *The Abundant Community*. San Francisco: Berrett-Koehler, 2012.
Meilaender, Gilbert. *Should We Live Forever? The Ethical Ambiguities of Aging*. Grand Rapids: Eerdmans, 2013.
Millon, Theodore, and George S. Everly, Jr. *Personality and Its Disorders: A Biosocial Learning Approach*. Hoboken, NJ: Wiley & Sons, 1985.
Moltmann, Jürgen. *The Church in the Power of the Spirit*. New York: Harper & Row, 1977.
———. *The Coming of God: Christian Eschatology*. Minneapolis: Fortress, 1996.
———. *The Crucified God*. Minneapolis: Fortress, 1974.
———. *In the End—The Beginning: The Life of Hope*. Minneapolis: Fortress, 2004.
———. "The Resurrection of Christ and the New Earth." *Communio Viatorum* 49.2 (2007) 141–49.
———. *The Source of Life: The Holy Spirit and the Theology of Life*. Minneapolis: Fortress, 1997.

BIBLIOGRAPHY

Morris, Randy. "Therapeutic Approaches to Extinction Anxiety: Apocalypse as a Rite of Passage." Lecture, Care of Souls Conference, Tacoma, WA, February 22, 2019.

Morse, Christopher. *The Difference Heaven Makes: Rehearsing the Gospel as News*. London: T. & T. Clark, 2010.

Moses, Joy. "COVID-19 and the State of Homelessness." *National Alliance to End Homelessness*, May 19, 2020. https://endhomelessness.org/blog/covid-19-and-the-state-of-homelessness/.

National Coalition for the Homeless. "Education of Homeless Children and Youth." July 2009. https://www.nationalhomeless.org/factsheets/education.html.

―――. "Health Care and Homelessness." July 2009. https://www.nationalhomeless.org/factsheets/health.html.

―――. "Homeless Families with Children." July 2009. https://www.nationalhomeless.org/factsheets/families.html.

O'Connor, Kathleen. *Jeremiah: Pain and Promise*. Minneapolis: Fortress, 2011.

Oswalt, Roy M., and Arlyn Jacobson. *The Emotional Intelligence of Jesus: Relational Smarts for Religious Leaders*. Lanham, MD: Rowman & Littlefield, 2015.

Palmer, Parker. *On the Brink of Everything: Grace, Gravity, and Getting Old*. Oakland, CA: Berrett-Koehler, 2018.

Parnell, Whitney. "Knowledge Is Dangerous to Institutionalized Power." *Sojourners*, October 7, 2020. https://sojo.net/articles/knowledge-dangerous-institutionalized-power.

Parsons, Stephens. *The Challenge of Christian Healing*. Nashville: Abingdon, 1986.

Patton, Natalie. "8 Sayings Christians Use to Let Ourselves Off the Hook." *Sojourners*, August 29, 2017. https://sojo.net/articles/8-sayings-christians-use-let-ourselves-hook.

Peters, Ted. *God—The World's Future*. Minneapolis: Augsburg Fortress, 1992.

―――. "The Terror of Time." *Dialogue* 33.1 (Spring 2000) 56–66.

Peterson, Eugene. "Spirit Quest." *Christianity Today* (November 8, 1993) 27–30.

Piatt, Christian. "Five New Christian Clichés to Avoid." *Patheos*, October 26, 2012. https://www.patheos.com/blogs/christianpiatt/2012/10/five-new-christian-cliches-to-avoid/.

―――. "Nine (Final) Christian Clichés to Avoid." *Patheos*, July 10, 2012. https://www.patheos.com/blogs/christianpiatt/2012/07/nine-final-christian-cliches-to-avoid/.

―――. "Ten Clichés Christians Should Never Use." *Sojourners*, July 6, 2012. https://sojo.net/articles/christian-cliches/ten-cliches-christians-should-never-use.

―――. "Ten More Clichés Christians Should Avoid." *Sojourners*, July 9, 2012. https://sojo.net/articles/christian-cliches/ten-more-cliches-christians-should-avoid.

Prieto, Jaime L., Jr. *The Joy of Compassionate Connecting: The Way of Christ through Nonviolent Communication*. Scotts Valley, CA: CreateSpace, 2010.

Rohr, Richard. *Divine Dance: The Trinity and Your Transformation*. New Kensington, PA: Whitaker House, 2016.

―――. *What the Mystics Know: Seven Pathways to Your Deeper Self*. Chestnut Ridge, NY: Crossroad, 2019.

Ross, J. Robert. "Journey in Egypt." *Sojourners* 5.5 (May/June 1976) 22–23.

Sanders, Bernie. "Bernie Sanders Urges Supporters to Vote for Biden." *New York Times*, October 3, 2020. Video, 1:25. https://www.nytimes.com/video/us/elections/100000007376473/sanders-biden-campaign.html.

Sandlin, Mark. "10 Things You Can't Say While Following Jesus." *Sojourners*, January 21, 2014. https://sojo.net/articles/10-things-you-cant-say-while-following-jesus.

BIBLIOGRAPHY

Semega, Jessica, et al. "Income and Poverty in the United States: 2018" *United States Census Bureau*, September 10, 2019. https://www.census.gov/library/publications/2019/demo/p60-266.html.

Shook, Jill Suzanne. *Making Housing Happen: Faith-based Affordable Housing Models* Nashville: Chalice, 2006.

Shostrom, Everett L., and Dan Montgomery. *Healing Love: How God Works within the Personality.* Nashville: Abingdon, 1978.

Sider, Ronald J. "Economic Inequality: Should We Call It Sin?" *Sojourners*, March 19, 2013. https://sojo.net/articles/economic-inequality-should-we-call-it-sin.

———. *Rich Christians in an Age of Hunger.* Nashville: Nelson, 2010.

Smedes, Lewis. *Standing on the Promises.* Nashville: Nelson, 1998.

Snodgrass, Klyne R. *Who God Says You Are: A Christian Understanding of Identity.* Grand Rapids: Eerdmans, 2018.

Snyder, C. Arnold. *Following in the Footsteps of Christ.* Maryknoll, NY: Orbis, 2004.

Sölle, Dorothy. *The Silent Cry: Mysticism and Resistance.* Minneapolis: Fortress, 2001.

Southwick, Stephen M., and Dennis S. Charney. *Resilience: The Science of Mastering Life's Greatest Challenges.* Cambridge: Cambridge University Press, 2018.

Speerstra, Karen, and Herbert Anderson. *The Divine Art of Dying: How to Live Well While Dying.* San Francisco: Divine Arts, 2014.

Stasha, Smiljanic. "The State of Homelessness in the US—2022." *Policy Advice*, last modified July 30, 2022. https://policyadvice.net/insurance/insights/homelessness-statistics/.

Swartley, Willard. *Covenant of Peace: The Missing Piece in New Testament Theology and Ethics.* Grand Rapids: Eerdmans, 2006.

———. *Health, Healing and the Church's Mission.* Downers Grove, IL: InterVarsity, 2012.

Taylor, Barbara Brown. "Let There Be Night." Interview by Elizabeth Dias-Clarkesville. *Time* (April 28, 2014) 38–41.

UNESCO World Heritage Convention. "Auschwitz Birkenau: German Nazi Concentration and Extermination Camp (1940–1945)." https://whc.unesco.org/en/list/31/.

UNICEF. "Levels and Trends in Child Mortality 2014." https://data.unicef.org/resources/levels-trends-child-mortality-report-2014/#:~:text=September2014..

Vance, Eric. "Mind over Matter." *National Geographic* 230.6 (December 2016) 30–56.

Verhey, Allen. *The Christian Art of Dying: Learning from Jesus.* Grand Rapids: Eerdmans, 2011.

Wadell, Paul J. *Becoming Friends: Worship, Justice, and the Practice of Christian Friendship.* Grand Rapids: Brazos, 2002.

Weddell, Kendra. "Biblical Friendship in an Age of Loneliness." *Christian Century* 136.3 (January 30, 2019) 30–31.

Weingarten, Kaethe. "Reasonable Hope: Construct, Clinical Applications, and Supports." *Family Process* 49.1 (2010) 5–25.

Willard, Dallas. *Knowing Christ Today: Why We Can Trust Spiritual Knowledge.* New York: HarperCollins, 2009.

Williamson, Marianne. *A Return to Love: Reflections on the Principles of* A Course in Miracles. San Francisco: HarperOne, 2012.

Wilson, Jonathan R. *Gospel Virtues: Practicing Faith, Hope and Love in Uncertain Times.* Downers Grove, IL: InterVarsity, 1998.

Wink, Walter. *Engaging the Powers.* Minneapolis: Fortress, 2017.

———. *Jesus and Nonviolence: A Third Way.* Minneapolis: Fortress, 2003.

Witherington, Ben, III. "God Wants to Heal Us." *Christianity Today* 60.3 (April 2016) 60–63.
Wolsterstorff, Nicholas. *Justice: Rights and Wrongs*. Princeton: Princeton University Press, 2010.
World Health Organization. "Children: Improving Survival and Well-being." September 8, 2020. https://www.who.int/news-room/fact-sheets/detail/children-reducing-mortality.
Wright, N. T. *Surprised by Hope: Rethinking Heaven, the Resurrection, and the Church*. San Francisco: HarperOne, 2008.
Yancey, Philip. *Prayer: Does It Make Any Difference?* Grand Rapids: Zondervan, 2006.
Yoder, John Howard. "Exodus: Probing the Meaning of Liberation." *Sojourners* (September 1976) 27–33.
———. *The Original Revolution: Essays on Christian Pacifism*. Scottsdale, PA: Herald, 1971.
Yoder, Perry B. *Shalom: The Bible's Word for Salvation, Justice and Peace*. Nairobi: Evangel, 1987.

Subject Index

abandonment, 57, 63, 67, 172–73
absence of God, 26, 67, 68, 146
abundance, 72, 94, 109, 110
aging, 182–83, 185
Abraham and Sarah, 127
Adam, 55, 160
amazement, 108
anger
    alleviation of, 77
    burden of, 73
    difficulty expressing, 70
    and false hope, 162
    of God, 68, 71, 74–75
    as primary emotion, 64, 67, 69, 183
    handling, 7, 134
    and victimhood, 12
    while caring for others, 8
Anthony, Susan B., 119
anxiety
    and attachment, 92
    author's experience of, 103, 110, 175, 178
    in being vs. doing, 43
    chronic, 8, 59
    egocentric, 106, 186
    overcoming, 60
    over physical appearance, 53
    as primary emotion, 64, 181
    and suffering, 106
assets, 85–86
attachment styles, 91–92
attitude(s)
    as asset, 48
    in caregiving, 8
    changes in, 10, 88, 101, 128
    cultivating hopeful, toward dying, 187
    in healthy spirituality, 110
    about mortality, 128
    toward pain, 192
    shown toward us, 42
    unconscious, 87
attunement, 44
Auschwitz-Birkenau, 122, 174

Babylonian exile, 20
being
    vs. beliefs, 105
    and dehumanizing, 140
    and divine breath, 100
    vs. doing, 74, 182, 188
    and emotional health, 81
    given by God, 114
    human and divine, 102
    human vs. spiritual, 99, 164
    new way of, 41–50
    as social, 90
    sustained by God, 135
    Trinitarian, 56
beliefs
    changing or challenging core, 87, 88
    and distorted spirituality, 105
    and following Jesus, 189–90
    about prayer, 160
    revealed in emotions, 64
    role of, in helping caregivers cope with secondary trauma, 8n8

SUBJECT INDEX

Berrigan, Daniel, 4
Bible, the
   author's experience of reading, 103
   and character, examples of, 114
   composition of, as unfolding story, 20
   and despair, 68
   on the human relationship to God and creation, 54
   and justice, 142, 149
   and neurotic fear, 68–69
   and the poor and homeless, 141, 145, 150
   and trauma, 19
blame, 45, 51, 53, 83, 140, 157, 165
body, the human
   acceptance of, v. alienation, 52–54, 105
   changes in, related to hope or hopelessness, 51
   compassion for, 56–59
   in connecting us to the world, 54–55
   designed for healing, 158
   as gift/gifts of, 48, 55, 56, 59, 198
   image, 54
   language, 65
   practical exercises to care for, 59–62
   and resurrection, 182
   role of, in eliciting suppressed emotions, 77
   sensory stimulation of, 61
   as temple of the Holy Spirit, 59
   See also human personhood: six dimensions of; Jesus: his life in a human body
body of Christ, 130, 133, 145
Bonhoeffer, Dietrich, 119, 125
brain, the human
   activity of, 54, 58, 59, 79, 91
   and the body, 51
   and change, 132
   conditioning of, 60
   in dying, 192
   in relationship to mind, 79
   structure of, 79–80
   and trauma imprints, 21
breath, 44, 60–61, 100

Calhoun, Alice, 134
cancer, author's experience of, xv, 9, 175–76, 195–98
caregivers, 8n8, 37, 50, 91
character, 48, 54, 94, 112–21 123. *See also* human personhood: six dimensions of
charity, 44, 143, 151–54
chemotherapy, xv, 9, 175–76, 196–97
childhood/children
   attachment experiences in, 14, 91, 92
   and beliefs about God, 87
   borrowing the earth from our, 49
   in family discussions about illness, 163
   and growing into hope, 15
   and healthy ways of handling pain, 46
   and homelessness, 138
   and messages received from authority figures, 87
   in parable of social change, 152
   personality formation in, 91
   in poor countries, 166
   and relational poverty in adulthood, 94
   suppressing emotions in, 6
   and wonder, 108
   See also Jesus: and children
children of God, 114
chronos, 187
circumstances, 8–9, 36, 70
community, 49, 124, 126, 129, 131–35
compassion
   in community, 153, 165
   generated by hope, 71
   of Jesus, 73–75, 96, 161
   for others, 65, 89, 96, 97, 109, 120
   for our physical bodies, 56–59, 62, 176
   practicing, 44, 115, 119
   self-, 67, 85
compulsive behaviors, 67
confidence, 34
Corrigan, Marie, 119
counseling, 8n8
covenant, 50, 128–31

SUBJECT INDEX

creation
  beauty of, 58
  God's love for, 115
  human body embedded in, 57
  the new, 33, 35, 71, 125
  out of nothing, 30
  as sanctuary of God's presence, 57
cross, the. *See* Golgotha; Jesus: death and crucifixion of

Day, Dorothy, 119
death and dying
  author's personal experience of, 191
  Christian church's handling of, 186–87
  Christian perspective on, 30, 183–85
  facing it, overcoming its opposition, 35, 178–79, 184
  fear of, 27, 179–82
  hopeful process of, 167, 182, 186–87, 191–93
  living with, 189–90
  as ministry opportunity, 169
  preparing for, 187–88
depression, 8, 23, 68, 106
despair
  coexistence of, with hope, 4–5
  as emotion and mindset, 67–68
  leading to new possibilities, 29
  and relational poverty, 94
  relationship of to human freedom, 19
  and society's weakest parts, 136
  tolerability of, 8, 47
  and unhealthy patterns, 83, 100–101
dignity, 49–50, 98, 109, 137, 141, 174
disciples of Jesus, 23–26, 24n12. *See also* followers of Jesus
doubt, 126, 148, 170, 171

Eden, Garden of, 31
emotion(s)
  in decision-making, 65–67
  defined, 63–64
  health of, in Jesus, 71–74
  in human development, 64
  strengths of, 48
  in struggle and hope, 67–71
  managing/working with, 70, 75–77
  in unhealthy thinking, 81–83
  See also human personhood: six dimensions of; healing: of emotions.
emotional intelligence, 64–65, 72
emotional reasoning, 83–84
empathy
  in community, 97
  defined, 65
  development of, 92, 182
  and emotions, 48
  and ethics, 118
  in facing despair, 84
  importance of, in relationships, 96
  learned in childhood, 92
  in relation to the poor, 139–40
  See also Jesus: empathy of
environment, 42, 55, 169
Erasmus, 187
evil
  as attack on the body, 86, 198
  never brought by God, 164
  not the final word, 26
  reality of, 180
  in suffering, 106, 171
  social dynamics of, 108
  systemic, 22–24, 142, 163, 173
  as temporary burden, 47
  triumphs of, 47, 176
  victory over, 32, 172, 174
exercise. *See* physical exercise

faith, 88, 103–8, 169–70
false hopes, 5–6, 36, 162
fear
  acknowledging, 7
  as biggest enemy, 86, 168–69
  and bodily illness, 52, 192, 197
  and community, 126
  and control, 180
  of death, 27, 178, 180, 184–85, 188, 198
  and emotions, 63–64, 67–69, 77
  encouraging resistance to, 17
  and establishing justice, 142
  and false hopes for healing, 162

SUBJECT INDEX

fear *(continued)*
    freedom from, 89
    generated by underlying assumptions, 88
    overcoming, 8, 47, 77, 86–87, 93–95, 174, 180, 187
    sharing in friendships, 115
    as societal state, 93
    and thought patterns, 88, 102
Finch, John, 108
Finney, Charles, 119
followers of Jesus
    confidence of, in God's culminating work, 35
    effect of Jesus' death on, 23–24, 185
    and facing death, 70, 187–88
    and joy, 77
    and paradox of Christian discipleship, 167
    and positive emotions, 70
    as representatives of humanity's future, 50
    as social misfits, 34
    as witnesses to the resurrection, 24–27
    See also disciples of Jesus
forgiveness
    and character, 119
    characterizing Jesus' relationships, 22, 73, 189
    difficulty receiving, 87
    in friendship, 115, 183
    in the new creation, 47
    in rebuilding relationships, 96, 191
    self-, and shame, 69
Francis of Assisi, 119
Frederickson, Barbara, 64
freedom
    from addictions, 44
    and Christian hope, 33, 114, 193
    in community, 127
    described, 19, 23, 29, 41, 122, 124, 148, 186
    emotional, 67
    and faith, 78, 80
    and God's actions, 166
    of learning to let go in facing death, 186–87
    in living with aging and illness, 163, 182–83
    of reflection on self and others, 6, 49
    self-directed, 46
    from self-inflicted demands, 110
    and the Spirit, 125
    vs. slavery, 18
friendship, 45, 53, 56, 92–93, 95, 97, 115–17
future. *See* God's future

God's authentic work in our lives, 106–8
God's future
    anticipated in hopeful community, 128–31
    coming to us in Christ, 22, 37
    coming to us now in the present, 47
    definition and mental pictures of God's, 30
    as our citizenship, 110
    our vision of, bringing hope, 22
    promises of, 31–33
    perspectives of, in relationship to hope, 17–18
Golden Rule, the, 72
Golgotha, 74, 102
grace
    and accepting limitations, 97
    availability of, to all, 164–65
    and being vs. doing, 43
    difficulty receiving, 87, 193
    as divine action superseding human law, 26
    in forgiveness, 109
    in friendship, 45, 117
    in healing, 73, 158, 161, 163, 170
    vs. human effort, 33
    vs. human righteousness, 32
    of Jesus, 22, 189
    in relationships, 94, 96, 130–34, 147
    resting in, 44–45, 59
    resurrection, 33, 69
    vs. shame, 64, 69, 76
    and surrendering the past, 96

SUBJECT INDEX

grief
- and blame, 85
- effect of hope on, 29, 31
- of God the Father, 146, 173–74
- God's involvement in, 175
- and human free will, 19
- and letting go in dying, 186–87
- and prayer, 162
- protesting and loving God simultaneously in, 192
- temporary nature of, 191
- traumatic, 23, 24

group development, 134

Hammarskjöld, Dag, 69n5, 119
healing
- acts of Jesus, 22, 73–74, 162, 173, 189
- of broken communities, 137–53
- in community practices, 133–34
- vs. cure, 191
- described in diverse ways, 158–59
- from difficult relationships, 46–47, 89
- of emotions, 15, 73
- in global perspective, 166–67
- God's actions in, 106, 114, 157, 165–66, 167–68
- inner, xvi, 45, 69, 70
- and love as most important ingredient, 169
- in meditation exercises, 86
- motivation for, 3, 36, 68
- of past events, 76
- places, 116
- potential for, 28
- praying for, 159–63, 167–70
- and self-awareness, 107, 180
- as spiritual work, 100
- recommended prayer for, 170
- of spirit, 100–103
- of the world, 130

heaven
- and earth, in the new creation, 32–33, 34, 36, 48–49, 110–11, 113, 191
- and earth, in relationship to each other now, 22, 27, 55
- in John's vision, 31
- kingdom of, 144
- less about afterlife than about life now, 33
- made by God, 131
- sermons on, 178

hell, 13, 26, 82, 147, 178, 183
Hillesum, Etty, 122
Holy Spirit
- empowering Jesus' followers to kingdom witness, 130, 135
- human body as temple of, 59
- as mother, 126
- in natural processes of healing, 158
- new age of righteousness in, 173
- in relationship with human spirit, 100
- role of, in covenantal community, 128–31
- work of, in Trinitarian relationship, 125

homelessness, 72–73, 136–39
hope
- and the big picture, 9–10
- biblical, generated out of human struggle, 19
- both individual and communal, 50
- our capacity for, in choices we make, 15–18, 42
- choosing to step forward in, 47
- Christian, in uprising of liberation and freedom, 33–34, 190–91
- Christian, radical origins of, 27
- communities of, 136
- cultivating, 15, 47, 50, 116, 121–23, 136
- descriptions of, in common usage, 3
- development of, in childhood, 14
- durable, 46
- and God's future, 22, 30–35
- as God's hope in us v. our personal effort, 34
- vs. hopelessness, 81–83, 87
- how it works, 8–10
- inside out, outside in, 46–47, 48
- intended for everyone, 136
- most important truths about, 28
- vs. optimism, 6–7
- reality of, 193
- in relationship to faith, 88

SUBJECT INDEX

hope *(continued)*
    of an entire society, 136
    sureness of, 70
    transcendent v. proximate, 36.
    See also false hopes.
human personhood
    development of, 54–55
    six dimensions of, 48, 50
    stewardship of, 42–43
humanity, 49, 50
hurt
    and anger, 69–70, 134
    and difficult emotions, 64–67
    differences in expressing, of women and men, 70
    fear of being, 89, 93–96
    helping children process, 46
    healing from, 47, 77, 87

identity, 50
illumination, 109
Ignatius, St., 193
illumination, 109
image of God, the, 55–56
imagination, 33, 44, 80, 102, 111, 168, 178
intimacy, 71, 98–99

Jeremiah, 20–22
Jerusalem, 20–23, 31, 74–75, 110, 129, 145
Jessica (author's client), 11–13
Jesus
    absorbing all our faults, 69
    abundance mentality of, 72
    and average lifespans, 185
    and children, 73–74
    death and crucifixion of, 23, 32, 56, 74, 128, 171–74, 184
    and fear, 71, 72
    as God's weapon against death, 189
    emotional experiences of, 35–36, 71–74
    empathy of, 72–75, 96
    and eschatology, 28, 35, 47
    his hopefulness, 121–23
    his life in a human body, 56
    and the kingdom, 22, 28, 35, 49, 72, 128, 130, 185
    and the paradox of God's absence and presence, 67
    on religious hypocrisy, 22
    resurrection of, 20, 22–24, 24–27, 56, 101, 106, 128, 184
    second coming of, 33
    theology of, 173
    victory of, over suffering and evil, 29, 32
    his vision for a new social order, 22
    See also body of Christ; followers of Jesus
John, 31–32
joy
    and belonging, 17
    brought by hope, 71
    in character traits, 123
    and dying, 191
    and emotions, 64, 77
    experiencing, 110, 161
    of God, 19, 32, 63, 72, 99, 106, 140
    in God's future, 31
    and God's love, 93, 125
    and healing, 28, 160
    and illumination, 109
    of Jesus, 74–75, 113, 189
    longing for, 99
    and peace, 28–29
    and sorrow, simultaneously, 170
    in the face of suffering, 147
journaling, 76
justice. *See* social justice

kairos, 31, 187, 191
King, Martin Luther, Jr., 119
kingdom of God, 49, 114–15, 166–67. *See also* Jesus: and the kingdom
Kohlberg, Lawrence, 117–18
koinonia, 130

lament, 21, 68, 74, 166, 192
Lazarus, 73–74
living with illness, 163
loneliness, 16, 67, 106

SUBJECT INDEX

loss
  in community, 133
  and despair, 67, 68, 85
  in dying, 180, 181, 184, 187, 191–92
  facing, 166
  fear of, 72
  and feeling powerless, 4–5, 15
  of personal integrity, 131
  and renewal, 182
  solidarity with those who struggle with, 49
  in surviving trauma, 21
love
  capacity for, when others don't love us, 47
  in community, 35, 103–4
  and dignity, 49
  and emotions, 64, 70, 77
  of enemies, 131
  experience of, in suffering and illness, 167
  despite pain, in dying, 186
  in facilitating healing, 169
  for the flourishing of all things, 193
  of God, 93, 109, 166, 174, 193
  and group worship, 134
  and human freedom, 19, 44
  humans created for, 41, 70, 93
  hope empowered by, 193
  and hopeful personalities, 89, 93–94
  of justice, 142
  as key ingredient of healing, 169
  learning to, 109, 121
  living in, instead of fear, 94–95. 97
  motherly, from God, 126
  of the needy, 154
  of neighbor, 151
  nonviolent, 26
  vs. performance, 106
  questioning God's, 171
  and protesting against God while loving God, 192
  in relationship to personal values, 122
  and relinquishment, 186
  saying yes to, 102
  for self and others, 45–46, 107, 123, 131

  between Son and Father, 71, 72, 74
  for the struggling, 172
  and transformation, 127, 175
  in triumphing over hate, 173
  unconditional, 8, 13, 31–32, 36, 42, 72, 96, 105, 189

Mandela, Nelson, 119
Mary, mother of Jesus, 23–24
May, Gerald, 108
medical providers, 184
meditation, 59, 98, 102
Menchu, Rigoberta, 119
Merton, Thomas, 119
mind, 48, 79–81. *See also* human personhood: six dimensions of; thinking
morality, 64
Mother Teresa, 167
mystery, 45, 181, 183–84

nature (the natural world), 35, 49, 54–55, 57–58, 87, 114, 160
Nero, 190

optimism, 6–7
oppression, 73
overeating, 65–67

pain
  the body's ability to function in, 48, 51
  causes of, overcome by Jesus' resurrection uprising, 106
  in childbirth, 181
  contextualized in God's larger story, 122, 191
  of creation's labor, 106, 114
  in dying, 192
  emotional, 15, 46, 85
  endured by Jesus, 56, 173, 175
  and fearful images of the future, 68
  God's involvement in our, 28, 31, 175, 176
  of grief, 162
  in Jesus' violent death, 172

SUBJECT INDEX

pain *(continued)*
   in Kohlberg's stages of moral development, 117
   and the logic of true hope, 36
   modern medicine attitudes toward, 6
   not the final word, 173
   from the past, released in forgiveness, 96
   personal and subjective, 192
   physical, 46, 76, 192
   in the present, while anticipating a better future, 36
   processed differently by women than men, 70
patience, 15, 16–17, 114–15, 123, 167
Paul, the apostle, 26, 56, 129
peace
   as character trait, 123
   in detachment, 110
   in dying, 45, 187–88
   and emotions, 46, 64, 67
   experiencing, 103–4
   generated by hope, 71, 122
   in the healing process, 159, 176
   and justice, 5, 22, 101
   and meditation exercises, 60–61
   in the new creation/God's future, 35, 111, 114, 127, 142, 175, 189
   with our past, 46
   with ourselves, 43, 105, 109, 167
   potential for, in every circumstance, 28, 29, 99
   as Shalom, 43, 77
   as state of grace, 45
personality, 48, 54, 89, 91–92. *See also* human personhood: six dimensions of
physical exercise, 52, 57, 59–60, 62, 67, 87–88, 198
positive emotions, 64, 70
positive thinking, xvi, 6, 17, 81–83, 84, 88, 92
post-traumatic stress disorder, 23
power
   over death, 34, 170, 184, 188, 190
   divine, intervening in human events, 145, 146
   for emotional transformation, 70
   of evil, 173
   God's, experienced in our lives, 30, 35, 98, 107, 129, 130, 163
   in healing, 158, 168
   over others, 101, 181
   of prayer, 159
   v. privilege, 101
   redemptive, in overcoming negative circumstances, 86, 114, 121, 186
   of resurrection hope, 27–29, 31, 33, 47, 113
   as sacrificial, 174
   as security in human institutions, 124
   shared, 94
   in social relations, 190
   of tyrannical authority structures, 22–23, 71, 125, 127, 142, 150–51, 165, 189
   through weakness, 26, 28, 169
powerlessness, 4, 12, 23, 34, 67, 72, 187
prayer
   and Christian clichés, 164–66
   defined, 102
   for healing, 157–59, 160, 162–63, 168–69
   intercessory, 134, 158, 168
   and the mind, 102
   with others, 115
   practicing, 59, 102, 103, 166–70, 182
   seeking answers to, 5, 21, 157, 159
   types of, 178, 180
psychotherapist(s), 95, 171
purgation, 108

Rachel (of Bethlehem massacre), 23
radiation therapy, 176
reality, 49
real world, the, 34, 48–49
redemption, 49, 114, 134–35, 187, 192
relationship(s)
   assumptions about, in hopeful personalities, 92
   based in love, 93, 96
   childhood expectations of, 87
   in dating, 53
   empathy in, as key ingredient, 96

SUBJECT INDEX

as eternal, 191
with God, nature of, 41–42
healing from difficult, 45, 96
and identity, 90
intentional, in God's community, 131–35
with others, 45–46, 95–97
with ourselves, 42–45, 69
resilience/resiliency,
  and adversity, 36, 90, 183, 198
  author's experience of, in chemotherapy, 176
  and changed perspective, 22
  in children, 92
  communal, 20
  in cultivating hope, xv, 7–8
  and friendship, 117
  of hopeful people, 70, 71
  of Jesus and his followers, 74, 77
  praying for, 170
  in surviving trauma, 13
  and temporary hopes, 35
resurrection
  coming of, for Jesus' followers, 70
  coming through suffering, 168
  as God's insurgency over death, 184, 190
  hope, 135
  power of, in new life vs. old life, 29
  See also Jesus: resurrection of
Roman Colosseum, 190
Romero, Oscar, 119
ruach, 55

Saunders, Cecily, 119
salvation, 20, 23, 25, 124, 127, 187
Scriptures. *See* Bible, the
self, 42–44, 57
self-awareness, 41
self-talk, 70, 83, 84, 87
sensory stimulation, 61
shame, 69
sin
  and death, 178
  defined as disconnected and shut-down, 126
  as economic injustice, 149–51

Jesus' forgiving of, 190
and power structures, 23
taken on by Jesus, 32, 69
social justice, 28, 104–5, 190
Sölle, Dorothee, 108
sorrow, 16, 21, 29, 74, 166, 170, 192
soul, 37, 50. *See also* body, emotions, mind, spirit.
soul work, 50
Spirit. *See* Holy Spirit
spirit, 48, 100, 108–111. *See also* human personhood: six dimensions of; Holy Spirit
spirituality, 55, 98–99, 105–7
strengths, personal. *See* assets
suffering
  and character development, 121–23
  Christian hope stereotyped as escape from, 19
  community support in, 168
  in dying, xvi
  experiencing hope in extreme, 22, 176
  and fearful images of the future, 68
  from lack of medical care, 148–49
  of God, 146, 147, 173–74, 176
  and hope may go together, 192
  meaning or meaningless of, 5, 75, 114, 180
  and oppressive power structures, xi, 15
  our responses to, 6, 34, 101, 106, 171–73
  as path to resurrection, 168
  physical, 61
  power to endure, 121–22, 128, 158, 176–77, 186
  prayer for, 170
  questioning God in, 171–72, 176
  relief of, vs. extension of life in medical treatment, 181
  solidarity in, 165–66
  transformed in God's future, 31, 34, 189
  from worries, 180
  See also Jesus: death and crucifixion of

SUBJECT INDEX

surrender
    in acknowledging simultaneous suffering and hope, 192
    in author's experience of radiation, 176
    vs. control, 102
    in dying, 181, 186, 189, 193
    God as author of, 107
    to God's coming kingdom, 74
    God's power made perfect in, 28
    God's self-, 174
    in healing prayer, 167
    of Jesus and his early followers, 75, 185
    in letting go of false gods and hopes, 109
    in meditation exercise, 68
    of the past, to God's grace, 96
    posture of, in healthy spirituality, 99

thinking, 81–85, 87–88. *See also* mind
time, 31, 33
trauma, 15, 21, 23–24, 74
Trinitarian God, 32, 56, 125–26, 174
Truth, Sojourner, 119
Tutu, Desmond, xi

unification, 109
vulnerability, 17

war, 48–49
Wiesel, Elie, 174
Willard, Frances, 119
worship, 98, 123, 127, 129, 134, 142, 159

Author Index

Abraham, William J., 184
Augsburger, David, 18n9

Barth, Markus, 129–30
Bauckham, Richard, 24n12, 126n5
Benner, David, 100n4, 101–2, 105
Berger, Peter, 14
Berry, Wendell, 182
Block, Peter, 124nn1–2
Blount, Brian K., 184nn11–12, 189–90
Bonhoeffer, Dietrich, xiv, 110n22, 145–46
Brown, Warren S. and Brad D. Strawn, 55n3, 91n3, 92n4
Brueggemann, Walter, 63, 157
Burns, David, 83, 84n5

Calhoun, Alice, 134n32
Callahan, Daniel, 181
Carbon, Claus-Christian, 65n4
Carr, David M., 19n1
Chen, Dr. Nick, 197
Claiborne, Shane and Tony Campolo, 131n30
Collins, Chuck and Mary Wright 153n59
Cousins, Norman, 51
Craddock, Fred, 185n13
Cullane, Dennis, 138n2

Davies, Katie, 7–8
Dicken, Thomas M., 145n32, 146nn35–36, 147n38

Dossey, Dr. Larry, 158
Duffin, Erin, 149n44

Eagleton, Terry, 6n4, 7
Elliot, David, 178
Erikson, Erik, 3

Finch, John, 109n21
Fischer, Kathleen R., 182n5, 186n18
Foster, Richard, 168n30
Frankl, Viktor, 5, 10
Friedman, Zach, 150n54

Gandhi, Mahatma, 148
Gonzalez-BeHass, Alyssa R., and Patricia P. Willems, 117n14
Gushee, David, 141n7, 144n26

Hart, Tom, 108n18
Hauerwas, Stanley, 114n6, 121n15, 158, 182n4
Hauerwas, Stanley and Will Willimon, 125n3
Hays, Richard B. and Judith C. Hays, 185n14
Helverson, R. N., 98
Hilfiker, David, 152n58
Hunter, Rodney J., 41

Johnson, Lynn, 61n11
Johnson, Samuel, 79

AUTHOR INDEX

Jones, James W., 130, 131n29
Jones, Serene, 23n10

Kalb, Claudia, 159n7
Kearney, Melissa, 150n55
Kelly, Orville E., 163n20

Lemon, Jason, 148n42
Lenoir, Frédéric, 122n16
Lewis, C. S., xv, 89
Lifton, Robert Jay, 4–5n2
Linn, Matthew, 159n5, 169n32
Lopez, Shane, 51n1

May, Gerald, 109n21
McKnight, John and Peter Block, 124nn1–2
Meilaender, Gilbert, 180n2, 181n3
Merton, Thomas, 48
Millon, Theodore and George S. Everly, Jr., 90n1
Moltmann, Jürgen
   on the relentless coming of God's kingdom, 27, 115n10
   on the Spirit, 55n6, 126, 128n18, 129n20, 130n28
   on suffering, 174n4
Morris, Randy, 54n2
Morse, Christopher, 28n23, 33n13, 35n20
Moses, Joy, 149n47
Mueller, Kayla, 112

National Coalition for the Homeless, 137n1, 138nn3–4

O'Connor, Kathleen, 20–21n3
Oswalt, Roy M. and Arlyn Jacobson, 65nn2–3

Palmer, Parker, 183
Parnell, Whitney, 150n56
Parsons, Stephen, 158
Patton, Natalie, 164n22
Peters, Ted, 30n1, 47, 49, 50n3
Peterson, Eugene, 100n6
Piatt, Christian, 164n22
Polkinghorne, John, 30

Prieto, Jaime L., Jr., 97n10

Rohr, Richard, 99nn1–2, 100n5, 101nn10–11, 102nn13–14. 103n15, 108n17, 126
Ross, J. Robert, 130n24

Sanders, Bernie, 150nn49, 53
Sandlin, Mark, 164n22
Schweitzer, Albert, 15–16n3
Semega, Jessica, 149n43
Shook, Jill Suzanne, 143n14, 147n39
Shostrom, Everett L. and Dan Montgomery, 71n7, 72nn10–11, 73n15
Sider, Ronald J., 145n31, 147n39, 150nn48, 50–51, 57
Siegel, Bernie, 169
Smedes, Lewis, 18
Snodgrass, Klyne R., 80–81
Snyder, C. Arnold, 132n31
Sölle, Dorothee, 11, 109n21
Southwick, Stephen M. and Dennis S. Charney, 80n1
Speerstra, Karen and Herbert Anderson, 191n27, 192nn28–29, 193n33
Stasha, Smiljanic, 149n46
Swartley, Willard, 77n30, 158n3, 164n21

Taylor, Barbara Brown, 101n7

UNESCO, 174n5
UNICEF, 166n25

Vance, Eric, 168n28
Verhey, Allen, 184n9, 187n19, 188n20

Wallis, Jim, 22n8
Wadell, Paul J., 115nn11–12, 116n13, 134n33
Weddell, Kendra, 16nn4–5
Weingarten, Kaethe, 124
Willard, Dallas, 99n3
Williamson, Marianne, 93n5, 94nn6–8
Wilson, Jonathan R., 114n6
Wink, Walter, 73n17, 73n20, 161n15
Witherington, Ben, III, 161n13

AUTHOR INDEX

Wolterstorff, Nicholas, 147n40
Wright, N. T., 24n13, 27n22

Yancey, Philip, 158n4, 159n8, 161n16
Yoder, John Howard, 127n13, 128nn16–17
Yoder, Perry B., 43n1, 77nn29–30

Scripture Index

Genesis

2:7	55n4, 160n9
3	160n11
3:19	160n10
12:1–3	127n10

Deuteronomy

10:17–19	140n6
16:20	142n8
21:33	172n2
30:15, 19	127n14

Joshua

24:24	127n12

Psalms

33:6	55n5
46:10	43
103:13	88n6
111:10	109n20
139:8	147n37

Isaiah

5:7–9	142n12
5:8	142n9
10:1–3	145n30
10:1–2	142n11
26:2–10	142n10
26:19	25
53	25
58	142n9
58:3–7	142n13

Jeremiah

4:17	20
5:26–29	145n30
7:32—8:3	20n2
17:9	113n2
19:9	20n2
20:3	22n7
20:7	21n6
28:14–18	21nn4–5

Lamentations

5	20n2

Daniel

12:1–3	25

Amos

5:22–23	142n9
6:4, 7	145n30

SCRIPTURE INDEX

Micah

2:2	145n30

Matthew

5—7	22n9, 144n23
5:6	109n19
5:45	72n13
6:31–34	88n6
7:7	72n14
7:12	72n12
11:28–30	73n16
14:13–21	72n8
18	90n2
23	143n16
25:31–46	90n2, 144n24, 146n35
25:35–37, 40	144n25
26:38	74n24
27:46	171n1

Mark

1:14	128n15
1:15	22, 189n24
1:27	73n20
1:35–42	73n19
3:15	73n20
3:31–35	130n26
6:4–6	161n19
6:5–6	161n14
6:30–44	72n8
8:34–35	167n26
10:14	74n23
10:17–27	144n18
11:15–19	73n21
12:13–17	143n17
14:33	74n24

Luke

1:46–56	23n11
4:18–22	74n27, 136, 143n15, 145n31
6:24–25	144n18
7:8	73n20
9:12–17	72n8
12:13–21	144n19
12:15–21	72n9
12:27	72n14
16:19–31	144n19
17:5–10	170n33
18:18–28	144n20
18:25	144n21
19:1–10	144n20
20:25–37	144n22
22:44	74n24
23:26	74n26
23:34	73n19
24	25n14
24:11	24n12

John

3:3–6	126n7
3:16	88n6
6:1–15	72n8
	14:2–3, 34n18
14:26	126n6
14:30	165n23
20:18	24n12

Acts

2:44–47	129n19
5:41	77n31
7:59	193n35
9:3–22	26n16

Romans

5	75n28
5:5	64n1, 113n1
5:8	88n6
6:3–4	188n22
6:19	56n9
8	161n17
8:11	56n8, 191n26
8:18	34n19
8:19–25	114n7
8:23, 26	192n30
8:28	88n6, 113n1

8:35–39	88n6	\multicolumn{2}{c}{**Ephesians**}
12:1–2	80n2, 88n6		
12:1	57n10	2:13–22	101n9
12:11–12	71n6	3:10	168n29
13:12	33n12	4:20–24	160n12
14:7–8	188n21, 193n34	6:12	165n24
15:13	71n6		

1 Corinthians

1:27	146n34
2:9	19
6:15	56n7
8:6	114n8
10:13	88n6
12	168n31
15:1–8	26n17
15:10	34n16
15:42–49	161n18
15:45	129n20

Philippians

1:6	193n32
2:5–11	96n9
3:10	185n16
3:13–14	113n4
3:13	30
4:5	33n12
4:8	88n7

Colossians

1:15–17	101n8, 114n9
1:17	34n15
3:17	125n4

2 Corinthians

4:8–12	171
4:8–11	26n18
4:8–10	188n23
4:10–11	167n27
5:17	123n17
5:18–19	146n33
6:19	173n3
11:23–29	26n18
12:7–10	26n19

1 Thessalonians

4:13–14, 18	185n17

Titus

3:4–7	88n6

Hebrews

6:5	33n11
8:8–13	128n15
11:1	xi
11:9	127n11
12:1–2	113n3
12:2	113n5
13:1–3	34n17

Galatians

1:4	192n31
1:13	26n15
1:22	130n25
2:20	110n23, 123n18
3:13	172n2
3:28	88n6, 101n9, 129n23
4:19	130n25
5:22–23	71n6. 123
5:22	64n1

James

5:8	33n12
5:13–18	157n1

1 John

1:9   88n6

Revelation

1:5   130n27
5:10   130n27
20:6   130n27

www.ingramcontent.com/pod-product-compliance
Lightning Source LLC
Chambersburg PA
CBHW020408230426
43664CB00009B/1228